1/14/88

For Larry –
who introduced me to
Garrison Keillor, (and a lot of
your own rather profound thoughts
and observations) and who I
admire, respect and adore without
reserve!

love,
Geena

(my new life philosophy is the
bottom 2 lines on page xv)

Leaving Home

LEAVING HOME

HOME

Garrison Keillor

VIKING

All of these stories were performed, in slightly different form, on
"A Prairie Home Companion," a production of Minnesota Public
Radio. Many thanks to Jennifer Howe for her inspired hard work
and to editor Kathryn Court for her savvy and strength of spirit.
The mouse episode in "New Year's" was taken from an account
by Joe O'Connell, and the bus story in "Aprille" came from
my wife, Ulla Skaerved.—G.K.

VIKING
Viking Penguin Inc., 40 West 23rd Street, New York, New York 10010, U.S.A.
Penguin Books Ltd, 27 Wrights Lane, London W8 5TZ (Publishing & Editorial),
and Harmondsworth, Middlesex, England (Distribution & Warehouse)
Penguin Books Australia Ltd, Ringwood, Victoria, Australia
Penguin Books Canada Limited, 2801 John Street, Markham, Ontario, Canada L3R 1B4
Penguin Books (N.Z.) Ltd, 182–190 Wairau Road, Auckland 10, New Zealand

First published in 1987 by Viking Penguin Inc.
Published simultaneously in Canada

"A Trip to Grand Rapids," "The Killer," and "Chicken" first appeared in *The Atlantic*.

Grateful acknowledgment is made for permission to reprint an excerpt from "The Road Not
Taken," from *The Poetry of Robert Frost*, edited by Edward Connery Lathem. Copyright 1916
by Henry Holt and Company; copyright 1944 by Robert Frost. Reprinted by permission of
Henry Holt and Company, Inc.

LIBRARY OF CONGRESS CATALOGING IN PUBLICATION DATA
Keillor, Garrison.
Leaving home.
I. Title.
PS3561.E3755L43   1987   813'.54   87-40219
ISBN 0-670-81976-X
ISBN 0-670-82011-3 (Large Print Edition)
ISBN 0-670-82012-1 (Limited Edition)

Printed in the United States of America by
Arcata Graphics, Fairfield, Pennsylvania
Set in Century Expanded at NK Graphics, Keene, New Hampshire
Designed by Amy Hill
Photograph by Thomas Frederick Arndt

To my mother and father,
John and Grace

One more spring in Minnesota,
To come upon Lake Wobegon.
Old town I smell your coffee.
If I could see you one more time—

I can't stay, you know, I left so long ago,
I'm just a stranger with memories of people I knew here.
We stand around, looking at the ground.
You're the stories I've told for years and years.

That yard, the tree—you climbed it once with me,
And we talked of cities that we'd live in someday.
I left, old friend, and now I'm back again,
Please say you missed me since I went away.

One more time that dance together,
Just you and I now, don't be shy.
This time I know I'd hear the music
If I could hold you one more time.

Contents

Contents

A Letter from
Copenhagen

Here in a little room at the back of a flat in Copenhagen, full of boxes full of wreckage from the collapse of an American career, I imagine a girl slept who came from Jutland a century ago to work as a maid to the tea merchant and his wife whose apartment this was. I imagine she was fourteen, a quick bright girl who sent a krone home every week and intended to go home herself someday, but the merchant's wife was a shrewish old harridan who shrieked at the girl and wore out her good humor, and one Sunday afternoon, enjoying her few hours of freedom with a walk through Langelinie park along the harbor, the girl saw a tall sailing ship loading up with barrels and crates of provisions for a long voyage and people giddy from excitement who were laughing and weeping and young sailors at the rail whom she suddenly envied, and in that moment she started to dream about America.

Some days it seems that I am living the immigrant dream in reverse, starting with success in America, then the voyage, then the life of servitude in the Old World. It's hard work setting up housekeeping in a foreign language. But then I take my shopping bag down to the open market on Frederiksborggade and one look down the avenue of booths heaped with crates of produce and I'm home in Lake Wobegon, back in the land of tomatoes and cucumbers. Cucumbers are *agurker* in Danish, but tomatoes are *tomater* and I see *meloner* and *nektariner, bananer, radiser, broccoli, selleri,* and plenty of *aebler* (both "Golden Delicious" and "Granny Smith"). For *vandmelon,* you pay ten kroner, almost $1.50, and they're as big and thump as well as what I remember from our *vandmelon* patch at home. *Mais* is ten kroner for three ears, a little expensive, but when it comes to *mais* who counts the cost?

Back home, our fridge was getting full in July. We took tomatoes to church to give away, as Christ said we should do, and arrived late and in the cloakroom we found paper sacks full of Christian tomatoes and cucumbers. It was like heaven will be, excessive, so much that we'll have all we can handle, we'll be filled. We'll eat creamed peas and onions, beet greens with butter, fresh carrots (*gulerødder*), and tomatoes, and cucumbers, sliced in vinegar, and *mais.*

Sweet corn was our family's weakness. We were prepared to resist atheistic Communism, immoral Hollywood, hard liquor, gambling and dancing, smoking, fornication, but if Satan had come around with sweet corn, we at least would have listened to what he had to sell. We might not have bought it but we would've had him in and given him a cup of coffee. It was not amazing to learn in eighth-grade science that corn is sexual, each plant containing both genders, male tassel and female flower, propagating in our garden after dark. Sweet corn was so delicious, what could have produced it except sex? Sunday after church, when the pot roast was done and the potatoes were boiled and mashed and a pot of water was boiling—only then would Dad run out with a bushel basket and pick thirty ears of corn. We shucked it clean in five seconds per ear and popped it in the pot for a few minutes. A quick prayer, a little butter and salt, and that is as good as it gets. People have searched the world over for something better and didn't find it because it's not there. There's nothing better, not even sex. People have wanted sex to be as good as sweet corn and have worked hard to improve it, and afterward they lay together in the dark, and said, "Det var dejligt." ("That was so wonderful.") "Ja, det var." "Men det var ikke saa godt som frisk mais." ("But it wasn't as good as fresh sweet corn.") "Ney."

If I had eaten more sweet corn, maybe I'd still be in Minnesota, sitting between the wall and kitchen table, munching away line after line like a typewriter, but I lost touch with people who raised corn and with their church and wasn't invited to Sunday dinner anymore and slowly lost my bearings, and felt lost at home. In Minneapolis, they tore down Met Stadium for a polyester ballfield with a roof over it, a ghostly greenish plastic baseball mall, and all those lovely summer nights were lost. The night train to Chicago was taken off, another broken romance, and all the little truck farms around the Twin Cities disappeared that sold fresh tomatoes, squash, and sweet corn at roadside stands or off the tailgate of a truck. Immense shopping malls sprang up in their place like fungus on the grass. One Christmas, after I wrote a book, I stood autographing copies of it for six hours at a chain store in the Ridgedale complex, as large and bewildering as an Air Force base, and felt its peculiar dementia, low and steadily throbbing from fluorescent lights, air conditioners, and electronic systems including synthesized violins playing homogenous hymns to the anesthetized people, and knew that somewhere we had gone wrong. But all that was off to the west in Hennepin County. Saint Paul, my home, seemed to be, like Lake Wobegon, a gentler place, shaded from predators—and then the worst occurred. The hometown newspaper decided that, being a published author, I was a credit to the community and should be paid close attention, so it announced my romance with my wife and published a photograph of our house, our address, and interviews with the neighbors. I felt watched. Felt mistaken for somebody else. It dawned on me that life might be better elsewhere. That winter it was warm, there was no snow, the landscape was dry and brown and bleak. We left Saint Paul in June, as soon as school was out.

Life is complicated and not for the timid. It's an experience that when it's done, it will take us a while to get over it. We'll look back on all the good things we surrendered in favor of deadly trash and wish we had returned and reclaimed them. We may sit in a cool corner of hell and wish we had kept the ballpark, built the shops elsewhere, and not killed off all those cornfields.

I don't know whether anyone killed radio or it simply died and became a phonograph, but I was privileged to get a chance to reclaim a slice of it thirteen years ago and did my best for that grand old cause, the live broadcast. In fact, the stories in this book were written for performance on the radio, on "A Prairie Home Companion," as you may see from the tone of them. They were written for my voice, which is flat and slow. There are long pauses in them and sentences that trail off into the raspberry bushes.

When I burst upon the radio business in 1963 as the friendly announcer of "Highlights in Homemaking," I badly wanted my voice to sound like that of Orson Welles, as rich and smooth as my mother's gravy on Sunday pot roast, and I succeeded so far as to sound at least brown and thick and lumpy, and then the pretense was too hard to keep up, and by the time "Prairie Home" rolled along, my voice had drifted back toward center and sounded more like my dad's.

The show ran from 1974 to 1987, from a series of theaters and auditoriums in and around Saint Paul, at 5 P.M. on Saturday night, two hours of music and comedy. The last live show on June 13 was pretty typical. Chet Atkins and Leo Kottke played guitar, a Hawaiian school choir sang in Hawaiian, Jean Redpath sang and Stevie Beck played the Autoharp and I sang with Rich Dworsky's Orchestra, Tom Keith and Kate Mackenzie starred in an episode of "Buster the Show Dog," and Vern Sutton sang "Stars and Stripes Forever" with the mighty white Wurlitzer played from the pit by Philip Brunelle as Tom made excellent rocket sounds and the audience clapped and at the climax Vern crashed a pair of cymbals—classic American entertainment, in other words— and in the third half hour, I strolled out and told a story as per usual. I stood at the microphone, looked up into the lights, and let fly. If the crowd got restless, I sat down on a stool, which caught their interest, and if they rustled again, I stood up. After twenty minutes or as soon as the story came to an extremely long pause, I stopped and said, "That's the news from Lake Wobegon, where all the women are strong, the men are good-looking, and all the children are above average," and walked off.

The World Theater, our home for half of those thirteen years, was the right place for that sort of séance, a classic Shubert two-balcony house from 1905, inhabited by two bats and the ghost of a stagehand, all seats within eighty feet of the stage, closer than first base to home. Standing at stage center with your toes to the footlights, you're as close to a thousand people as you can conceivably be. Out there on the prairie where even close friends tend to stand an arm's length apart, such intimacy on such a grand scale is shocking and thrilling and a storyteller reaches something like critical mass, passing directly from solid to radio waves without going through the liquid or gaseous phase. You stand in the dark, you hear people leaning forward, you smell the spotlights, and you feel invisible. No script, no clock, only pictures in your mind that the audience easily sees, they sit so close. You come to be so calm out there, it is more like going to bed than going out to work. It is like crawling under a quilt that my grandma Dora Keillor made for me from scraps of clothes worn by my aunts and uncles, which is soft and thin from years of sleep, which comes easily to me when I lie under a smell that goes back to my earliest times lying in bed between my mother and father.

This lovely smell is one of a broad group of delicate smells that were lost to me for twenty-four years because I was addicted to cigarettes. The sense of smell is not an intellectual sense such as sight and hearing. We have so much language to describe how things sound and look—and so few words for how things smell and feel to our touch, our animal senses—so a smart guy like me thinks he can give up smell for the pleasure of smoking. Tobacco smoke overpowers and deadens about two-thirds of a smoker's sense of smell, and a few days after I stopped, I began to notice the vast realm of smells that were lost all those years. I began breathing in a life I hadn't felt since I was seventeen, like seeing grass after a quarter-century at the South Pole.

I smelled creamed peas and onions, wood smells, dirt smells. Walked into an old garage, and a hundred smells jumped out, the spirits of a hundred old men in undershirts mixing shellac and sanding a screen door and oiling a rifle and patching an innertube. A hidden life came back to me, the ordinary days of long ago when I sat with the others and talked on the porch and had a little chow. Bushes baking in the sun, us in the cool porch. An American flag hanging from a pole, a dog, old people in cane chairs, all dead now but that day they were just tired, their feet hurt—"Boy, these dogs are killing me," but it wasn't their feet that killed them. They said, "Here, rub my feet for me, wouldja." A pitcher of cold green nectar with chunky ice cubes from ice trays. Red roses on the pitcher, green leaves, and rocks of ice floating in the roses. White wicker chairs, old people with sore feet, a dog with long hair, miserable in the heat, he sighs and crawls under the porch, and here we sit, hot and moist. This old man smells like a garage. A sweet single-minded man who works when he works and when he sits down to eat he eats, no fooling around. When he's angry he is nothing but angry for one minute and then it's over. He isn't sweet on the outside, angry inside. He says "dangblast it" and slams a door into next week. Sits down to eat, first he prays in his prayer voice, like putting on a suit ("Our Lord and Father, we would come before Thee now . . ."), and then talks in his regular voice: "So what was that you was sayin' about that friend of yours then, he knew where he could get you a Chevy engine for *how* much? Mary, get us a dishrag then, this milk is leaking outta here." All of it comes back from the smell of cut grass and fried potatoes.

When I was four years old, I fell through a hole in the haymow into the bull pen, missing the stanchion and landing in his feed trough full of hay, and was carried into the house and laid on my grandma's sofa, which smelled like this quilt, and so did a warm shirt handed down to me from my uncle. When I was little I didn't think of grownups as having bare skin; grownups were made of wool clothing, only kids were bare-naked; now I'm older than they were when I was little and I lie naked under a quilt made of their clothes when they were children. I don't know what makes me think I'm smarter than them.

Every time I read a book about how to be smarter, how not to be sad, how to raise children and be happy and grow old gracefully, I think, "Well, I won't make *those* mistakes, I won't have to go through that," but we all have to go through that. Everything they went through, we'll go through. Life isn't a vicarious experience. You get it figured out and then one day life happens to you. You prepare yourself for grief and loss, arrange your ballast and then the wave swamps the boat.

Everything they went through: the loneliness, the sadness, the grief, and the tears—it will all come to us, just as it came to them when we were little and had to reach up to get hold of their hand, when we knew them by the shape of their legs. Aunt Marie had fat little legs, I held her hand one cold day after a blizzard, we climbed snowdrifts to get to the store and buy licorice whips. She said, "Come on, we can make it, don't slip," and soon she was far behind, a fat lady in a heavy coat with a fur collar, leaning into the wind, wheezing from emphysema, and sometime later she died. She knew that death was only a door to the kingdom where Jesus would welcome her, there would be no crying there, no suffering, but meanwhile she was fat, her heart hurt, and she lived alone with her ill-tempered little dogs, tottering around her dark little house full of Chinese figurines and old *Sunday Tribunes*. She complained about nobody loving her or wanting her or inviting her to their house for dinner anymore. She sat eating pork roast, mashed potato, creamed asparagus, one Sunday at our house when she said it. We were talking about a trip to the North Shore and suddenly she broke into tears and cried, "You don't care about me. You say you do but you don't. If I died tomorrow, I don't know as you'd even go to my funeral." I was six. I said, cheerfully, "I'd come to your funeral," looking at my fat aunt, her blue dress, her string of pearls, her red rouge, the powder on her nose, her mouth full of pork roast, her eyes full of tears.

Every tear she wept, that foolish woman, I will weep every one before I'm done and so will you. We're not so smart we can figure out how to avoid pain, and we cannot walk away from the death that we owe.

My uncle Lew was the storyteller of my family, who loved to drive his big Chrysler around and visit with us and talk about the old days. He drove it right up into his nineties, when he finally wore out and died. I have a picture of him and me from years ago when I had a beard, sitting together on folding chairs in a front yard eating hotdish off paper plates, he is leaning toward me and saying, "I remember when our house burned in Charles City, Iowa, it was the first cold day of fall, and I was in the third grade, home from school, sick with the gripes in the big bed, looking at Mother's photo album and the smoke and flames come out of the damper on the stove and we both dropped everything and ran for our lives, I dropped the pictures and afterward Mother said, 'It's all right, it's all right, we can get along without pictures, we still have each other,' but she was crying and I felt so bad, they were gone and it was my fault. Some of those pictures were of Mother's family, her old aunts who had died—a picture was all she had left. We stood looking at the ashes of our house and Dad raking through them for those photographs. She said, 'Oh well, we'll see them in Heaven,' and I stood and bawled. . . ." He told this story so well that he made himself feel bad all over again and he had to stop and wipe away a tear.

These stories are not about my family, and yet I hope they carry on our family tradition of storytelling and kitchen talk, the way we talk and what we talk about. I believe in reincarnation only as we may experience it through our children; I hope my parents recognize themselves in me, just as I see myself in the tall young man upstairs playing the blues on his pink electric guitar; and I hope that our old radio show lives on in the homes of a few people who recognized the people in the stories. We had to stop short of the destination we dreamed of and we have to look to others to cross those mountains that stopped us and make the home that we tried so hard to reach.

Our people aimed for Oregon
When they left Newburyport—

Great-grandma Ruth, her husband John,
But they pulled up in Wobegon,
Two thousand miles short.

It wasn't only the dangers ahead
That stopped the pioneer.
My great-grandmother simply said,
"It's been three weeks without a bed.
I'm tired. Let's stay here."

He put the horses out to graze
While she set up the tent,
And they sat down beside their blaze
And held each other's hand and gazed
Up at the firmament.

"John," she said, "what's on your mind
Besides your restlessness?
You know I'm not the traveling kind,
So tell me what you hope to find
Out there that's not like this?"

The fire leaped up bright and high,
The sparks as bright stars shone.
"Mountains," he said. "Another sky.
A green new land where you and I
Can settle down to home.

"You are the dearest wife to me.
Though I'm restless, it is true,
And Oregon is where I'd be
And live in mountains by the sea,
But never without you."

They stayed a week to rest the team,
Were welcomed and befriended.
The land was good, the grass was green,

And slowly he gave up the dream,
And there the journey ended.

They bought a farm just north of town,
A pleasant piece of rolling ground,
A quarter-section, mostly cleared;
He built a house before the fall;
They lived there forty years in all,
And by God persevered.

And right up to his dying day
When he was laid to rest,
No one knew—he did not say—
His dream had never gone away,
He still looked to the west.

She found it in his cabinet drawer:
A box of pictures, every one
Of mountains by the ocean shore,
The mountains he had headed for
In the state of Oregon.

There beside them lay his will.
"I love you, Ruth," the will began,
"And count myself a well-loved man.
Please send my ashes when I die
To Oregon, some high green hill,
And bury me and leave me lie
At peace beneath the mountain sky,
Off in that green and lovely land
We dreamed of, you and I."

At last she saw her husband clear
Who stayed and labored all those years,
His mountains all uncrossed.
Of dreams postponed and finally lost,

Which one of us can count the cost
And not be filled with tears?

And yet how bright those visions are
Of mountains that we sense afar,
The land we never see:
The golden west and golden gate
Are visions that illuminate
And give wings to the human heart
Wherever we may be.
That old man by dreams possessed,
By Oregon was truly blessed
Who saw it through the eye of faith,
The land of his sweet destiny:
In his eye, more than a state
And something like a star.

I wrote this poem in Oregon,
Wanting the leaden words to soar
In memory of my ancestor
And all who lie along the way.
God rest their souls on a golden shore,
God bless us who struggle on:
We are the life that they longed for,
We bear their visions every day.

Leaving Home

A Trip to
Grand Rapids

It has been a quiet week in Lake Wobegon. It was chilly on Tuesday and Wednesday, as a cold front moved through, and the tomato growers stayed up late debating whether to cover plants for frost or not. "Naw," they decided about ten o'clock, and hit the hay and lay thinking about it: the humiliation of getting froze out, the shame of eating store-bought tomatoes, or, worse, going on tomato relief. "Here, Clarence, have a couple bushels of these—we got plenty. No, really. Bud covered ours that night in June, of course, when it froze—you remember—it was that night, you could tell by the birch leaves it was going to get below freezing . . . you didn't know that?"

It rained Wednesday night. Roger Hedlund lay worrying about his unplanted corn and thinking about his daughter Martha's new black kitten. Roger had laid down the law that a cat stays outdoors, even when it's cold: That's what it has fur for, put it outside, it'll take care of itself. She looked up at him, pleading. He said, "Now. Just do it." She put the kitten out. On her way upstairs she whispered, "Murderer." He heard her. When he went up to bed, he heard the kitten crying on the back step. Well, he thought, it'll go away. It cried pitifully and then it did go away, and after a while he went out to look for it. "Kittykittykittykitty." He walked naked except for his long T-shirt, barefoot across the cold wet grass, his big dog, Oscar, with him. He pulled the T-shirt down to make himself decent, and thought he heard the kitten under the house. Bent over to look, and Oscar sniffed him. Roger jumped straight into the side of his house, hitting the faucet with his thigh. He groaned and sat down in the grass. "*Ohhhhhh.*" And saw the flashlight. "Dad?" she said. "Dad? Is that you?"

"Go back to bed," he said, "everything is all right." But his voice sounded funny, like a man who'd run into a faucet. "What's wrong, Dad? Are you all right?"

No, he wasn't. Much later he was not so bad, after the pain subsided and he had a shot of bourbon, but he wasn't all right. He lay awake listening for the kitten. He fell asleep, and in his dreams something chased him to hell and back—it might have been a cat. In the morning the kitten came back. Martha said, "Don't you think it'd be less trouble if we kept him in the house? Then you wouldn't have to get up in the middle of the night and go find him, Dad. You see, if you keep something—" "All right," he said. "—if you keep something indoors, then you know where it is." "All right," he said, "we'll try it and see how it works."

Thursday night he was glad the kitten was in. It rained buckets, one of those summer thunderstorms when the sky turns black and clouds boil up and the wind blows the grass flat. Trees bend in half and sheets of rain fall like in the Old Testament, and then it's over.

The wind took hold of the Quaker State oil sign at Krebsbach Chev, the one that hung on the Pure Oil sign, and ripped it from the bracket and whipped it down Main Street like a guillotine. It sliced into the ground in front of the Unknown Norwegian and buried itself halfway in. When it came whistling down the street, Mr. Lundberg had just emerged from the Sidetrack Tap to make sure his windows were rolled up. The wind almost bowled him over, and then he heard a hum like a UFO and ran inside. It was the sign whizzing past so fast he only saw a blur, it could've cut someone in two. Such as him, for example. He is a hefty man and half of him would be almost as much as all of just about anyone else you could think of, but that sign would've done the job. It had not been a good week for him anyway, and then to get sliced in two on top of it—not a week you'd care to live through again.

Tuesday night a chunk of plaster fell from the bedroom ceiling, crashing on the bureau dresser and waking him and Betty out of a sound sleep. It was a chunk they have noticed for two years— first its outline, shaped like the state of Illinois, then the shadows where it pulled away from the lath. The force of gravity being what it is, it was clear what would come next, and they both looked up and said, "Looks to me like that plaster's coming off." So when it finally fell on the bureau, there were recriminations on her part, after they got over the scare. They lay in the dark, little bits of plaster falling, and she said, "If you'da just done it when you said you were going to." He knew better than to reply. She said, "I kept telling you to."

He lay, smelling the perfume on the bureau that got busted by the chunk. A dozen different perfumes, sickening, and when he opened the window, the wind blew all the perfumes directly at him. She said, "But oh no, you wouldn't listen to me, would you. Oh no. You wouldn't listen to me for one minute."

He lay and listened to her, remembering the awful nights out when she wore the perfume he bought her, such as the Sons of Knute Syttende Mai Ball, which he spent in a suit at least three sizes too small for him. He was too proud to have it let out, although it meant he couldn't dance, couldn't sit, had to stand, and when he dropped his wallet he had to kick it into a closet and close the door and ease himself down so he could pick it up, but when he eased back up, his pants split anyway, and then he could only stand in certain areas.

She said, "Well, maybe you'll listen to me the next time. I'm not wrong about everything, you know."

The perfumes were gifts from him, bought at K Mart in Saint Cloud for anniversaries and birthdays, in a panic at the last min- ute, him sneaking over to Notions while she was in Women's Wear and asking the clerk to give him something nice. He should have known, looking at the clerk, that her taste wasn't right on the mark. She looked like someone he played football with, except she piled her hair up high on her head and sprayed it to stay, so when she gave him a bottle of Nuits de Oui, he might've guessed it wasn't what Betty would wear. Smelling the perfumes made him think what a dope he was, and he couldn't even fix a ceiling before it fell either.

He lay in the dark thinking it over. Her last words were "And you can clean it up too." At six-thirty he got up and made toast and coffee and brought it up to her in bed. To confuse her. Then he got the vacuum out. He picked up the big pieces and the broken bottles, vacuumed the plaster bits and dust on the floor and under the radiator and on the bureau, as she sat and drank her coffee, speechless. He swooshed around with the vacuum, a new Japanese-made model more powerful than what he was used to, and it sucked up some money off the bureau, including a few quarters that banged around in its bowels, and it almost swallowed a picture of Donny Lundberg. As he rescued Donny from the vacuum's maw, it ate a tiny plastic bottle of superglue that clattered around inside it and then made a popping sound. He felt something wet on his bare foot. He wiped it off with his hand. Then it dawned on him that it was superglue. He said, "Oh for dumb," and clapped his hand to his forehead.

He was in that pose when Betty drove him to the hospital: *The Thinker*, hand to his forehead. He remained in serious thought until the nurse found the correct solvent and sat with a Q-tip and slowly pried his hand loose from his forehead and the bedspread from his foot. He had gotten so mad about putting his hand to his forehead, he kicked the bed with his sticky foot, and the spread came along attached to his ankle.

The hand-forehead separation, the bedspreadectomy, were carried out with professional gravity befitting an open-heart operation. Betty drove him home without a word about anything except the rainy weather and things other than getting stuck to yourself, but still he had to go to work at the Co-op elevator with an angry red mark on his forehead and another on the heel of his palm. They said, "What happened to you?"

He said, "I hit myself in the head with my fist."

"Boy, you hit pretty hard."

"Yeah, I guess I don't know my own strength."

It was a week when a person would rather not be sliced in half, because you'd want your family to remember you as a better man than what you were most recently.

The rain was good news for lawns and gardens; some of them turned so green, you look at them and see green for the rest of the day—your kids look green, your food, even your thumb.

Some kids turned green Friday night after the Junior-Senior Prom. The theme was "Caribbean Escapade," and the gym was decorated to look like a beach house under palm trees and an illuminated tropical moon. And a Plexiglas lagoon on a night in June. With a macaroon by the old spittoon. Couples of seventeen-year-olds in evening dress, dancing close, and the visions of elegance led to delusions of invincibility when the bottle was passed in the parking lot. Some kids learned that although vodka-and-apple-juice is tasteless going down, it's quite memorable on the return trip. That night, in and around town, a few sailors had to weather heavy seas. If any preachers had been awake at 3:00 A.M., they could've converted them to temperance, Methodism, Masonry, yoga, or Japanese yen; the fields were ripe for harvest.

The rain was more than farmers needed and came at the wrong time, keeping them out of the fields, and now planting is late. Farmers are in enough trouble as it is, and even if they could run the weather as they please, they still might not make it. Roger got so nervous he couldn't sit down for two minutes. He'd start to say something, jump up in the middle, look out the window, and forget what he said. Cindy said, "You're driving us crazy, let's get out of here. You can't do anything until it dries up, so let's go away and do something this weekend." He said, "You must be crazy." "No," she said, "not yet."

Leave before we get the corn in? "We'll go to Grand Rapids and stay with my sister," she said. What about Cathy and Martha? "They're old enough," she said, "it's only for a couple days." "Yeah," the girls said, "you need a break, Dad. You ought to go."

It was the eagerness in their eyes that Roger kept thinking about as he and Cindy drove north toward Grand Rapids Thursday evening, and how pleasant his girls were, how helpful as they saw their parents out to the car. "Here, Dad, let me carry that. In you go. Okay, you two have a good time and *don't worry about us*." Driving north, he could hear Cathy's voice saying, "Don't worry about us, don't worry about us," and just north of Aitkin he turned around and headed south. "Are you crazy?" Cindy said. "Yes," he said—"as the father of two teenage daughters, I'd be crazy not to be crazy."

When they turned onto the county road a half-mile east of their place, they noticed more cars than you normally see, all heading west. They came over the hill. Up ahead their house was blazing with lights. All the traffic was turning in at their driveway. They could hear the music quite clearly from the road as they cruised past. "You don't want to go in?" she said. Roger said, "I don't know. Maybe it's something we don't want to know about." "Then let's turn around and forget we ever saw this, whatever it is. God help us, I hope it isn't what I think," she said.

At the crossroad, he parked on the shoulder and they got out and looked at the farm. Across the muddy field, with so much standing water the house looked like a cruise ship with a big party on board. More cars drove up the gangplank.

"Probably it's not what we think," she said. "If we're going to trust them, then we have to trust them and not go around spying on them to see if they do what we want or not."

"I'm curious. I'm going over and see what's going on. Want to come?"

"Of course I do," she said.

It was hard going. They took off their shoes and socks and waded through mud up to their ankles, straight across the field in the dark, toward the carnival in their farmyard. Headlights, loud music:

he didn't know there were this many teenage kids in the county. They got to the edge of the windbreak. It didn't seem like their place with the music blasting. Voices screeching, drums pounding. "My gosh, they're going to kill the chickens," she said. She looked in the coop, and the chickens did look dazed. Some of the hens seemed to be turned upside down in their nests. Where was Oscar the faithful watchdog? Oscar, who goes crazy when the mailman turns around in the yard.

Roger peeked around the corner of the coop. Kids milled around, went in the house, came out. More cars pulled up, kids got out. Two kegs of beer by the back door. Kids moved around, restless, hanging around, watching other kids hanging around, watching to see if there was more fun somewhere else, boys circling, girls waiting—a lot like a party he sort of remembered from twenty-five or so years ago.

Oscar lay by the back steps, an empty beer cup by his head, his head on his paws. Some kids lit cigarettes, took long drags, big clouds of smoke. Lighting up—Roger remembered that. Kids passing their cigarettes around. That's generous, he thought. And there was his own little girl, Martha—reaching for a cigarette. No! No! he thought. *Don't.* She put it in her mouth, his sweet little daughter. Oh darling child, don't. A boy lit it and out of her sweet lips came smoke. Roger had taken two steps out from behind the coop. He wanted to run to her and yet he really didn't.

Cindy was right behind him, her hand on his back. "This is ridiculous. I can't believe they'd do this. Are we going to allow this?"

"I don't know."

"You don't? No? Well. I don't know either," she said. "I was hoping you'd know. You're always so—so—"

"Strict?"

"Yes."

"You know something?" he said. "I'm getting tired of being a dad." He didn't want to march in and be the cop, have everybody get quiet and him make a speech while sullen kids slink away cursing him under their breath. He wanted to take his lovely wife by her cool hand—Come away, come away, my love, my sweet slim darling, mother of my children, come away. . . . She said, "Look! They're tramping on my petunias."

"Come," he said.

"You're going to just walk away and leave them?"

"Yes."

"Are you sure this is right?"

"No."

He took her hand and they stepped carefully over old lumber in their bare feet and past the wreck of the old corn planter under the box-elder trees and Grandpa Steen's Model A, sunk down to the hubcaps.

"You know, that party at the gravel pit was like this," she said.

"What party?"

"Roger, honey, you know very well."

There were fast footsteps behind them, and a snarl and a bark. It was Oscar coming straight at them—"*Oscar! Good boy!*" Oscar stopped, growling. "*Oscar! Oscar—easy boy, good boy.*" Roger took a step toward him; the dog barked. He backed up and barked and barked. He followed them across the field, barking.

How strange! To spy on your own house and be chased away by your own dog and then—to find that your own car is parked too far down in the ditch, and when you put your foot on the gas to come away my love, come away my dear one, your rear end slips to the side and you're stuck. What then?

They made it to Grand Rapids at 4:00 A.M. and tumbled into bed. Before he went to sleep, he saw it all over again: his long hike back to the house, up the driveway; the silence when he came around the corner; someone shut off the tape, there was a lot of shuffling and muttered hellos, and he said, "Can somebody give us a push?" And when Martha said, "What were you doing parked on the road?" and he said, "None of your business," she said, "Oh Daddy, you didn't," and he said, "Well, I'm just human, you know," and she said, "You're so sweet. I had no idea," and smiled at him. "Huh?" he said. He said, "I meant that—you mean you thought that—you really thought that your mother and I—?" And then, after the Tollerud boy pulled them out with his old pickup, Roger had a bad feeling in his rear end: no billfold. He must've dropped it when they ran through the mud with Oscar on their tails. Maybe it was in the field, but he didn't think he'd look for it right then. He said to Cindy, "You got some money?" She said she thought that he had money. So he said to Martha, "Would you happen to have some money you could let me have until Monday?" "Hey!" she said. "My dad needs some money." They passed a hat and collected sixty dollars. "I'll pay you back!" he said to them all. "No problem, don't worry about it," they said. And the quiet ride to Grand Rapids in the middle of the night. He thought Cindy was asleep and then she said, "Sure, you remember that party, that's where we met. You were with your cousin, and he spilled beer on my pedal pushers, and you wiped it off with your hankie. I had beer running down my leg and you tried to clean it up."

Later she said: "What do you think your grandpa would have thought if he'd come home and found a hundred kids hanging around his house?" He said, "He woulda been darned surprised to be alive in 1986, I'll say that."

Her sister left a note on the door: "We went to bed. The rollaway is made in the basement, help yourself to anything in the fridge. Will wake you up at 7. XXX Gloria."

Settling down on the rollaway, he thought again: I'm getting tired of being a dad. Love my girls, but I've been a parent long enough, I did what I could. I can't go on being in charge much longer. These kids, this world, are going to continue long after I'm gone, and I should get used to that and even enjoy it. I can't run them. I can only love them and this good life.

Thank you, God, for this good life and forgive us if we do not love it enough. Thank you for the rain. And for the chance to wake up in three hours and go fishing: I thank you for that now, because I won't feel so thankful then.

Good night, my sweet wife, sweet dreams. He kissed the back of her neck and lay, full of love, and fell asleep.

A Ten-Dollar Bill

It has been a quiet week in Lake Wobegon. Senator K. Thorvaldson writes from Florida that he is coming home. He had trouble with his prostate last fall and now he's having more and he'd like Dr. DeHaven to fool with it and not somebody he doesn't know. A prostate is personal. He had to decide by March 1 whether to keep his condo for April or lose $215 in deposit, and he decided to keep it. But now he's thinking $215 is cheap, he'd rather get out of there and escape his three roommates, his cousin Frank and Frank's wife, Eunice, and their mangy spaniel, who bit him in the Greyhound bus depot one sweltering day when Senator was returning from a trip to the dog track and was groggy from the long ride. When the dog sank his teeth in his calf, the old man folded up and fell down, but Eunice said, "Oh, it's not all that bad, it's only a scratch," and gave the beast a tug and said, "Oh, Nicky. Shame." In the car driving out to the condo, she said, "It takes him a while to get used to people." That was in January.

Two weeks ago, Eunice's aunt came to stay for an unspecified length of time in the two-bedroom condo, and, without so much as a beg-your-pardon, Eunice moved Senator's clothes to the hall closet and made up the hide-a-bed for him. She said, "Aunt Louise is depressed from her blood-pressure pills, I couldn't ask her to sleep in the living room," so there he was, paying $215 a month for a couch and one-fourth of a bathroom, and enduring a surly dog, now surlier because the couch had been his bed. Aunt Louise took long hot tub baths to treat her depression, so Senator couldn't get in the bathroom until late at night, when, even if he hadn't drunk a drop of anything, he felt like his prostate was coming off at the hinges. When he got back to his bed, he heard an embittered growl from Nicky, who had crawled into it. He said "Get out!" and folded up the bed on top of the dog to get the message across. But the dog seemed satisfied with that, even pleased, and finally Senator sat on top and squeezed the dog and (probably) squeezed the dog's prostate to where he yelped and crawled out. Senator got in, but it wasn't a happy night of sleep, lying in a bed where an old dog had been. It felt damp and hairy and rank, like the floor at the bus depot. The dog lay on the carpet and ever so often he'd hoist himself up and growl in a strange, dreamy way; Senator was afraid the dog might have a dream and do some sleepwalking and sleep-biting, so he was awake most of the night, listening to the mutt's heavy stuffed-up breathing and feeling the hide-a-crossbar in the small of his back, unless he turned over onto his stomach, when it caught him right smack across the prostate.

So he's thinking of coming home early. His grandnephew Jim Tollefson was the one who got this news from him, in a letter, along with a money order for a hundred dollars for his birthday, though Jim's birthday—his eighteenth—is in July. Senator K. said, "Just in case this dog goes for my throat and I die in my sleep, I want you to have your birthday present." But really he sent it because he knows Jim's dad is such a tightwad. Every time the boy collects his allowance, Byron peels off the ten like it's the last one around. He says, "I don't know where you think this stuff comes from, but it sure doesn't grow on trees, I'll tell you that."

There is a photograph on the wall over Byron's chair of a husband and wife perched on white kitchen chairs in a dirt yard in front of a sod house, and eight children, one tall boy with shoes on and five little barefoot kids and twins, a boy and a girl, on their mother's lap. On *his* lap the father holds a portrait of a girl who died a year before of influenza. Next to the tall boy is his dog, who jerked his head as the lens opened, and so in the picture he has two heads, and there is a cow grazing on the roof. It was the summer of 1876. In August the twins perished of diphtheria. To look at the parents, you might guess their ages as late fifties, but Karl is twenty-eight and Sophie is two years younger. He is her second husband, the first (who was the tall boy's father, Bjorn) died six years before. Sophie was Bjorn's second wife, the first (the tall boy's mother) having died in childbirth. The tall boy is Jim's great-grandfather, Jacob. The youngest ones in the family have no blood relation to the oldest. You can see from the picture where people got their philosophy that life is hard.

"Dad," Jim says, "I need some money." It's after supper, his dad is eating a bowl of ice cream.

"What do you need money for? I gave you money a couple weeks ago."

"I spent it."

"What for?"

"Things. You know."

"No, I don't know. Tell me."

He bent over the kitchen table, clearing the dishes. "Well, I went out with some people and we went into Saint Cloud and we went to a movie and we had pizza."

"Pizza! I buy food for the house and then you want me to pay so you can go out to restaurants—?"

"Well, there were ten of us, so we couldn't very well eat here."

"Who were they?"

"Just some kids from school."

"Don't they have names? Or you ashamed of who you're keeping company with?"

"No."

"I don't see why you expect me to fork over cash every time you decide you want some—"

It was a ballet, not a movie and pizza, that Jim had gone to with his friend Stanglund and Stanglund's girlfriend, Susie, driving to Minneapolis and back on Tuesday night. A memorable night. It cost almost the entire hundred dollars. His down jacket was shorter than his sportcoat, which looked dumb. He pronounced ballet "ballot" and tried to convince Susie he'd been to numerous ballots—"What kind of dancing do they do?" she asked. "Oh, a lot of different dancing. Different styles. You know. Spanish and French, Italian, Mexican." The ballet was good. He sat in the dark and never took his eyes off it. One ballet after another, short ballets, and the lights came up and people clapped. He didn't know how much to clap, so he did what the people behind him did, though they didn't like it as much as people ahead who shouted and whistled. The people behind said, "They don't have the sense of line they used to." Everything he saw went into his memory whole. One dance: a man in black tights, a woman in tights and skirt; when they danced together, the way he held her and lifted her and she arched her long back, and the way when he danced by himself, so alone—so graceful and full of tears—he took three steps and a tremendous leap and hung in air and you saw his face so clear, illuminated by grief, and then he vanished.

"Why can't you look at me when you talk to me? What's the matter with you?"

He looked at his father's forehead.

"When I was your age, I sure never went looking for a handout and I'll tell you why—because I knew that the world does not owe you a living. Do you know that?"

Jim said that, yes, he did know that, but Byron wasn't sure. He peeled off the ten and talked more about having a sense of responsibility. A young cat sat on the chair next him, fascinated by the ten-dollar bill that swooped overhead when Byron, gesturing broadly, said, "My father never woulda put up with one-half of what I put up with from you, not for one minute." The green bird fluttered and the cat crouched.

"There was discipline then, I'll tell you, and a willingness to sacrifice, to wait for what you wanted, not to have everything handed to you right away on a silver plate." The bird dove and fluttered and the cat—waiting for what he wanted, not expecting it to come on a silver plate—tensed for the leap, winding his mainspring, as the bird flung itself through the air. "I don't know how many times I have to say this before you finally get it through your head—" Byron shrieked.

It was a tremendous leap for a little cat. He hung in mid-air and then hung on to the man's hand—and then flew, catapulted halfway across the room, landing perfectly on his feet, to dash away into the dark.

Easter

I**t has been a quiet week in Lake Wobegon.** The children are back to school after a riotous week of Easter break. The weather was so lovely when the children were released from confinement, the fresh air went to their heads. Air has a different effect on children: what we merely breathe, children are ignited and launched by. At Our Lady on Sunday morning, Father Emil felt as if he was speaking to a convention of rabbits instead of the usual herd of turtles. Constant movement in the pews. The homily was on new life and it was all around to be seen.

When I was a kid, we sat quietly on Sunday morning sometimes for forty or fifty seconds at a stretch. Fidgety kids were put between two grownups, usually your parents or sometimes a large aunt. Like tying a boat to a dock. Every time you moved they'd grab your shoulder and give you a sharp shake and hiss at you, *Sit*. Death will be like that. I'll be in bed and think, "Well, I think I'll get up and live a little," and death will grab me, shake me, say, "Shhhh. Be quiet. Lie still." I used to think about death on Sunday morning. How hard it would be to lie in your coffin for years with nothing to read, nothing to do, but some grownups I knew probably could manage quite well.

Some former children returned for Easter, bringing their children with them, and some children were shipped earlier to spend the week with grandparents, some of whom are starting to recover to the point where they can sit in a chair and sit back all the way, not lean forward ready to jump when they hear the crash. The grandparents imagined the kiddos leaning against them on the sofa listening to Uncle Wiggily: they forgot how explosive kids can be. Something in the air sets them off. A kid can go all day and hardly eat, then the moon shifts and he's eating like a farmhand. You served baked horse and he eats all of it. Children can lie around for a long time, then a herd of them bursts in the front door and gallops through the kitchen and outside. Children are always on the verge of bursting. They burst six, seven times a day and think nothing of it.

Virginia Ingqvist had two grandkids with her last week, Barbara's two oldest, Doug and Danielle. Hjalmar worked late at the bank. He loves them, but he knows his limit, and it's about thirty minutes. One is four and the other five, an age when you want to find out everything in one day. "Why don't buildings fall?" asked Doug two minutes after he arrived. "Because," Virginia explained, "because they're built to stand." "How?"

Thirty seconds, and already she was into architecture, and knew that biology and astronomy and physics were coming right up. Then theology. "Who's God?" "God is God." "Yeah, but who?" It's never a subject you know something about, such as etiquette.

Barbara came up on Friday with her two-year-old and took all three of them to her friend Ruthie's house to visit. Ruthie has three of her own. Her three and Barbara's three sniffed each other for a moment and then two cats made the mistake of coming around the corner of the house into the backyard. The cats realized it was a mistake and backed away, saying, Uh, sorry, didn't know you were here. We'll come back later. But the kids grabbed them, hauled them indoors, got them dressed and into a doll buggy, two little cat children. The cats went limp, waiting for a chance to break out, which they did—two cats in full regalia, one up the tree, one on the garage roof, trying to remove their clothes, five children in pursuit, and the two-year-old investigating the back porch.

Barbara and Ruthie sat in the yard talking about child rearing. Barbara's philosophy is more relaxed than her mother's, less restrictive, a hands-off approach, allowing children freedom to explore and find their own boundaries. As she said this, she watched the little boy climb the porch steps, stand at the top, turn around, and when he took a step forward straight out into space, she leaped up and made a dash for him, too late to catch him, but she almost stepped on his head. When she scooped him up, she came close to spraining his neck. A major cause of injury to children is parents rushing to the scene. The panic reflex. Some children love to scream for the thrill of making immense people move fast. I remember that, on a quiet day, my sister and I in the backyard wondered, "Where's Mom?" Upstairs, we thought. So I screamed, "*MOM*." She made it down in two seconds. A good pair of wheels for an old lady.

Grandma Tollefson turns off her hearing aid when descendants are around, so a crash is only a whisper to her, boys thundering around upstairs are a distant tapping. One afternoon a sound came out of her house like jets taking off, her grandson practicing his guitar. She was there, knitting, rocking, saying to him, "You know, there was a boy I knew who played the guitar—what was his name? Oh dear. He moved away in 1921, I think. He played his guitar on his porch, and I sat in our porch and listened. I don't think he knew. The screens were so dark, and I could hear him so clear, just like I can hear you. I was in love with him for a whole summer and he didn't know it." Kevin didn't hear a word she said, and she didn't know the music was blowing her hair back.

Selective ignorance, a cornerstone of child rearing. You don't put kids under surveillance: it might frighten you. Parents should sit tall in the saddle and look upon their troops with a noble and benevolent and extremely nearsighted gaze.

The Buehler boy celebrated a birthday last night and ten of his closest friends came over for a party. They danced to alarming music and ate an alarming amount of pizza and told alarming jokes and there were periods of alarming dead silence, which the Buehlers heard from the kitchen, where they remained in quarantine. They whomped up armloads of chow, and passed it to their son, who carried it to his guests. Stayed in the kitchen for five hours, except for one trip to the bathroom, averting their eyes, and the mister snuck up front once to have a look, and when he looked he wished he hadn't. He was dying of curiosity. The party was so quiet and then burst into laughter, and then silence and then whispering and screams of laughter. He tiptoed down the hall and peeked and saw they were huddled over the Buehlers' wedding album. Nineteen fifty-nine was a funnier year than he had realized and he was a little hurt. He was quite handsome then in those half-rim glasses, his hair carefully oiled and combed back on the sides, like an ocean wave about to break, and piled high in front. He misses that pompadour. There's not much left where it rose from his head, a little tuft as a souvenir of what a stylish devil he used to be. He was hurt when he heard them laughing about his hair. He thought, "What are these people doing in my house? Why am I feeding them?"

Nothing you do for children is ever wasted. They seem not to notice us, hovering, averting our eyes, and they seldom offer thanks, but what we do for them is never wasted. We know that as we remember some gift given to us long ago. Suddenly it's 1951, I'm nine years old, in the bow of a green wooden rowboat, rocking on Lake Wobegon. It's five o'clock in the morning, dark; I'm shivering; mist comes up off the water, the smell of lake and weeds and Uncle Al's coffee as he puts a worm on my hook and whispers what to do when the big one bites. I lower my worm slowly into the dark water and brace my feet against the bow and wait for the immense fish to strike.

Thousands of gifts, continually returning to us. Uncle Al thought he was taking his nephew fishing, but he made a permanent work of art in my head, a dark morning in the mist, the coffee, the boat rocking, whispering, shivering, waiting for the big one. Still waiting. Still shivering.

Corinne

It has been a quiet week in Lake Wobegon. Senator K. Thorvaldson arrived home from Florida on Tuesday morning. He wanted to come sooner but he was flying on a special low rate for old Norwegian bachelors and the ticket had complicated restrictions, so he could only fly on a Monday or a Thursday after sunset by way of Dallas, Texas. In Dallas he got bumped and his bag went to Phoenix. He got on a later plane that sat at the gate for an hour and a half, so the trip took eleven hours, and when the old man landed in Minnesota at 8:45 A.M., most of the Christian patience and good humor were drained out of him. When Corinne Ingqvist picked him up at 9:30, he was mumbling to himself. "What's the matter?" she said. "You look like you're about to shoot somebody."

She looked fresh and lovely. She had come from teaching her poetry class. She is Senator K.'s second-niece once removed on his mother's side of his father, she lives near the airport, and she was going up to Lake Wobegon anyway to ask her father for a loan.

They got in her red VW and headed north on Lyndale Avenue,

through the city of Minneapolis, and he said he would never patronize that airline again or speak to anyone else who did. They coasted along the West River Road, through the cornfields and truck farms, the long plots of rich black dirt plowed toward the Mississippi, and saw a girl and her father trotting down a road on two black horses. In Anoka they turned left onto Highway 10. She stopped for ice-cream cones at Santa Claus Land and by Monticello he was cooling down. Through Saint Cloud he was telling her how young and beautiful she looks and if she's been waiting all these years for him, she shouldn't wait any longer.

She said, "What happened to that lady from Maine you were in love with?" She turned and looked at him. "Are you going to marry her or not?" He said, "Keep your eyes on the road. You're the pilot, I'm the copilot, I'm the one who gets to look at scenery."

He said, "Look at that. The Holiday Inn sign says 'Congratulations Myrna and Marvin.' You don't think that could be your cousin Marvin, do you? He still lives in Tulsa, I thought. So why would the Holiday Inn here know about him? But I suppose maybe he's traveling and he's a guest here tonight. But I thought his wife's name was Marcie, so why would it say Myrna and—unless he's traveling with another woman, of course! But then why would they say 'Congratulations'? It doesn't seem to me like the sort of thing that a national motel chain should be encouraging, does it, Corinne?"

"You go right ahead and have your fun," she said. "And someday you're going to need my advice in matters of the heart, and I may not be there to give it to you. So tell me. You going to ask her to marry you or not?"

"I already asked," he said, "and now it's up to her, I guess. Funny, when I was young I thought a lot about love, thought too much—at least I think I did. I loved so many women, all so splendid and lovely, and I thought about each one and how she might not be the one for me, and eventually convinced myself. Now I'm older and wiser, I finally fell in love and didn't think about it, just asked her to marry me, and now she's thinking about it."

The sky was turning dark with clouds as they drove north. She put her foot on the brake and veered left onto the turnoff toward Lake Wobegon. The turnoff is just before a sharp bend in the highway and when you brake for the turn, you think of the speeding truck that might leap from the bend and roll you flat as a pancake. This turn might be your last. You brake and at the last moment you hit the gas and swerve left, as if crossing a forbidden border. Where the county road leaves the highway, there's a dip in the road and a bump that lets you know you're back in the land of where you come from. You hit the bump and see George Washington's face on the schoolroom wall and hear the Nicene Creed, "I believe in one God the Father Almighty, Maker of heaven and earth, and of all things visible and invisible," and smell tunafish casserole.

Corinne doesn't believe in God, but there is some evidence to show that God believes in her. She has a gift to teach, a sacred gift. Fifteen years in dreary bluish-green classrooms, pacing as she talks, this solid woman carries a flame. She cares what she says, if it is precisely truthful and if it can be heard correctly; her dark eyes flash, her hands flutter, she lifts her head and stands on tiptoe to give the sentence coming out of her mouth a little more arc. Now she is driving home to do research on her dad. She wants him to loan her fifty thousand dollars to buy a house. Hjalmar is president of First Ingqvist State Bank, and he and his daughter have had their differences. Some of their arguments made the glasses rattle in the pantry and the family dog cringe behind the couch.

"So how's your dad doing?" Senator asked as they came over the hill and around the curve into town. She said, "He looks a lot older all of a sudden. He's got me worried. He's so stubborn, he won't see a doctor." Senator is a year older than Hjalmar. He sat up straight. "Anyway, I hope he gives me this loan. If he doesn't, I'm going to marry some rich old man—some rich old black man—some rich old black gay man—and buy the house next door to him."

Past the grain elevators and over the tracks and into town they cruised, past the traffic light, flashing amber, and she dropped him at his sister-in-law's little green house. "Good luck, goodbye, God bless you," he said, and ducked his head and trudged up the walk toward bed.

Hjalmar was waiting for her in his office, sitting in his swivel chair, his skinny old legs up on his desk, the pink socks and two-tone shoes. His thin white hair was combed across his old pink head. She pushed the application across the desk and he studied it. "Is all of this, what you list here, is that *credit-card* debt? Mmmm-hmmmm. You made a mistake here—nine times eight is seventy-two, not twenty-seven." He swung his legs down and sat up. "Is this all your income? Mmmm-hmmmm. I thought I gave you some bonds about five years ago."

"I sold them."

"Mmmmmm. Emergency?"

"No, I went to France for the summer. Remember?"

No, he didn't. *You sell bonds to go to France? It doesn't make sense, does it? You sell bonds to buy other bonds. Bonds don't have anything to do with France. To go to France you save money in a Vacation Savings Account, you don't sell your securities to take a trip.*

He grunted, *hnnnh.* "What's this house like?"

"It has big windows across the front of the living room," she said, smiling beautifully. "Actually, it's like one big window that looks down the hill toward the river. Actually, the hill is two hills, with a big lawn between, like a terrace. There's an old stone water tank by the house, a handsome stone tower like something the Romans might have built except newer. It's covered with vines, and birds nest there. Toward the road is a field, already fenced in almost, I could keep a horse there. There are eight or ten magnificent oak trees. It's peaceful and gorgeous. The river flows by—"

"How old is the furnace?" She didn't know. "How about the plumbing? Good water pressure? How old is the roof? Any leakage in the basement?" The house was in reasonably good shape, she thought. It wasn't sound plumbing that attracted her to it, however. "Of course not," he said.

"So? Do I pass?" she asked.

"Well, I don't know," he said, "I have to make sure it's a good loan." He hesitated. He had the check in his pocket, made out to her. He intended to give it to her. He was unsure of his timing. Should he seem more reluctant? Was he being too easy on her? Would she respect him more if he made her wait until tomorrow?

"I guess I could try a bank in the Cities," she offered.

"It's too late to take your business elsewhere," he said. "I'm your father. It's too late to shop for another one." He gave her the check. A personal check for fifty thousand. "Pay me back when you can," he said, the old smoothie. He offered his hand. They shook hands. And he took her out to lunch. Meat loaf, whipped potatoes, string beans, bread, and tapioca pudding—a lunch you can seal a bargain on and know it'll stay sealed.

A Glass of
Wendy

It *has been a quiet week in Lake Wobegon.*
It was awfully quiet Tuesday when the news got out that Father
Emil is stepping down as pastor after forty-some years at Our
Lady of Perpetual Responsibility. He didn't mean to announce it
until further on into Lent, afraid people might slack off with a
lame-duck priest, but the DeMolay was going around selling garden seeds on Tuesday to send themselves to summer camp and
Father Emil, always a great customer of theirs, said, "Boys, I
won't be planting a garden this spring," and they went home and
told their parents. In Lake Wobegon, if a person doesn't plan to
garden in the spring, they plan to be planted themselves. Margaret
Krebsbach called him up and said, "You're not putting in a garden;
what's wrong?" He said, "I'm retiring on the 31st of March, the
day after Easter."

"Oh," she said, "you're just tired. You feel bad, you need a
vacation. You can't leave us." "You know," he said, "this last
January I baptized the child of a girl who is the child of a couple
I married. Three generations is about enough. When I get to
where I'm burying people I baptized, I don't know but what I'll

get confused and mix em up." He said, "People here need some-body who's got all his marbles, because, God knows, a lot of them don't. So it's time to retire."

Margaret told her mother-in-law, Myrtle, and then the news spread across town within an hour. Myrtle is one of the mass media. Father Emil retiring—amazing news: a man there so long, like part of the landscape, a work of architecture, a tree, in a town where tradition is important and sometimes all that we have. To think of him being gone—it's hard to imagine. Even if you're not Catholic, and here, if you're not Catholic, you're *absolutely* not Catholic. We don't go in for nondenominationalism and tolerance. In the Bible we don't find the word "maybe" so much, or read where God says, "On the other hand, uh, there could be other points of view on this." So we go in for strict truth and let the other guy be tolerant of us. But even if you're not Catholic, in a town like Lake Wobegon, when the priest clears his throat, the dogs stop barking. When the priest walks down the street, every-body's quiet.

Clarence Bunsen stopped by to visit him. Clarence had been in the Cities over the weekend, attending a Ford dealers' banquet where Bunsen Motors got a plaque as one of the oldest Ford agencies in Minnesota. It was a seventeen-pound bronze plaque you could put on your front step and use for a boot scraper. Clar-ence said, "I don't know why I went or why I brought it back, I hate to die and leave this junk for my kids to think about. We got a wallful of plaques for being one of the oldest, and as long as we stay around we'll get more of them. To me they're no more at-tractive than a concrete block. I know that when I'm dead my kids are going to want to heave this junk into a hole but they'll feel guilty, so they'll keep it in a box somewhere and pass it on to their kids. Damn souvenirs are like mercury in the bloodstream, except they're hereditary too. You suffer from it and then give it to your kids."

"Oh I don't know," said Father Emil, "it may be ugly to you but tastes change. . . ." He knew it wasn't true: he only said it in his pastoral capacity. He squinted at the plaque. It was ugly all right. "I hope they're not going to give me one of these," he said.

"We'll give you a trip to Florida."

"Why not Jamaica?"

"I don't think old priests are supposed to go farther south than Florida. Unless they're missionaries, of course."

"Then maybe the parish would send me to Florida, and you Lutherans could pay the freight from there to Jamaica and I could be a Lutheran missionary."

"You'd make a good one, Father. You sure have the intelligence for it. With your background, we could probably train you in a couple of years."

Father Emil smiled a sweet tolerant smile. "Being a Lutheran is my idea of a vacation," he said. "I can't imagine anything more relaxing. To take those truths that are too hard for you and change them a little to make it easier on yourself—just like, if you're tired of falling down, you turn down the force of gravity—I tell you, Luther was a great man all right."

On the way home Clarence dropped in at the Sidetrack to see if Wally was there. Wally was, of course. Being the proprietor, he had to be. He said, "Clarence, what can we get you?"

"Oh nothing for me, Wally. I just dropped in to see if you were here."

"Of course I'm here. Where else would I be?"

"Well, I wanted to make sure. But as long as I'm here, I might as well have a beer."

"You want a Wendy?"

"Of course I want a Wendy. What else would I have?"

"Just wanted to make sure."

Saint Wendell's beer, brewed by the Dimmers family at the old Dimmers Brewery in nearby Saint Wendell's for five generations, since their ancestor evaded the selective-service system of the Prince of Prussia and fled to the New World. He also skipped out on some debts in the process and broke the hearts of three young women who had the impression they would become Mrs. Dimmers as soon as he paid his debts and finished military service. The young rounder came to Minnesota and became rich and distinguished making beer. He thought at first of calling it Dimmers beer but listened to good advice and called it Saint Wendell's. For as long as anyone remembers, men in the little taverns around Mist County have said, "Gimme a Wendy," and some bartenders don't ask, they just give you a Wendy, and if you say, "I didn't ask for that," they say, "Where'd you say you were from?"

"I don't believe I said."

"Good. I don't want to know."

Wendy's is the beer a man drinks because it is the best. It's made from the deep wellwater from the town of Saint Wendell's, there's no water like it. People from all over the world have said so: it's good water. Saint Wendell's has a municipal faucet, and people drive up with a trunk full of plastic bottles and get a month's supply. A Frenchman came and got two gallons and took it home. This is true. French customs wasn't going to let him take it through, but then they tasted it and said "Ahhhhh," and those men were French, and the French make great water themselves. Wendy's is made from it, using an old German recipe, by people who have worked for Dimmers Brewery so long they don't remember if they were hired or if they took a vow. The old brick brewery was supposed to resemble a Bavarian castle, but when it was built, in 1879, bricklayers had beer rights: there was two-fisted day-long drinking on the job. When the layers got on high scaffolding, it made them dizzy. So the building starts out to be a castle and rises royally for two stories and then it quits and becomes a sort of barn. The bricks for the towers were used to make a brick road because the layers felt more comfortable on their hands and knees. The brick road is a hundred feet wide for about seventy-five feet and then it's seventy-five feet wide for one hundred feet and then it becomes a path.

You think of this as you sit in an old dim bar and drink a Wendy, and you think of how the beer wagons kept rolling in Saint Wendell's through Prohibition. They trained the horses to make the deliveries, and these smart Percherons memorized complicated beer routes—stop here, skip two houses, stop there—and when they stopped, a guy ran out of the house and grabbed his beer.

The horses didn't make change but they did everything else, but of course if a horse got on the sauce himself, he might get mixed up, but usually they did the job and if the sheriff came, all he found was a wagon and a horse with red eyes and bad breath.

A man thinks of the Dimmerses' history when he drinks a Wendy, especially the first Dimmers, who ran away from responsibility, shirked his duty to his country, reneged on his debts, seduced women and lied to them—but, hey, who's perfect? Those are the very sins a man goes into a tavern to contemplate committing.

You think of history while sitting in a bar unchanged in your lifetime, and you feel peaceable: the long mirror, the neon beer signs, the old oak back bar with glass doors and columns and dark figures (angels or trolls) at the top, brooding, and below them the Minnesota Twins scoreboard (that's what they're brooding about) and the old Swancrest radio, the fancy cut glasses in the cabinet for drinks nobody knows how to make, drinks with swizzle sticks— they don't use those here. Wally's nephew tended bar once and put ice and sweet vermouth in Mr. Berge's whiskey and said, "Here, try this." Mr. Berge didn't see the swizzle stick, though it had a big fleur-de-lis on the end. When Mr. Berge removed the fleur-de-lis from his left nostril, he bled a little, but he was peaceable. He only said, "Sonny, don't do that again unless you tell me, and then don't do it anyway. Gosh, it hurts."

In Minneapolis, you go to any hotel or shopping mall and find an English pub or a Western saloon or small-town tavern with a name like BILLY BOB'S, but the antiques come from the antique factory and the concept was developed by a design team—the city is full of new places made to look old, but those aren't the same as a joint where people have sat for fifty years, and all of them people you know. It's the difference between a lie and the truth. It's not true that Wendy's is the best beer in the world, actually it's not that good. And it gives me terrible gas. The fact that we can sit and say it's the best and defend it against superior brews is one more reason why it *is* the best, and maybe the gas helps us do that.

Father Emil appeared in the Sidetrack once, when Wally and

Evelyn celebrated their twentieth anniversary. He walked in, wished them well, had a sip of brandy, and said goodbye. That was twenty-seven years ago. Wally kept the glass and wrote *Father Emil* on it and put it on the shelf. One day he was washing glasses and left it sitting two minutes on the counter and somebody saw *Father Emil* and put in two bits, so there it sat, a collection glass, for years and years. If you told a priest joke you had to put a quarter in the glass, and for Norskie jokes, moron jokes, jokes about drunks, any bad joke, the jury at the bar assessed a fine, and so, over the years, comedy helped support the church.

"So, Clarence," Wally says. "We should go in on a gift for him— maybe some kind of a . . . What's the word I'm trying to think of?"

"A plaque."

"Yes, a plaque. We could glue the Father Emil glass onto it, and think of a humorous inscription. You're humorous. You should do it."

"Naw, we oughta send him on a trip to someplace like Jamaica. Or just send him to Jamaica itself."

"How much would that run us, do you think?"

"I don't know. Couple thousand, maybe."

"Gosh, you'd have to tell some pretty rank ones to get a couple thousand. You care for another?"

"No, I'm going to have to get on out of here, it's getting late."

The
Speeding Ticket

It *has been a quiet week in Lake Wobegon.* The only news was that Gary and Leroy gave out a speeding ticket last week, their first in a month or more. If there was a law against pokiness, they could have made a mass arrest of the entire town—people have been feeling low since the Swedish flu struck. It's the usual flu with chills, fever, diarrhea, vomiting, achiness, and personal guilt, but it's accompanied by an overpowering urge to put things in order. Before you collapse into bed, you iron the sheets. Before you vomit, you plan your family's meals for the upcoming week.

The Bakkes got back from two weeks in Florida. Jeanette said it was cold and miserable there and they almost went crazy staying with Jack's sister Judy and her husband D.J. and their four kids in their mobile home near Winter Green. D.J. smokes so much Jeanette said it was like she was smoking herself. It made her nervous and she ate more greasy food and gained six pounds and split a seam on her new red Spandex bathing suit. That depressed her, so she gained three more. The food tasted of smoke. She could smell every puff coming from Judy and D.J.'s bedroom at night, and she could hear them fighting like they were in the room with her. So Jack and Jeanette couldn't sleep. Their mattress smelled of smoke too. Judy's oldest boy worked in a supermarket until 3:00 A.M. and the youngest one sleepwalked and was a bed-wetter (as Jeanette and Jack discovered one night when he crawled in with them). On the drive home from Minneapolis, they had the bitterest fight of their eighteen-year marriage over whether it had been a good vacation or not and why, and it upset her so she started coughing and she could see *smoke* coming out of her mouth, but, she told Dorothy when she got back, that wasn't the worst of it. The worst was that she set off the metal detector in the Miami airport. So it's true what she read, that a faulty can opener makes steel filings that fall in your food. She's had the same opener since 1969. Jack's mother gave it to her, along with a sarcastic remark about cooking. Shards of steel in her tunafish, creamed corn, mushroom soup, for eighteen years: how was she supposed to know? If you can't trust your can opener, then what? Is your wastebasket going to get you? Your slippers give you a disease? (Deadly Foot & Mouth Virus Traced to Pink Scuffs, Doctors Reveal.)

"If you set off the metal detector, how'd you get on the plane?" asked Dorothy. "Oh, when I took off my cinch belt, it didn't buzz anymore, but that cinch belt never used to set off alarms. It's these filings building up that finally pushed me over the limit," Jeanette explained. "Good gosh! how could I eat for all these years and not notice pieces of steel? I must not've been chewing my food good enough."

So she ate more potatoes to try to absorb the filings, although the same magazine that warned about can openers also warns about a virus from unclean potato eyes that can cause hair loss, and now Jeanette has gained so much weight she's afraid to climb on a scale.

Jack is still mad at her. As Justice of the Peace, he married a couple last Sunday that looked so happy he told Jeanette he wanted to tell them what it was really like. "If they'da stayed around here fifteen minutes, they'da changed their minds about matrimony," he said sardonically. It was an older couple, in their fifties. They drove up during breakfast. Jeanette was still in her bathrobe. She could tell by their embarrassment that they'd come to get married. When she got them a cup of coffee and they said they were from Grand Forks, North Dakota, and she said, "Oh. That's a long way to drive, isn't it. Where'd you spend the night?" they looked down at their shoes, like teenagers. He was heavy, bald as a bowling ball, and perspiring, and she was skinny and had a little mustache, and the backs of her hands were red and flaky. Jack called up Leroy, who lives next door, to come over and witness. He said to the man, "That'll be twenty-five dollars. I always ask for it in advance because, you know, some people are in a hurry to get away. Heh heh heh heh heh." The man turned crimson and fished out the money. Leroy came over. He was sick, he said, so if he had to depart suddenly, that was why. They got married and Jeanette put on a record of Perry Como singing "True Love" and Jack said good luck to them, and out they went, another story that we'll never know the ending of.

Leroy was sick, he thought, because of exhaust fumes in the police car, a 1984 Ford. He and Gary sit in it with the engine idling and they get severe headaches. Clint Bunsen checked it and said it was perfectly all right. But Clint himself has been under the weather, so maybe he missed something. Clint is the sort who doesn't get sick until everyone else has had their turn, then if he has a day or two free he'll be sick too but not quite as much.

They had just had the car checked and resumed patrol when they gave out the speeding ticket to a green 1987 Lincoln Continental. Leroy said it was going at least sixty-five down Main Street and never even touched its brakes. Myrtle Krebsbach was about to cross the street in front of the Clinic and heard the engine whine and looked up, and a sheet of water hit her amidships. She thought it was a heart attack. Gary and Leroy tore after it, almost running into the rear end of Rollie Hochstetter's manure spreader, and it took them two miles to catch up. They pulled the Lincoln over and walked up alongside and the man rolled down the window and said, "Just a moment. I'll be right with you." He was talking on his car telephone. They had never seen one before.

They waited. Leroy stood, his arms folded, and Gary leaned

down by the window, looking in. The man was about sixty, with silvery hair and blue suit. He was talking in numerals, it was amazing, the figures he had in his head. They couldn't figure out what he was saying. A minute passed and Gary cleared his throat. "Let's go, we don't have all day," he said. But he wasn't quite as angry as he was before.

They told him what he'd done and he almost collapsed from horror. "Oh no," he said over and over, "oh my gosh—thank goodness nobody was hurt. I don't know what happened to me. I didn't even see a stop sign. I don't remember seeing stores or anything. Houses. Schools. I was concentrating on—you see, I have a carton of belostalone I'm supposed to deliver to the University of Chicago tomorrow—that's who I was talking to—but I should've been paying attention. It's my own fault. Take me in, it's all right. I'll get these drugs there some other way. It's my responsibility."

Gary rode in the Lincoln, Leroy following in the cruiser. Leroy noticed that Gary and the guy were talking pretty friendly when they arrived at the Chatterbox. They all sat down in a back booth and Leroy called Jack to come. A lynch party had gathered, including Myrtle and Dorothy, but it didn't hang him right away. It asked questions, that was its first mistake. "Who in the hell are you?" said Myrtle.

He gave them his card: Dr. Walter W. Ingersoll, Saint Luke's Biomedical Laboratory, Saint Francis, Ontario. *A Canadian!* "That's right," he said.

Leroy said, "What do you think you're doing, going sixty-five miles an hour through a town with children! You're a doctor! A doctor ought to have some sense!"

"You're absolutely right," he said, "and there is no excuse for what I did. All I can say is that I'm supposed to be at the U of Chicago hospital at eight tomorrow morning with a carton of belostalone. It's an experimental drug that we've been testing in Canada and now they're about to introduce it in America. I don't know how to explain it to you, it's kind of technical for the lay person."

Jack and Jeanette had arrived. Jeanette said, "Well, I think you'd better explain, and, you know, we're not as dumb as you might think. We know about medicine."

"Well, then, you've probably heard of the experiments with Compazine in Alaska—" Yes, she'd read a little bit about that. "Well, fine, Compazine was a chemotherapeutic drug that showed some effectiveness against myoplasmia, but it made people lose their hair, so belostalone was developed to combat that side effect, and it turned out that not only did people not lose hair, it . . . I don't know how to say this," he said, "but if Chicago knew I was telling you this, I'd lose not only my license to practice medicine but my doctorate in genetic cybernetics as well—so you have to promise . . ." They promised. "Belostalone not only prevented hair loss, it also reversed the effects of aging in every respect."

"It makes you younger?" said Jack.

"No, sir. I didn't say that. Your chronological age cannot be changed. But you don't have to show it. I'm seventy-two. But you'd think I was sixty-five, wouldn't you?"

Actually he looked more like fifty-five.

"If anyone got hold of that carton in my trunk, it would have a street value of approximately sixteen million dollars." He looked them straight in the eye. He said, "I know that what I did was terribly wrong, and I don't think I'm going to sleep well for a long time thinking about how I could've killed someone, a child. . . . There's only one way I can make it up to you, and it's wrong too, I suppose, it's stealing, but it's the lesser of two evils—I'll give you each a bottle of belostalone. It's in my trunk."

His trunk was full of blank brown cartons and a black bag and boxes marked "Fragile: Pharmaceuticals." It smelled of disinfectant, the kind you find in doctors' offices.

"How long did it take to develop this, Walter?" Gary asked, putting a big foot up on the Lincoln's bumper.

"It was found utterly accidentally," he said. "The amazing advances all come about that way. They were looking for a simple booster for spring chicks and started with root extract from Jerusalem artichokes and— This is all natural, by the way. . . ." He fished out a box of tiny glass bottles carefully packed in cotton.

He handed a bottle to each of them: Gary, Leroy, Jack, Jeanette, Myrtle, Dorothy, and Floyd, Dorothy's son-in-law, who was helping her paint the cafe. Everyone looked embarrassed. "Listen," Gary said, "we can't have you stealing these for us. Let us pay you something." Walter wouldn't hear of it, but they insisted. "At least your cost."

"Well," he said, "that's the thing, it's so expensive, medical research, these new drugs are sky-high: just the cost on this is twenty dollars a bottle."

To reverse the effects of aging, this seemed like a good deal.

They pressed their money into his hand and he gave it back and they handed it to him again but he waved them away and finally they stuck it in his shirt pocket. There it stayed. They stood by the green Lincoln and talked for a while about Canada and good fishing places up there, and finally he drove off. Only then did Leroy realize that he had never actually written Walter the ticket for speeding.

When Clarence heard the story from Leroy, he almost lost his balance and fell over. "Reverses the effects of aging!" he said. "Oh that's good. That's just about perfect. I guess we know what his monologue is going to be about this week. You boys ought to copyright this yourselves, so you can charge royalties."

Yes, they knew it themselves: they were had, in broad daylight, swindled by a smooth talker into buying twenty dollars' worth of swampwater, and they were ashamed of it, but the odd fact is that they all look better this week. Jeanette feels terrific. No more flu, and she's losing weight, and her skin color is back. Leroy's headaches have stopped. Gary had another problem from sitting too much in the patrol car, and those have cleared up too.

Jack called the University of Chicago hospital and they'd never heard of Dr. Ingersoll or belostalone, and neither had anyone in or around Saint Francis, Ontario. Who else could he call? The problem with a fake like Dr. Ingersoll is that when he does you good and you want more medicine, you don't know how to reach him. There is no place to go. A fake takes you to where you start to get well and then leaves you there, on your own.

Seeds

It has been a quiet week in Lake Wobegon. It was cloudy most of the week, and a cold wind blew in off the lake and picked up some dust off the street and blew it right in your face. You walk around in dim light carrying ten pounds of wool and look down a cold gray street lined with miserable yards and taste dust in your mouth and then get some dirt in your eyes, it brings your life to a halt. You've got to find your mother, your teacher, Sister Arvonne, to wipe your eyes, but you can barely see, standing helpless, weeping, cold; it's no wonder at that moment you think, "Albuquerque. Why didn't I think of Albuquerque? Why didn't my parents think about Albuquerque before I was born? I'd be a native Albuquerquian, or Albuquerquer. I'd be an Albuquerquite." It never gets cold and you don't grow old because you just stay young lying in the sun, oh the sky is never murky in Albuquerque.

Do Albuquerquians ever long for Minnesota? I imagine they do. I imagine they would envy us even more than they do if they knew more about us. I imagine that atheists like it fine in Albuquerque, but the ones who know God and talk to God have asked God, "God, what is your country?" And God told them, "Well, I don't like to single out one place over another, because of course there are good people everywhere, but if I had to pick one place, based on what I know, which is everything, I guess I'd have to say Minnesota." Those Albuquerquians (and God knows there must be a few of them) must want to live here in the worst way. And March is a month when you can do that.

It was a quiet week. Josh, a salesman for Inspirational Systems, visited Pastor Ingqvist's tiny office in the Lutheran annex on Wednesday, selling a worship program for Advent called "Actualizing the Child in Ourselves." Bud took the snowplow off the truck Wednesday evening, being tired of driving around with it banging up and down. He said, "It's sure to snow now, but it'll just have to melt, I'm through thinking about it."

My attitude exactly. I put away my parka in April and put on a jacket. If it turns cold, that's not my problem, I refuse to accept winter anymore. If we get a blizzard, let someone else worry about it, I won't. There comes a point where you have to stand up to reality and deny it. Rain, rain, go away, come again another day. O-U-T spells Out. When I got fed up with weeding the garden, I'd look at the weeds and say, "That's not weeds. I say that's spinach, and I say let it stay where it is."

When Ruthie had her baby out of wedlock (actually not "out" of wedlock, just not quite far enough into wedlock, about six and a half months), as the wedding approached people said, "Oh, I don't think she's heavier. She always was big-boned, you know." As if we had bones in our bellies. When the baby came, people fussed over it and said, "My, I can't believe how big it is." At eight pounds, four ounces, it was the most gigantic baby ever born two and a half months premature.

Aunt Mary Thorvaldson, the sister-in-law of Senator K., ventured downtown on Thursday, seeing the ice is gone. Senator went to Johnsville, Florida, in January to pick up seashells and suck on oranges, and he offered to take her, but she said it wouldn't look right, a widow on a trip with her brother-in-law, what would people think? For one thing, they would think she was seventy-nine and it was awfully nice of him to take her. But she stayed home.

She gets around in most weather, but she keeps off ice. When it's icy, Ralph sends one of his boys up to her little house with her groceries, but she looks forward to when the sidewalks are clear and she comes down to shop, which she likes to do every day. She brings her five or six things to the counter and Ralph rings them up and says, "Nine dollars and eighty-four cents, Mary." She looks down at the little group of things and says, "Nine eighty-four? Are you sure?"

"You got $1.19, 1.59, 2.79 twice, 1.25, and 13 cents: $9.84."

She can see all the numbers of the prices on the labels. But $9.84? For these few things? Two jars of Taster's Choice, a can of tuna, a can of pears, a can of corn, and a packet of marigold seeds. It's impossible for this to cost $9.84. She looks at Ralph. She surveys the labels. He counts the items on the register slip, and the items on the counter. But $9.84? How can that be?

Ralph has acted in this play for years. He knows his part. He waits as she goes down the list again, adding it up slowly in her head. Then Ralph says, "Ah! That should be $1.49. That's $9.74." *Well.* That's more like it. "I'm sorry. This is one of those days." She gets a quarter and a penny change. She puts the goods in her shopping bag. She walks home, feeling a little better.

Down the block, at the Feed 'N Seed, Harold has set up the old wooden bins to put seed packets in that've arrived from the Milton Seed Co. in Northrop, South Dakota. Big corn and bean packets, plain yellow envelopes, and this year he's ordered more of the packets with color pictures on them and is even hanging up green and yellow crepe paper that the Milton salesman gave him and signs saying "Festival of Gardens" and "Top Quality, Best Value." The salesman, Ritche, says this could almost double seed sales, he's seen it happen. He says to Harold, "You got to build excitement, make a visual appeal to the passer-by, and your walk-ins, you got to make them think *seeds* the minute they come through the door. Did you know that one-third of all seed sales is pure impulse? People walk in—BAM—they gotta have some seeds right now!" Mass displays, more color, and these new seed packets with the Scratch 'N Sniff pictures: they were a big hit in the test markets last year.

But seeds are all the Feed 'N Seed sells—that and feeds—so if you weren't already thinking seeds you probably wouldn't come in unless it was to hang around with Harold and talk about the basketball tournament. Anoka won, and Harold won twenty-four dollars when they did. It's spring itself that builds excitement and makes a visual appeal for the passer-by, and if prospects of spring don't excite you, probably crepe paper won't have a big effect. But Ritche believes this is going to be it, the big year, the great garden boom, when Milton triples tomato-seed sales—big growth in the carrot-and-beet sector, cucumbers up this year, beans up, pole beans way up, gross national kohlrabi, eggplant, everything up this year. Ritche is twenty-five. Already he is one of Milton's best. Richard is his name but he uses Ritche because it gets noticed. People see it, they remember you. Name recognition is important in sales.

He lives in Marshall: he and Cindy bought a town house on the edge of town; they're expecting a baby in July, and he believes that in seed sales and in his own life, things are starting to turn around. Driving on to the next call, ten, twenty, thirty miles away, he gets excited when he sees the town, its big grain elevator on the horizon. He says, "Come on. Let's go. Let's go, big team. Let's go, sales!" He's on the road for Milton six days a week, crisscrossing the district in his '78 Rambler wagon. It's full of crepe paper, Styrofoam cups, and burger cartons. The carpet is ripped and the floorboards are mulched with dirt from a hundred little towns. Old seed samples take root there. The Rambler has almost a quarter-million miles on it, and soon it'll go to a junkyard and sit. Corn and beans will grow up in it and muskmelon vines come out of the seats. All the seeds he spilled in there will blossom into a little forest of flowers on wheels, vines trailing out of it. The plants will reproduce for years. All the old seed salesmen's cars become pots for plants. And the most luxuriant ones grow on the seat where he sat. It's all waiting for spring to happen.

Chicken

It has been a quiet week in Lake Wobegon. It was cool and rainy, no good for farmers to pick corn, so some of them came and sat in the Chatterbox Cafe for a while and tried to be a comfort to each other by telling a few familiar jokes. Roger and Rollie and Harold and Virgil Berge, sitting in the back booth, began with a few clean ones about animals walking into a bar and asking for a drink, and a cannibal joke, and the pig-in-the-apple-tree joke, and the ventriloquist who spends the night at the sheep farmer's, and the one about the Norwegian trying to get into heaven. Then Harold started one about a seed salesman who was traveling through. His voice dropped as he came to the part where the lady tiptoes out to the privy in the moonlight and her dog follows her, and everyone leaned in close, and Mr. Lundberg and Bud and Russell came and huddled over the booth, waiting to be killed by this beloved old classic, and he said, "So Clarissa seen a petunia growing near the path and bent down to pick it up . . . and the dog he . . ." and Harold, who has been under a lot of pressure lately, began to slowly explode. He leaked air out of his nose and his ears. He gasped and whinnied, tears running down his face,

he grabbed on to the table, out of control, he stood up and motioned
to be let out, but they were starting to leak too and couldn't move.
He attempted to climb over them but was too weak. He tried to
say the punchline, but it wouldn't come out. So he fell down on
the floor and crawled out under the table.

Uncle Al was there, having a bite of meat loaf. He told me later,
"You know, some people only know how to tell a joke, but Harold
knows how to make people laugh."

Strange for my uncle Al to eat in a commercial establishment,
seeing as he is married to Aunt Flo, whose cooking can make the
lame walk, but this was a cool fall day when we were butchering
chickens in her backyard, and Uncle Al is a gentle man who has
no stomach for killing. He loves to eat fried chicken but not one
whom he knew personally, so he killed a couple hours uptown as
the rest of us executed forty-seven chickens that Dad brought in
from Uncle Larry's farm the night before. There had been forty-
eight chickens but one got loose when we emptied them out of the
gunny sacks into Al's garage to spend their last night. She flew
up in my face, a burst of feathers that made me let go, and took
off like a bat out of hell. Dad went after her but he is seventy
years old. The chicken tore around the trash barrel and down the
alley. The others milled in the garage all night, mumbling to themselves—that it wasn't fair that *she* got to go when *they* had to
stay, that if *anyone* got to go, then *everyone* should go—and finally
the sun came up and a young rooster sang and about nine o'clock
we arrived and sat down to have coffee. My mother had been up
since four and had drunk three cups of coffee already, on account
of a dream in which someone was chasing her. "I always have bad
dreams when we butcher chickens," she said.

"Your problem is, you drink too much coffee," said my dad.
"Coffee makes you sleep light, so a bad dream wakes you up. Me,
I sleep right through my bad dreams, they don't bother me at all,
not even the worst nightmares."

But it isn't that. My mother feels bad about butchering and so
do I. Dad and Aunt Flo are country people, and in the country
you do as you like, but Mother and I grew up in town, so we

worry more about what people think, and when you have forty-seven chickens in the garage, you know the neighbors are talking. People in Lake Wobegon don't slaughter chickens anymore, not in their backyards; it's not considered decent. Oh, you might do one or two, in the evening, but forty-seven in broad daylight, a chicken massacre—people would think you're common. People buy chickens at Ralph's; they come in plastic bags, big white cold oblong things.

For our sake, to accommodate squeamishness, Aunt Flo tried to give up butchering and be content with store-bought chicken, but it was against her principles. She cooks to bring happiness, it is part of her ministry, so to put tasteless chicken on the table is to preach false doctrine. She believes in the goodness and worth and beauty of chicken. Any fool can cook a hunk of cow, whack off a slab, slap it on a platter, and call it dinner, but chicken is delicate and has got to be done right. The chickens in the store were pumped full of feed and kept drugged and in the dark and you could taste the misery of the bird in its meat. Aunt Flo's philosophy is to let them run free, to feed them table scraps and delicacies and talk to them while you feed them, to keep them in chicken bliss right up to the moment their heads hit the block.

Once, on a trip to Minneapolis to visit relatives, she was dragged by them to a swank restaurant where she sat dazzled by crystal and silver and white linen, and ordered . . . chicken—or La Poulet Alla Cacciatore de Jardinera à la Estragon con Piña Colonna—and it was borne to the table in a golden dish and served with a flourish, but underneath the hoopla and publicity was a pitiful corpse of an unhappy creature, which to her represented the wretched dishonesty of these times, and she pushed it aside and decided it would either be vegetarianism or butchering. And there we were on a fall morning about to do business in the backyard.

"Well," Aunt Flo said, standing up to rinse out her coffee cup, "I don't think those chickens are going to butcher each other."

My mother already had two big pots of water on to boil, my dad had sharpened the ax blade, and out we went, into the wet cold yard. The chickens fell silent in the garage when the back door slammed. I looked in the alley for the forty-eighth chicken. "Well," we said, "we might as well get started."

My parents and Aunt Flo have been butchering chickens since long before I was around to help, so they don't really need me. My dad kills them, my mother plucks them, and Aunt Flo cleans them. When he's done killing, my dad helps with the plucking, and then they all help clean. My job hasn't changed since I was a child: I help out here and there doing this and that, but mainly my job is to select the chicken and catch its legs with a long wire hook and grab its ankles and carry it to my dad, who takes care of the rest.

When I opened the side door of the garage, a volunteer chicken flew up and I grabbed it and there was the first one. I turned and walked back to the garage and put my hand on the knob and heard the *whack* and went in for the next one.

All the chickens had to die, so it wasn't like I had any real power; I was only a lower-level bureaucrat trying to keep things going smoothly. I didn't have the power of clemency, so why did they look at me that way—why did I feel cheap? I closed the door behind me and stood in the dim light with my hook and work gloves, the chickens milling away from me, and I took a deep breath and snagged one and it cried out, "Oh no, gosh no, please no, don't do this," and I took it to my dad and handed it over and turned my back, not wanting to watch as this creature, who had been alive in my hands just a moment before, now—*whack*—was gone. I didn't want to see the blood or watch my mother at the big boiler on the back step or smell the hot wet feathers when she dipped the carcass in boiling water, the hiss, the ripping of feathers. Didn't want to look and didn't want the neighbors to see me, so I strolled back and forth from the garage to the block, as if I was taking them to the doctor, as the crowd in the garage got smaller and smaller, and then I thought: You really ought to kill one yourself before they're all gone. This is something you should know how to do if you eat meat, otherwise you better stick to celery. You're dishonest, I said to myself: you come from an honest family that faces life and death, but you live like it's a story and you made it up—it's time you become an adult and kill a chicken. Eight chickens left, and then six, and the fifth one, I watched my dad do it.

He's a one-handed butcher. Holds it by the legs in one hand, flops it down, and the ax in the right hand is already up high on the backswing and down *whack* and the head drops like a cut flower and the blood runs out in the dirt. My uncle Larry paints a line on the chopping block and places the chicken gently down on its belly with its beak on the line, and that line hypnotizes the chicken—it lies very quietly, staring cross-eyed at the yellow line, thinking about infinity, and then suddenly it stops thinking. Uncle Larry likes to swing the ax with two hands. My dad uses one.

We were down to two chickens unless No. 48 walked in, so when I took out the next-to-last one, I said, "Maybe I'll do the next one." Okay, he said. I caught the last chicken. I was glad to be getting rid of it, the last witness to the massacre. My dad said, "Want me to hold it for you?" I shook my head. My mother said, "You be careful, now." Imagine going to bat against your first chicken, you cut your own foot off, and walk funny the rest of your life, a stiff walk, like a chicken.

I got a grip on the chicken's legs and swung it up on the block and hauled off with the ax and hit down hard and missed by two inches. I had to pry the ax out of the wood and now I was mad. I swung again and down it came dead center *whack* and at the same time I let go and the chicken took off running. It had no head. It dashed across the yard and out in the street and was gone—I never saw a chicken move so fast. I guess without the extra weight they can really go.

My dad explained afterward that when I missed the first time and planted the blade in the block, the blade got hot. So when I cut the chicken's head off, the blade cauterized the wound and stopped the flow of blood, and you had a running chicken in pretty good shape except with no brain.

We took off after it down the street and around the corner and up and across the neighbor's yard. A high-speed chicken. It raced through flower beds and bounced off fences, pure energy, no thought, kept going—fast. Ran over two little kids in a sandbox. Ran past a couple of dogs, who looked up and decided not to get involved with it. My dad and me trotting along far behind. We heard the squeal of brakes when two cars stopped and the headless chicken tore across Main Street by Bunsen Motors, just as Harold came tottering out of the Chatterbox Cafe, weak from his privy joke. It sped past him and he vowed to give up coffee from now on. It went up behind the cafe toward Our Lady Church, losing speed. Mrs. Mueller was standing by her garbage can and she has a face that would stop a clock. It slowed down the chicken to where she was able to trip it and grab it. She took it in and rebutchered it and plucked and cleaned it and put it in her fridge, but my dad and I didn't know that until hours later. So when we came wheezing along the alley and saw a chicken walking toward us with its head on its shoulders, we were momentarily confused.

It was the forty-eighth chicken, of course, and we chased it in behind the church and cornered it against the fence and snatched it and took it home. Then Mrs. Mueller called. We said, "You can keep it." We put on a pot of water to boil and drove out to a cornfield my dad knows about where it's shady and the corn has matured more slowly. We picked three dozen ears of sweet corn and raced home to the boiling water and put in the ears and had a wonderful vegetable dinner along with potatoes and beets and some squash. It was delicious. That was Thursday. I imagine that tomorrow we may try some fresh chicken.

How the
Crab Apple Grew

▤ *t has been a quiet week in Lake Wobegon.*
It was warm and sunny on Sunday, and on Monday the flowering crab in the Dieners' backyard burst into blossom. Suddenly, in the morning, when everyone turned their backs for a minute, the tree threw off its bathrobe and stood trembling, purple, naked, revealing all its innermost flowers. When you saw it standing where weeks before had been a bare stick stuck in the dirt, you had to stop, it made your head spin.

Becky Diener sat upstairs in her bedroom and looked at the tree. She was stuck on an assignment from Miss Melrose for English, a 750-word personal essay, "Describe your backyard as if you were seeing it for the first time." After an hour she had thirty-nine words, which she figured would mean she'd finish at 1:45 P.M. Tuesday, four hours late, and therefore would get an F even if the essay was great, which it certainly wasn't.

How can you describe your backyard as if you'd never seen it? If you'd never seen it, you'd have grown up someplace else, and wouldn't be yourself; you'd be someone else entirely, and how are you supposed to know what that person would think?

She imagined seeing the backyard in 1996, returning home from Hollywood. "Welcome Becky!" said the big white banner across McKinley Street as the pink convertible drove slowly along, everyone clapping and cheering as she cruised by, Becky Belafonte the movie star, and got off at her old house. "Here," she said to the reporters, "is where I sat as a child and dreamed my dreams, under this beautiful flowering crab. I dreamed I was a Chinese princess." Then a reporter asked, "Which of your teachers was the most important to you, encouraging you and inspiring you?" And just then she saw an old woman's face in the crowd, Miss Melrose pleading, whispering, "Say me, oh please, say me," and Becky looked straight at her as she said, "Oh, there were so many, I couldn't pick out one, they were all about the same, you know. But perhaps Miss—Miss—oh, I can't remember her name—she taught English, I think—Miss Milross? She was one of them. But there were so many."

She looked at her essay. "In my backyard is a tree that has always been extremely important to me since I was six years old when my dad came home one evening with this bag in the trunk and he said, 'Come here and help me plant this'—"

She crumpled the sheet of paper and started again.

"One evening when I was six years old, my father arrived home as he customarily did around 5:30 or 6:00 P.M. except this evening he had a wonderful surprise for me, he said, as he led me toward the car.

"My father is not the sort of person who does surprising things very often so naturally I was excited that evening when he said he had something for me in the car, having just come home from work where he had been. I was six years old at the time."

She took out a fresh sheet. "Six years old was a very special age for me and one thing that made it special was when my dad and I planted a tree together in our backyard. Now it is grown and every spring it gives off large purple blossoms. . . ."

The tree was planted by her dad, Harold, in 1976, ten years after he married her mother, Marlys. They grew up on Taft Street, across from each other, a block from the ballfield. They liked each other tremendously and then they were in love, as much as you can be when you're so young. Thirteen and fourteen years old and sixteen and seventeen: they looked at each other a lot. She came and sat in his backyard to talk with his mother and help her shell peas but really to look at Harold as he mowed the lawn, and then he disappeared into the house and she sat waiting for him, and of course he was in the kitchen looking out at her. It's how we all began, when our parents looked at each other, as we say, "when you were just a gleam in your father's eye," or your mother's, depending on who saw who first.

Marlys was long-legged, lanky, had short black hair and sharp eyes that didn't miss anything. She came over to visit the Dieners every chance she got. Her father was a lost cause, like the Confederacy, like the search for the Northwest Passage. He'd been prayed for and suffered for and fought for and spoken for, by people who loved him dearly, and when all was said and done he just reached for the gin bottle and said, "I don't know what you're talking about," and he didn't. He was a sore embarrassment to Marlys, a clown, a joke, and she watched Harold for evidence that he wasn't similar. One night she dropped in at the Dieners' and came upon a party where Harold, now nineteen, and his friends were drinking beer by the pail. Harold flopped down on his back and put his legs in the air and a pal put a lit match up to Harold's rear end and blue flame came out like a blowtorch, and Marlys went home disgusted and didn't speak to him for two years.

Harold went crazy. She graduated from high school and started attending dances with a geography teacher named Stu Jasperson, who was tall and dark-haired, a subscriber to *Time* magazine, educated at Saint Cloud Normal School, and who flew a red Piper Cub airplane. Lake Wobegon had no airstrip except for Tollerud's pasture, so Stu kept his plane in Saint Cloud. When he was en route to and from the plane was almost the only time Harold got to see Marlys and try to talk sense into her. But she was crazy about Stu the aviator, not Harold the hardware clerk, and in an hour Stu came buzzing overhead doing loops and dives and dipping his wings. Harold prayed for him to crash. Marlys thought Stu was the sun and the moon; all Harold could do was sit and watch her, in the backyard, staring up, her hand shielding her eyes, saying, "Oh, isn't he marvelous?" as Stu performed aerial feats and then shut off the throttle and glided overhead singing "Vaya con Dios" to her. "Yes, he is marvelous," said Harold, thinking, "DIE DIE DIE."

That spring, Marlys was in charge of the Sweethearts Banquet at the Lutheran church. Irene Holm had put on a fancy winter Sweethearts Banquet with roast lamb, and Marlys wanted to top her and serve roast beef with morel mushrooms, a first for a church supper in Lake Wobegon. Once Irene had referred to Marlys's dad as a lush.

Morel mushrooms are a great delicacy. They are found in the wild by people who walk fifteen miles through the woods to get ten of them and then never tell the location to a soul, not even on their deathbeds to a priest. So Marlys's serving them at the banquet would be like putting out emeralds for party favors. It would blow Irene Holm out of the water and show people that even if Marlys's dad was a lush, she was still someone to be reckoned with.

Two men felt the call to go and search for morels: Harold put on his Red Wing boots and knapsack and headed out one evening with a flashlight. He was in the woods all night. Morels are found near the base of the trunk of a dead elm that's been dead three years, which you can see by the way moonlight doesn't shine on it, and he thought he knew where some were, but around midnight he spotted a bunch of flashlights behind him, a posse of morelists bobbing along on his trail, so he veered off and hiked five miles in the wrong direction to confuse them, and by then the sun was coming up so he went home to sleep. He woke at 2:00 P.M., hearing Stu flying overhead, and in an instant he knew. Dead elms! Of course! Stu could spot them from the air, send his ground crew to collect them for Marlys, and the Sweethearts Banquet would be their engagement dinner.

Stu might have done just that, but he wanted to put on a show and land the Cub in Lake Wobegon. He circled around and around, and came in low to the west of town, disappearing behind the trees. "He's going to crash!" cried Marlys, and they all jumped in their cars and tore out, expecting to find the young hero lying bloody and torn in the dewy grass, with a dying poem on his lips. But there he was standing tall beside the craft, having landed successfully in a field of spring wheat. They all mobbed around him and he told how he was going up to find the morels and bring them back for Marlys.

There were about forty people there. They seemed to enjoy it, so he drew out his speech, talking about the lure of aviation and his boyhood and various things so serious that he didn't notice Harold behind him by the plane or notice the people who noticed what Harold was doing and laughed. Stu was too inspired to pay attention to the laughter. He talked about how he once wanted to fly to see the world but once you get up in the air you can see that Lake Wobegon is the most beautiful place of all, a lot of warm horse manure like that, and then he gave them a big manly smile and donned his flying cap and scarf and favored them with a second and third smile and a wave and he turned and there was Harold to help him into the cockpit.

"Well, thanks," said Stu, "mighty kind, mighty kind." Harold jumped to the propeller and threw it once and twice, and the third time the engine fired and Stu adjusted the throttle, checked the gauges, flapped the flaps, fit his goggles, and never noticed the ground was wet and his wheels were sunk in. He'd parked in a wet spot, and then during his address someone had gone around and made it wetter, so when Stu pulled back on the throttle the Cub just sat, and he gave it more juice and she creaked a little, and he gave it more and the plane stood on its head with its tail in the air and dug in.

It pitched forward like the *Titanic*, and the propeller in the mud sounded like he'd eaten too many green apples. The door opened and Stu climbed out, trying to look dignified and studious as he tilted eastward and spun, and Harold said, "Stu, we didn't say we wanted those mushrooms sliced."

Harold went out that afternoon and collected five hundred morel mushrooms around one dead elm tree. Marlys made her mark at the Sweethearts dinner, amazing Irene Holm, who had thought Marlys was common. Harold also brought out of the woods a bouquet of flowering crab apple and asked her to marry him, and eventually she decided to.

The tree in the backyard came about a few years afterward. They'd been married awhile, had two kids, and some of the gloss had worn off their life, and one afternoon, Harold, trying to impress his kids and make his wife laugh, jumped off the garage roof, pretending he could fly, and landed wrong, twisting his ankle. He lay in pain, his eyes full of tears, and his kids said, "Oh poor Daddy, poor Daddy," and Marlys said, "You're not funny, you're ridiculous."

He got up on his bum ankle and went in the woods and got her a pint of morels and a branch from the flowering crab apple. He cut a root from another crab apple and planted the root in the ground. "Look, kids," he said. He sharpened the branch with his hatchet and split the root open and stuck the branch in and wrapped a cloth around it and said, "Now, there, that will be a tree." They said, "Daddy, will that really be a tree?" He said, "Yes." Marlys said, "Don't be ridiculous."

He watered it and tended it and, more than that, he came out late at night and bent down and said, "GROW. GROW. GROW." The graft held, it grew, and one year it was interesting and the next it was impressive and then wonderful and finally it was magnificent. It's the most magnificent thing in the Dieners' backyard. Becky finished writing 750 words late that night and lay down to sleep. A backyard is a novel about us, and when we sit there on a summer day, we hear the dialogue and see the characters.

Truckstop

It has been a quiet week in Lake Wobegon. Florian and Myrtle Krebsbach left for Minneapolis on Tuesday, a long haul for them. They're no spring chickens, and it was cold and raining, and he hates to drive anyway. His eyesight is poor and his '66 Chev only has 47,000 miles on her, just like new, and he's proud of it. But Myrtle had to go down for a checkup. She can't get one from Dr. DeHaven or the doctors in Saint Cloud because she's had checkups from them recently and they say she is all right. She is pretty sure she might have cancer. She reads "Questions and Answers on Cancer" in the paper and has seen symptoms there that sound familiar, so when she found a lump on the back of her head last week and noticed blood on her toothbrush, she called a clinic in Minneapolis, made an appointment, and off they went. He put on his good carcoat and a clean Pioneer Seed Corn cap, Myrtle wore a red dress so she would be safe in Minneapolis traffic. He got on Interstate 94 in Avon and headed south at forty miles an hour, hugging the right side, her clutching her purse, peering out of her thick glasses, semis blasting past them, both of them upset and scared, her about brain tumors, him about semis. Normally she narrates a car trip, reading billboards, pointing out interesting sights, but not now. When they got beyond the range of the "Rise 'N Shine" show, just as Bea and Bob were coming to the "Swap 'N Shop" feature, a show they've heard every morning for thirty years, they felt awful, and Florian said, "If it was up to me, I'd just as soon turn around and go home."

It was the wrong thing to say, with her in the mood she was in, and she was expecting him to say it and had worked up a speech in her mind in case he did. "Well, of course. I'm sure you would rather turn around. You don't care. You don't care one tiny bit, and you never have, so I'm not surprised that you don't now. You don't care if I live or die. You'd probably just as soon I died right now. That'd make you happy, wouldn't it? You'd just clap your hands if I died. Then you'd be free of me, wouldn't you— then you'd be free to go off and do your dirty business, wouldn't you."

Florian, with his '66 Chev with 47,003 miles on it, wouldn't strike most people as a candidate for playboyhood, but it made sense to her—forty-eight years of marriage and she had finally figured him out, the rascal. She wept. She blew her nose.

He said, "I would too care if you died."

She said, "Oh yeah, how much? You tell me."

Florian isn't good at theoretical questions. After a couple minutes she said, "Well, I guess that answers *my* question. The answer is, you don't care a bit."

It was his idea to stop at the truckstop, he thought coffee would calm him down, and they sat and drank a couple cups apiece, and then the pie looked good so they had some, banana cream and lemon meringue, and more coffee. They sat by the window, not a word between them, watching the rain fall on the gas pumps. They stood up and went and got in the car, then he decided to use the men's room. While he was gone, she went to the ladies' room. And while she was gone, he got in behind the wheel, started up, checked the side mirror, and headed out on the freeway. Who knows how this sort of thing happens, he just didn't notice, his mind was on other things, and Florian is a man who thinks slowly so he won't have to go back and think it over again. He was still thinking about how much he'd miss her if she was gone, how awful he'd feel, how empty the house would be with him lying alone in bed at night, and all those times when you want to turn to someone and say, "You won't believe what happened to me," or "Did you read this story in the newspaper about the elk in Oregon?" or "Boy, Johnny Carson is looking old, ain't he? And Ed too," and she wouldn't be there for him to point this out to—and he turned to tell her how much he'd miss her and she wasn't there. The seat was empty. You could have knocked him over with a stick.

He took his foot off the gas and coasted to a stop. He hadn't noticed her crawl into the backseat, but he looked and she wasn't there. She hadn't jumped—he would've noticed that. (Wouldn't he?) It couldn't've been angels taking her away. He thought of the truckstop. He was a good ways from there, he knew that. He must've gone twenty miles. Then, when he made a U-turn, he noticed he wasn't on the freeway anymore. There was no median strip. He was on a Highway 14, whatever that was.

He drove a few miles and came to a town named Bolivia. He never knew there was a Bolivia, Minnesota, but there it was. Went into a Pure Oil station, an old man was reading a Donald Duck comic book. Florian asked, "How far to the Interstate?" He didn't look up from his comic. A pickup came in, the bell dinged, the old man kept reading. Florian went down the street into a cafe, Yaklich's Cafe, and asked the woman where the Interstate was. She said, "Oh, that's nowheres around here." "Well, it must be," he said, "I was just on it. I just came from there."

"Oh," she says, "that's a good ten miles from here."

"Which way?"

"East, I think."

"Which way's east?"

"What way you come in?"

"That way!"

"That way is northeast. You want to go that way and then a little southeast when you get to the Y in the road. Then keep to your left. It's about two miles the other side of that old barn with

Red Man on the side. Red Man Chewing Tobacco. On your left. You'll see it."

There was a funny look about her: her eyes bulged, and her lips were purplish. Her directions weren't good either. He drove that way and never saw the barn, so he turned around and came back and looked for the barn on the right side, but no barn, so he headed back to Bolivia, but Bolivia wasn't there anymore. It was getting on toward noon.

It was four o'clock before he ever found the truckstop. He had a long time to think up something to tell Myrtle, but he still had no idea what to say. But she wasn't there anyway. The waitress said, "You mean the lady in the blue coat?" Florian didn't remember what color Myrtle's coat was. He wasn't sure exactly how to describe her except as *real mad*, probably. "*Ja,* that's the lady in the blue coat," she said. "Oh, she left here hours ago. Her son come to get her."

Florian sat and had a cup of coffee and a piece of apple pie. "Can you tell me the quickest way to get to Lake Wobegon from here?" he asked. "Lake what?" she said. "I never heard of it. It can't be around here."

But it was, not too far away, and once he got off the freeway he found his way straight home, although it was dark by then. He stopped at the Sidetrack for a quick bump. He felt he owed it to himself after all he'd been through and what with what he was about to go through. "Where's the old lady?" asked Wally. "Home, waiting for me," he said.

He headed south and saw his house, and kept going. Carl's pickup was in the driveway and he couldn't see facing the both of them. He parked on the crossroad and sat, just beyond Roger Hedlund's farm, where he could watch his house. It was dark except a light was on in the kitchen and one in the bathroom. Roger's house was lit up. What if Roger should see him and come out to investigate? Out here in the country, a parked car stands out more than a little bit, you might as well be towing a searchlight behind you. It's considered unusual for a man to sit in his car in the evening on a crossroad an eighth of a mile from his own house, just sit there. If Roger came out, Florian thought he'd explain that he was listening to the radio and it was a Lutheran show so the old lady wouldn't have it in the house—Roger was Lutheran, he'd like that.

He ducked down as a car came slowly past, its headlights on high beam. The preacher on the radio might be Lutheran, he didn't know. It sure wasn't the Rosary. The man was talking about sinners who had wandered away from the path, and it seemed to Florian to fit the situation. "Broad is the road that leadeth to destruction, and narrow is the path of righteousness"—that seemed to be true too, from what he knew of freeways. The preacher mentioned forgiveness, but Florian wasn't sure about that. He wondered what this preacher would do if *he* had forgotten his wife at a truckstop and gotten lost; the preacher knew a lot about forgiveness theoretically but what would he do in Florian's situation? A woman sang, "Softly and tenderly Jesus is calling, calling for you and for me. See by the portals he's waiting and watching. Calling, O sinner come home."

> Come home, come home—
> Ye who are weary come home.

Florian felt weary. Seventy-two is old to get yourself in such a ridiculous situation. He waited as long as he could for Carl to leave, and then the coffee inside him reached the point of no return and he started up the engine. Taking a leak in another man's field: he drew the line at that. He turned on his headlights, and right when he did he saw Carl's headlights far away light up and the beams swung around across the yard and Carl headed back toward town.

Florian coasted up his driveway with the headlights out. He still did not have a speech ready. He was afraid. He also had to pee. Outside, on the porch, he smelled supper: breaded fish fillets. He was surprised that the door was unlocked—they never have locked it but he thought she might if she thought he was coming.

He hung up his coat in the mud room and looked around the

corner. She was at the stove, her back to him, stirring something in a pan. He cleared his throat. She turned. She said, "Oh thank God." She dropped the spoon on the floor and ran to him on her old legs and said, "Oh Daddy, I was so scared. Oh Daddy, don't ever leave me again. I'm sorry I said what I did. I didn't mean it. I didn't mean to make you so angry at me. Don't leave me again like that."

Tears came to his eyes. To be so welcome—in his own home. He was about to tell her that he hadn't left her, he'd forgotten her; then she said, "I love you, Daddy. You know that."

He was going to tell her, but he didn't. It occurred to him that leaving her on account of passionate anger might be better than forgetting her because of being just plain dumb. There wasn't time to think this through clearly. He squeezed her and whispered, "I'm sorry. I was wrong. I promise you that I'll never do a dumb thing like that again."

She felt good at supper and put on the radio; she turned it up when she heard "The Saint Cloud Waltz." *Sometimes I dream of a mansion afar but there's no place so lovely as right where we are, here on a planet that's almost a star, we dance to the Saint Cloud Waltz.* That night he lay awake, incredulous. That she thought he was capable of running away, like a John Barrymore or something. Seventy-two years old, married forty-eight years, and she thought that maybe it hadn't worked out and he might fly the coop like people do in songs? Amazing woman. He got up at six o'clock, made scrambled eggs and sausage and toast, and felt like a new guy. She felt better too. The lump on her head felt like all the other lumps and there was no blood on her toothbrush. She said, "I wonder if I hadn't ought to call down there about that appointment." "Oh," he said, "I think by now they must know you're all right."

Dale

1.

It has been a quiet week in Lake Wobegon. Commencement was Wednesday evening at the football field, the eighty-seven members of the Class of '86 were ushered into the next chapter of their lives to the sweet strains of Elgar. Carla Krebsbach was one of them, and earlier that day, while she looked at the pictures of her classmates, autographed, in her copy of *The Shore*, she thought, "Wouldn't it be nice if there were eighty-six people in the Class of '86? It would be like a good omen," and then it struck her that she had wished someone dead, just as her eyes fell on Dale Uecker's picture, where he had written, "If you get to heaven before I do, just drill a hole and pull me through— Lots of love and good luck to a great kid, that's you!"

She thought, "Dale is going to die because of my terrible thought." With his black hair combed like he never combs it, serious eyes looking straight out, he looked like he might be dead already, hanging in his basement from a rafter, or drunk and crashed into a tree, or his head blown off. *Lord have mercy on me, a sinner.* She put on her eye shadow and prayed for God to save his life.

That night, at seven o'clock sharp, the eighty-seven moved in processional formation out of the gym door, across the dirt lot, and onto the cinder track around the field where the Leonards won two games last fall. To the sad and elegant cadence of "Pomp and Circumstance," the Class passed before the bleachers and the sharp tiny flashes of light here and here and here like parents' heads exploding, and filed into the eight rows of folding chairs between the forty- and fifty-yard lines, and, on a signal from Miss Falconer, they sat down in unison. She had them practice in the lunchroom on Tuesday. She said, "Don't flop down like that, don't just collapse like a pile of bricks—let yourself down gracefully— no, not like that!—you look like you're an invalid."

She worked with them on the correct method of sitting and they got worse at it, until she threw up her hands in despair. She is a small, utterly elegant woman, so perfectly groomed and neatly dressed that if she dropped dead the undertaker wouldn't have to fix her up a bit—she's ready to go right straight in the coffin for reviewal. So elegant, and she clapped her elegant hands and cried, "What's the matter with you people? This is simple! Don't flop, don't poke around or grope or waggle your seats, just—*sit*. Dale? Dale, are you part of this, or what is your problem?"

Dale had reason to be distracted. He was fairly sure that he'd flunked Dentley's final in higher algebra and that any moment there'd be a knock on the door, Mr. Halvorson would come in and say, "Dale, could I see you . . . out here . . . for a moment," and his classmates would turn and look and think, "Heroin. Heroin and car theft and sex acts too awful to mention." He'd follow the principal out to the hall and hear him say, "I have bad news, Dale. You can't graduate, you'll have to come back next year." He waited all day for the knock, he felt like he was floating. Tuesday afternoon they got their copies of *The Shore* and sat on the grass where they used to sit talking after lunch all those years and signed each other's yearbooks. He wrote, "Dear Allen, remember all the good times we had—"

"I will always remember this," he thought, "this very moment; years from now I'll always be able to remember exactly how this looked and how I felt. I'll remember her face" looking at Carla Krebsbach—and he looked where Carla had written in his book:

When darkest night surrounds you
Look up and see a star
And know that you have one true friend
No matter where you are.

Algebra ordinarily was a good subject for him but on Monday he couldn't remember anything the first twenty minutes. He kept saying, "Relax," and relaxed and got panicky in a relaxed sort of way. The last thirty minutes he wrote down anything he could think of that made sense. On the last problem, in the last panicky minutes of the hour, he caught a clear view of Barbara Soderberg's test—the problem solved in big block lettering—and looked up at the top of Dentley's head behind his desk, looked at Barbara's test again, and then looked up at the minute hand just about to jump to the twelve so the bells would ring, and thought, "This doesn't matter that much, it's just not that important to me." And set his pencil down. The bell rang and Dale stood up and walked away. That was Monday.

There are no Ueckers in *Who's Who*, Dale has checked. He imagined how his name'd look in there and wrote it down on an index card that is pasted inside his blue folder where he keeps his school stuff.

UECKER, DALE. b. Lake Wobegon, Minn. March 4, 1968. BA Harvard, 1990. MA Yale, 1991. Ph.D. University of Paris, 1993. Married, Danielle Monteux, 1992. Three children: Antoine, Mimi, and Doug. Elected to the Institute of Arts, 1994, and L'Institut Nationale Académie de la Honneur et Gloire et Héroisme, 1995. Author of numerous scholarly and artistic works, frequent lecturer here and abroad, recipient of more prizes than you could shake a stick at.

He thought of it again in the minute before the bell. He thought,

"Life is so wonderful that it is all we can do simply to experience it, and all the things people think are important—none of it matters if it makes us less able to live." Did I think of that myself? he wondered.

He wrote it on the front page of *The Shore* under a photograph of the school: I AM ALIVE. I AM A LIVING FEELING PERSON AND WHAT I USED TO THINK WAS SO IMPORTANT, IT ISN'T. TESTS AND GRADUATION DON'T MATTER BECAUSE NOW I KNOW WHAT I NEED TO KNOW, THAT THE IMPORTANT THING IS LIFE ITSELF.

How glorious to fail—and, in this moment of humiliation, discover the meaning of life.

It was the greatest day and a half of his life, and then it ended sadly. Dentley called him in and said, "Dale, your final wasn't so good but I've been looking at it and I'm going to give you a C minus on it and a C for the year—I think that basically you understand the material, you just didn't know exactly how to use it."

"But I didn't solve the problems," Dale said.

"Yeah, but I could see where you were headed on most of them, and anyway I'm going to give you some extra credit for class participation."

He looked up, a sad man with thin dry hair, smiling, and Dale said, "That's not right. I flunked your test. I don't want to sneak out of it. I failed."

"Dale, you had a bad day. I'm not going to nail you for that."

He didn't feel right about it but he let Dentley write down a C, then he felt worse. It was like he had refused to cheat, only to allow someone else to cheat for him. He talked to Mr. Halvorson, who thought Dale was complaining that the grade was low. He kept saying, "Dale, there's no shame in getting a C—it's a passing grade."

When he sat with the others Wednesday night, he felt good again. The night so clear, the smell of grass and damp, the music and voices drifting across the field, so many faces—how could a lover of life not be elated with so much to see as this? Carla won the Sons of Knute Shining Star scholarship and they all jumped up and clapped. She was valedictorian too. "When we look back on this night years from now we will see it as a great moment when our lives turned and our future course was determined," she said. At the end, the band played and they stood up together in a whoosh of gowns and walked out, heads high. Someone called, "Dale! Dale!" and the camera flashed. He went with Allen to Martha Hedlund's, whose parents weren't home, and drank beer and smoked a cigarette. Carla said, "Hi, Dale," and he put his arm around her. They talked about what they would do in life. "I'm going in the Navy," he said, which sounded good to him. A great night, drinking a can of beer, one arm around a girl, talking. And then she said, "I'm awfully glad you're alive."

"It's enough to be alive," he said, "a person doesn't need anything more."

"The Navy!" said Allen. "I thought we were going to go to Saint Cloud State together. How can you go in the Navy?"

"Just do it. That's how."

Drinking a beer, one arm around a girl, talking about life—on the verge of leaving all this behind, on the very edge, the last moment before the door shuts, the last trembling moment—when she said that strange wonderful thing, "I'm awfully glad you're alive."

So was he, so glad he was awfully sorry to say goodnight.

2.

Beautiful summer weather the week after graduation, a good week for fishing, when farmers got a lull in their field work and could go out and sit and rock in a boat and work on their sunburn. Rollie Hochstetter pulled in a stringerful of sunnies, fishing in Sunfish Bay, about twenty yards off the end of Kruegers' dock, not far from the weeds, with his brother-in-law Don Bauer in Don's aluminum boat (6½-horsepower motor), with 2½-to-3¼-inch worms, about two feet off the bottom using a ¾-inch red plastic bobber. Nearby sat Clint Bunsen in his boat, contemplating the sun on the cool water, the rod and reel in his hand. His serenity was disturbed by the activity at Rollie's stringer, so he called over, "You going to keep those puny things? I'm going for the big ones. I'm not sure those are legal-size, are they?"

Rollie said, "You know, to tell you the truth, I don't go for those big ones, they're too damn bony. These medium-size are the good eaters, you know that."

Clint contemplated the wisdom of Rollie: if you can't have something, find a reason why you wouldn't want it. He imagined Rollie as a monk in a boat, praying, "Lord, do not send me any of those big ones as they are too bony, Lord, as Thou surely must know. Grant Thy servant a little fish, one of the good eaters."

Clint knew why Rollie was out on the lake, though; it was because his heart was breaking. His grandson Dale Uecker decided to join the Navy, and who could say whether he'd come back or not?

"Why so soon?" his mother said. "How do I know you've even *thought* about it? Four years! Dale! What's the big rush? You haven't signed anything yet, have you? Honey. You didn't. Oh, Dale. How could you do this? Honey, you don't even know how to swim. You'd be out in the ocean someplace."

"Ma, they carry life preservers."

"How do you know that?"

"It's the law. They have to."

"Who's going to enforce it? This is the government, they make the law, they don't have to obey it, they don't hafta take care of you one bit—they could throw you over the side and who'd know it?"

Bobbie was scared and upset. Dale is her youngest boy, then it's Deb, and then they're all gone. She stood against the stove, crying into a dish towel. (This was a week ago Friday.) Everyone was there, an emergency family meeting, Rollie and Louise and

Jack and Bobbie and Dale's uncle Carl. Bobbie said, *"Talk to him, Jack."* "I can't tell him anything, I gave up telling him anything a long time ago," said Jack. Bobbie said, "Talk to him, Dad," and Rollie just looked away. He was hurt because Dale hadn't asked his advice.

Bobbie was making lasagna. "What am I doing this for?" she said through her tears. It was eight o'clock in the evening and everyone had eaten supper and she was making four big pans of lasagna, to freeze, she said, but with Dale leaving and taking his appetite with him, why such big pans?

"This is the craziest thing you ever did and you did some crazy ones," she said. She laughed. "Remember when you went after the groundhogs?" He certainly did. It was only a year ago. Something was harvesting their garden as the plants came up out of the ground, and one day Jack noticed six groundhogs hiking through the yard en route to the lunch program and thought, "Six is too many. One or two, yes (if they're married), but six is pushing charity too far," so he told Dale, "Dale, get out there and wipe out those groundhogs."

Dale got his .22 out of his closet and was coming downstairs when he caught sight of himself in the mirror. He wasn't wearing a shirt, and standing there, nice tan, fairly good pectoral development, rifle, he looked like a hero. He found a red bandanna and tied it around his forehead. Looked better.

Outside, leaning against the tree behind the corncrib, waiting for groundhogs in the scorching heat, he could imagine how good he looked, and he moved out through the weeds, imagining other men—Bravo Company—following him (though he couldn't hear them, that's how good they were). He nailed the first groundhog by the milkhouse. It flopped twice and he heard others scurry into the weeds at the end of the garden. One of them made a run for it. He fired and missed, and chased it, and then saw one at eight o'clock and turned and crouched and fired, but it was a big rock, not a groundhog, and the bullet hit it and then he heard a *chunk* and there was a hole in the side of their green Chevy.

She laughed at the thought of it, her boy at supper that night saying, "Dad, I was going after groundhogs today and I put a shell in the Chevy." The reason Dale waited until supper to confess was that his mom was weeding begonias on the other side of the car. He stood on the rock and looked at the hole and saw that if the car hadn't been parked there he would've killed her. He put the rifle back in his room.

She laughed. "Oh honey, I'm sorry, but it was so comical, the look on your face—" He might have killed her that afternoon and been in all the newspapers as a wacko teenager.

She said, "But what are you going to do with the nice car Grandpa gave you?"

"Well," he said, "it'll be just as nice in four years, except it won't have so much mileage on it."

Rollie didn't say much that night, because he felt too bad. He had looked after Dale since he was six—Rollie saw how those older brothers ganged up on the little boy and he knew what a hard man Jack could be, so he went out of his way for Dale and tried to show him things. He taught him how to drive a tractor when he was seven, and how to handle pigs, and took him fishing, and was close to him, as close as Rollie knew how to be, close enough that Dale came over to talk to his grandpa every single damn day, so he was hurt that the boy would now turn away and be secretive and, this Friday night, not even look at him. Rollie sat and studied his coffee. "You know," he said, "there never was a war we fought that we had a good reason for. None of them made sense. Not a goddamned one."

Jack cleared his throat. Everyone was quiet. Nobody spoke.

About eleven, Bobbie said she was going to bed. They walked out in the yard and stood around the cars for a while, talking. To Dale it was like a dream. Under the yard light and the stars in the sky, his family talking in the evening breeze, the big barn half full of hay bales like a cargo ship docked at the house, looming above them in the night.

Saturday he and his dad went out and cut more hay, and Sunday more relatives came over. He tried to call Carla but she was at her grandparents' fiftieth anniversary in Cold Spring, and in the evening she was gone, her mother said, to Saint Cloud with friends to see a movie. What friends? What was his name? Dale didn't dare ask, but he did drive past her house about eleven o'clock. The lights were on, but he didn't dare go in. He was afraid that if he said, "I came to say goodbye, I'm going into the Navy, who knows if I'll ever come back," she'd say, "Oh, that's interesting. Well, good luck."

Monday he cleaned out his room. He threw out all his school stuff, most of his letters, and his 4-H project on pork (Nature's Perfect Food), and selected the pictures he'd take along, including Carla's graduation picture, an enlargement. Most other people she gave a billfold-size but to him she gave an enlargement, one more way he knew she had feelings for him.

He called the Navy the next day and went to Saint Cloud and took all the tests and made up his mind that if they wanted him he was going.

"You seem almost happy about it or something," Allen said. "It's like you don't even care or anything."

The reason he felt happy was the Navy physical. As the doctor sat and asked him questions, Dale was making up his mind to ask him one, and finally, after he lowered his underpants and coughed and was checked for a hernia, Dale said, "I, uh, was always wondering why, uh, my pennis, you know, it hangs crooked. I always wondered what was wrong with it." The doctor looked. He said, "First of all, it's pronounced 'penis,' and secondly, it's perfectly normal."

Perfectly normal. What a gift. He took it home with him. *Perfectly normal.* He had worried about this since he was sixteen. He wanted to call Carla and tell her somehow, or at least be with her and feel perfectly normal. He was glad he had never discussed it with her and mispronounced "penis." Somehow the subject had never come up.

And suddenly it was Wednesday noon and Dale was leaving at one. His mother sat and wept over breakfast and then she got busy. Jack drove the Pontiac in to fill it up with gas, a sort of going-away present, a full tank. Dale sat in the living room. Debbie sat there, reading *Parents* magazine. Everyone came in for a little lunch, the Ueckers and Rollie and Louise and Carl. They squeezed in around the kitchen table, where his mother had laid out a big spread. She didn't use the dining room, because it wasn't Sunday and they weren't company. And she felt too bad. She felt so bad she had spent all morning fixing lunch. There were platters of meat, hot and cold, and tuna salad and potato salad and hamburger hotdish and tuna hotdish and breads and pickles—even Fran could see it was too much—and then she reached into the oven for the big one, a baking pan. She held it out to him—"For you, Dale"— and she took the tinfoil off. It was pigs in blankets, wieners baked into a biscuit crust. He had liked them when he was eight but she still thought it was his favorite dish. She watched him take two. She studied his face for signs of pleasure. "Mmmmmmmm, those are very very good. Thank you," he said.

And then it was one. "Well," he said. He stood up. "I can't stand it," she cried, and she ran into the bathroom. He hugged his grandpa and grandma, he shook hands with Uncle Carl, he looked at his dad and shook hands with him. He said, "Ma? Come on, Ma." And then he set down his duffel bag. "Did you give me back the car keys?" he said to his dad. Jack said, "I gave em to you, of course I did, you musta put em in the kitchen."

But they weren't anywhere in the kitchen. Everyone helped look except his mom, who was crying in the bathroom about her boy leaving. Except he wasn't leaving. "Look in your pants," Jack said. "Dad, I didn't *put* em in my pants. You had em."

"I gave em to you, Dale. I come home and got outta the car and come in and *give* em to ya. Look upstairs, look in the living room. Where were ya sitting? Try and think."

Grandma was crying now, and Debbie had an arm around her and was sniffling. Oh Dale, we may never see him again. Dale thought: *I may never get out of here.* His dad standing by the fridge saying: "This is stupid. This is the craziest thing I ever heard of." Carl: "Just calm down, Jack." Jack: "What are you talking about? I'm calm." Rollie: "Take it easy." Jack: "Why don't *you* take it easy, Dad?"

"Ma, come on out of there. Open the door."

"I can't. I feel too bad."

"Ma, are my car keys in there?"

"No."

"Ma, are you sure?"

"No."

"Ma, please. I got to go. Help me find them."

"But I don't want you to go."

"Ma, did you take my keys?"

"No."

"Ma!"

His grandma crying. "I just know I'll never see you again."

Debbie crying. "I'll be here, Grandma."

"Oh I know, honey, but it's not the same."

Debbie went up to her room to cry.

Jack said, "Maybe you gave em to someone. Maybe you left em out on the lawn somewhere. Maybe you left em in the *car*." When he said that, a thoughtful look came over his face. "You know," he said, "I wonder if they wouldn't be up over the visor."

And of course they were.

And so he left.

He drove past Carla's on the odd chance she'd be outside, and she was mowing the lawn and he got out to say goodbye and she hugged him. "I'll sure miss you a lot," she said, "so I hope you'll write me once in a while."

And away he went. It's a wonderful thing to push on alone toward the horizon and have it be your own horizon and not someone else's. It's a good feeling, lonely and magnificent and frightening and peaceful, especially when you leave someone behind who will miss you and to whom you can write.

And so the blue Pontiac rose over the rise and zoomed around the curve by the grain elevator and up the long grade to the hill and disappeared into the future.

High Rise

It has been a quiet week in Lake Wobegon.
It turned hot on Tuesday and Clarence got the Crosley electric window fan out from the basement. But it was cool in the basement, so he sat down for a while to catch up on some old magazines. 1958 was a hot year too. He brought the fan up and took the quilts down and read some more. Eisenhower: quite a man. And those tailfins. I don't believe you ever see a car in that exact shade of green these days. And white sidewalls. Do they still exist?

Questions like those keep him awake at night: Audie Murphy, alive or dead? What happened to Mary Miller of the 42nd Street Gang on "Sunday in Manhattan"? What a great show that was. It's hot and you kick off the blanket in your sleep and then you're aroused by your indecency and wake up and cover yourself and think about Mary Miller for a while and go to sleep.

There was a thin high-pitched whine in the air from clouds of mosquitoes and gnats, but we're used to that. It's summer and this is Minnesota, and mosquitoes are part of our heritage, going back to the seventeenth century when French explorers searching for the fabled oilfields of the north, canoeing through swamps and streams on the sweltering muskeg, stopped and looked at each other covered with black insects and red welts and dizzy from slapping their heads and said, "What do (you) say (we) try Quebec first and leave this for later?" And so our fabled oilfields remain safe and secure. Mosquitoes are what don't show up in the gorgeous color photographs of Minnesota, and we're not supposed to complain, but you ought to admire us for living here, it's an accomplishment, not everybody could do it.

Ella Anderson was in her garden digging up a patch of elderly irises, coated with mosquito lotion, Nuits de la Nord, which smells like ripe bananas. Father Emil was in the rectory garden putting in his onions—he has resigned as pastor of Our Lady and is only staying temporarily to help Father Wilmer get settled, but Sunday after Mass, Wilmer had his bags packed for two weeks of vacation. "How can you?" said Father. "You just started. I put in almost fifty years, I got to retire." Wilmer said he had thirty-seven vacation days coming from the diocese. Father never heard about a vacation policy. "Oh yes," Wilmer said, "and we got profit-sharing. IRAs for clergy. It's new this year." Father Emil thought, Next thing they'll have a Frequent Prayer program with prizes, put an odometer on the Rosary. So Wilmer went to San Francisco. He said, "No mosquitoes there, you know." Father Emil walked behind him out to the car, carrying Wilmer's gym bag. "They got sharks," he said, "they got snakes, they got mad dogs come down out of the hills on hot days and bite you in the hinder, you'll be sick for a week." Wilmer just laughed. No mosquitoes in California, and that's a vacation for him. That's why Father put in his onions. Green onions are a mosquito preventative. In forty-four years, he has yet to be bitten on the lips.

"It doesn't seem right," Myrtle said to Sister Arvonne, up in the Our Lady basement, planning the picnic for the Daughters of Martha in June, "that we have the God-given beauties of nature and can't even enjoy them for the Goddamned mosquitoes, it doesn't seem fair." Myrtle is seventy-three and she has talked that way all her life. Her husband, Florian, you couldn't get a swear word out of him if you squeezed him with a pair of pliers, but Myrtle has a gland in her neck next to the thyroid that secretes profanity, especially when mosquitoes get bad. She sits in her yellow lawn chair in the shade and slaps and swears, and now she's talking about moving to a senior citizen high rise in Saint Cloud. "Mosquitoes don't go higher than the third floor unless there's an updraft. I read an article on it. You live above the sixth floor, you're free and clear."

She's campaigned for the move to the high rise for almost two years, going back to when she got in a fight with her sister-in-law Beatrice over a blue Bavarian crystal vase Beatrice chose from Myrtle's mother's things after she died. Myrtle thought it was odd to let an *in-law* pick over Mother's things but she didn't want to say anything, and then Beatrice drew the short straw and reached out and picked the one precious thing out of the lot, the blue vase that to Myrtle had been since early childhood the most beautiful object she could imagine, left by a princess as a token of a gay life to come. Saturday, when the girls cleaned the worn-out little house, they shined up the crystal vase and walked around to see the diamonds that it made from a beam of light. It was magical. Fat Beatrice clutched it to her tremendous bosom and sighed for happiness, who knew nothing about this vase, hadn't grown up with it, she could buy one in a dime store and it'd be the same to her—but Myrtle didn't want to say anything, so she hauled off and slapped her across the face hard, and Beatrice squeezed the vase and it shattered and one shard pierced her left breast. She jumped up and tore off Myrtle's wig and the other sisters fell in between them. They cried and picked up the broken glass. They said they were sure glad Mother wasn't alive to see this, it woulda killed her. They made Beatrice and Myrtle kiss and make up. Myrtle gave Beatrice a peck on the cheek and whispered into Beatrice's right ear, "Jesus goddamn you fat old bitch." Six lowdown nasty words from the mouth of a grandma. There's been a poisoned courtesy between them ever since, fourteen years of saying hello between thin hard lips, and two years ago, when Beatrice became president of Catholic Mothers, Myrtle wanted to leave town.

Myrtle'd like to live someplace exciting. Lake Wobegon is boring. She almost moved to Minneapolis in 1937. She was going to
go and then she didn't and she's been talking about it ever since,
how she came *this close* to going and if only she had, well, she
wouldn'ta ever had to put up with this horseshit. Whenever her
kids were rotten, she told them how she'd almost gone away in
1937 and wished she had. She's been putting up with it for fifty
years. She's sick and tired of it.

To Florian, the idea of moving to Saint Cloud is unthinkable.
Myrtle says, "I seen a article in the *Times* about a new high rise
opening up. We oughta get our names in for that—you know some
people have to wait two years on the waiting list before they get
in, that's how much people our age want to live in one, two years
you got to wait. That's how desirable they are. Two years." Florian
gets up to put toast in the toaster, make another cup of Sanka,
stalling for time, wishing she'd forget it. "Well?" she says. "Well?"

"I just don't think it's realistic," he says. Living in a tall building,
seven, eight stories up: he went up the Foshay Tower once, thirty-
one stories, and couldn't stand near the edge because there was
suction from the ground trying to pull him off. So if you lived on
the eighth floor and couldn't go near the windows and had to walk
around next to the inside wall and maybe tie your left ankle to
the bedpost at night, what kind of life would it be?

He's lived there at the Krebsbach place since before he was
born. His mother had him in the downstairs bedroom, presumably
conceived of him there too and the six others before him, four of
them dead now. The latest one, dear Ruth, his favorite sister,
how funny and dear she was and yet her taste in men, my God!
four husbands, the first of whom was a disaster and they went
down from there. But as long as she lived and as bad as she felt,
she could always come back home because Florian lived here. He
rents out the land to Roger, but he still has the house and every
Thanksgiving and Christmas and Memorial Day and Fourth of
July there are some Krebsbachs there, depending on how they
feel about each other that year.

"Give me one reason," Myrtle says, "give me one *good* reason why we wouldn't be better off in an apartment in Saint Cloud."

That's why, a few years ago, Florian started raising ducks. At first a dozen and now a flock of thirty-six.

"It's good meat," he said, "and you know, they do eat mosquitoes."

"Ducks don't eat mosquitoes, don't be dumb."

"Oh yes, they eat their weight in mosquitoes. I read that in an article."

Myrtle looks at him. What is he talking about? She's the one who reads the articles. She never read word one about ducks.

"If they eat mosquitoes, how come we got so many we can't even sit in the backyard?"

"If they didn't eat them, we'd have a lot more, we wouldn't be able to sit, period."

Since Myrtle started talking high rise, Florian has bought a number of old Farmall tractors at auction and a corn drill and an old combine. He talks about fixing them up. Since she started talking about how nice a three-room apartment would be, he's been picking up old dressers cheap and antique bedsteads and washstands. As an investment. And expanding his duck herd.

So when she says to give her one reason, he says, "What can I do with the ducks?"

He takes a kitchen chair and sits in the yard and all the ducks come around. He holds up the cheese curls in one hand and caramel popcorn in the other and his audience looks up and he tells them a joke. He says: So one day a duck come in this bar and ordered a whiskey and a bump and the bartender was pretty surprised, he says, "You know we don't get many of you ducks in here." The duck says, "At these prices I'm not surprised." And he tosses out the popcorn and they laugh. *Wak wak wak wak wak.*

I was shot in the leg in the war.

Have a scar?

No thanks I don't smoke.

Senator K. Thorvaldson saw Father Emil planting onions behind the rectory, he walked over and said, "I thought you were retiring and moving South."

"Well, I thought you were going to marry that woman out in Maine and move East."

"Well, maybe I will, I don't know. It's hard to leave here though when I'm so curious to see what's going to happen to you. I want to find out how the story ends before I go away."

Father mentioned Myrtle and Florian. "Telling jokes to ducks!" says Senator K. "Has Florian lost his marbles or what, then?"

"He has forgotten an awful lot of jokes but the few he remembers the ducks enjoy them over and over."

Florian sits out back and just about falls over, some of them are so good.

Hey, call me a taxi.

Okay, you're a taxi.

"Give me one reason," she says, "why we shouldn't pack up and leave this town."

He says: So this couple went to get a divorce, she was eighty-nine and he was ninety-two—the judge said, "Why? You've been married seventy years and now you want a divorce?" "We hate each other," she said. "We haven't been able to stand each other since 1932." "Why did you wait so long?" he said. "We wanted to wait until the children were dead. This woulda killed them."

Collection

It has been a quiet week in Lake Wobegon. Sunday morning Clarence Bunsen stepped into the shower and turned on the water—which was cold, but he's Norwegian, he knows you have to take what you get—and stood until it got warm, and was reaching for the soap when he thought for sure he was having a heart attack. He'd read a *Reader's Digest* story about a man's heart attack ("My Most Unforgettable Experience") and this felt like the one in the story—chest pain like a steel band tightening. Clarence grabbed the nozzle as the rest of the story flashed before his eyes: the ride in the ambulance, the dash to the emergency room, unconsciousness as the heart team worked over him, the long slow recovery and the discovery of a new set of values. But as he imagined what was about to happen, the heart attack petered out on him. The story said it felt like an elephant stepping on you. This felt more like a big dog, and then somebody whistled and the dog left. So it wasn't a heart attack, there was no story, and Clarence felt better.

(The storyteller is disappointed, of course. A full-blown heart attack would be a reasonable test of his ability, perhaps leading to death itself, a narration of the last moments, the ascent of the soul through the clouds, an exclusive report.)

It wasn't a heart attack, but for ten or fifteen seconds it could have been one, and in the depths of his heart he thought it was—so in a way it was. When you believe you're dying, ten or fifteen seconds is like a lifetime, and when the false attack was over, he nonetheless felt he sort of had a new set of values. For one thing, he wasn't sure he should waste time taking a shower, life being so short, having come so close to death in the sense that when death comes it might come exactly like this. It was Sunday morning, but he wasn't sure he wanted to go to church and sit through a sermon, life being so short. If you knew you had twenty minutes left to live, why, then, church would be the place you'd head first; you'd turn yourself in, no more fooling around, no kidding, pour the sacred oil on me, Jack, say the words, and pluck your magic twanger—I don't have all day.

He thought instead of going to church he'd like to go for a walk (good for your heart) and worship God in the singing of birds, the sunshine, green grass, and flowers, which, this being Minnesota, we don't have yet. He thought: Life is short, so you should do something different. He dried his old body off and put on underwear—maybe, life being short, you ought to get new underwear, but what can an old man wear except boxer shorts? Can't go around in those bikini things you see in stores. What if a robber with a gun forced you to strip down to your underwear ("Hey you—old guy!—hear me? I said, *strip*"), and there you be, an old geezer in tiny purplish briefs, robber'd take one look ("Hey, man, you are ridiculous"), *bam*, you're dead. Dead because you did things different because life is short. He stood at the dresser, shopping for socks (black, brown, gray, gray-black, Argyle). Arlene called up the stairs, "It's almost nine-thirty!"

He wanted to yell back that he was feeling delicate from what he'd thought at the time was a heart attack, but it was hard to yell something so vague, so he yelled, "Be there in a minute," and in not many minutes he appeared in the kitchen in full Sunday regalia: brown suit, black shoes, white shirt, and one flash of color, the tiny red flecks in his dark blue tie. He appeared through the door in a cloud of bay rum, poured himself a cup of coffee, drank some, then kissed his wife (in that order—he is Norwegian), and looked in the frying pan on the stove and saw food that whenever you read about cardiovascular disease you read about that stuff.

He put a pan of water on to boil, for oatmeal. Arlene watched, spatula in hand. "What's the matter? Breakfast is ready. I got your eggs." Hard to explain: a semi–heart-attack. A heart that wasn't attacked but heard footsteps in the weeds. Maybe it was only a twig, maybe the whole aorta about to fall off.

"I don't feel like bacon and eggs this morning."

"Well, I guess I'll have to throw them out, then."

"Yeah . . ."

"Are you feeling all right? Are you sick?"

He's Norwegian; he said, "No. I'm just fine." A Norwegian's dying words: "I'm just fine." On the field of battle, torn to a red pulp except for your mouth: "I'm just fine." Wreckage of a car, smashed to smithereens, a bloody hand reaches out the window and writes in the dust: "O.K."

It was warm out, and on the way to church they smelled mud, a sweet smell of rot and decay, and a whiff of exhaust as the Tolleruds cruised by with their carload of kids. Clarence used to walk to Sunday school with his four little kids. Now, having almost had a heart attack, he misses their sweaty little hands for one heartbreaking instant and misses how, before going in to worship the Lord, he ran a quick bladder check and a nose check to see where blowing was needed. The kids always cured him of the sort of morbid mood he felt this morning—he never had these long grim thoughts about death when the kids were little, but then he was younger, of course.

Church was half full and restless. Pastor Ingqvist's Lenten sermons have gotten longer. Val Tollefson has been after him to liven up his preaching. Sunday morning before church, Val tunes in "Power for Tomorrow" on TV from the Turquoise Temple in Anaheim, and there is a gleam in Reverend La Coste's eye that Val wishes Pastor Ingqvist would emulate and also use more dramatic inflection, rising, falling inflection, cry out sometimes, use long pauses to give solemnity to the sermon.

Clarence checked out of Pastor Ingqvist's sermon early. It was about the parable of the laborers in the vineyard, the ones who came late getting the same wage as those who came early and stayed all day, a parable that suggests you need not listen carefully to the whole sermon from the beginning but can come in for maybe the last sentence or two and get the whole point. Besides, the pastor's long pauses were hypnotic. Clarence's mind drifted away to other things, until suddenly he was startled by his own heavy breathing: he opened his eyes; the sermon wasn't over, it was only a long pause. The pastor's inflection suggested he was coming toward the end and the offering was next. Clarence eased his wallet out and saw he had no cash. He got out a pen and hid the checkbook in his Bible (next to Psalm 101) and quietly scratched out a check for thirty dollars, more than usual, because he had almost had a heart attack and also because his offering was personalized. He wrote surreptitiously, trying to keep his eyes up and ahead—knowing you're not supposed to write checks in church, it isn't a grocery store.

He glanced to his right, and Mrs. Val Tollefson was glaring at him. She thought he was writing in the Bible. (In the old Norwegian synod you didn't write in a Bible, not even little comments in the margin like "Good verse" or "You can say that again," because every word in the Bible is true and you shouldn't add any that might not be true, not even in pencil, because it undermines the authority of Scripture.) Meanwhile, the sermon ended and Pastor Ingqvist launched into prayer. Clarence tried to tear the check quietly out of the checkbook. There's no worse sound in the sanctuary than a check ripping. His check wouldn't come quietly, the first half-inch rip sounded like plywood being torn from a wall, so he waited for the pastor to launch into a strong sentence of fervent prayer to cover up the check removal, but Pastor Ingqvist was pausing at odd points, so Clarence couldn't tell when it was safe or when suddenly he would be ripping in the middle of pure holy silence. Clarence folded the check back and forth until it almost fell off. Mrs. Tollefson was about to get up and snatch Scripture out of his hands. At prayers' end, as they said the Lord's Prayer, he eased the check out ("And lead us not into temptation, but deliver us from evil: For thine is the kingdom, and the power, and the glory, for ever. Amen"), and when Elmer passed the basket, Clarence laid down the check folded neatly in half in the basket and bowed his head and suddenly realized he had written it for three hundred dollars.

He had written with his eyes averted and he knew he had written three-zero-zero on the short line and three-zero-zero on the long line. Could a man sneak downstairs after church and find the deacons counting the collection and say, "Fellows, there's been a mistake. I gave more than I really wanted to"? He now felt fully alive for the first time all day. He felt terrifically awake. He had given all he had in the checking account and a little more. What would they do until the end of the month to keep body and soul together? Maybe they would have to eat beans and oatmeal. What's a man gonna do? A man's got to live.

Life Is Good

t *has been a quiet week in Lake Wobegon.*
Lightning struck the Tollerud farm Tuesday, about six o'clock in
the evening. Daryl and his dad were walking the corn rows, talking, and the clouds were dark and strange but it wasn't storming
yet, and Daryl said, "If I were you, I'd take Mother out to Seattle
tomorrow and enjoy the trip and not worry about this." Right
then it hit, up by the house: a burst of light and a slam and a sizzle
like bacon. They ran for the house to find her in the kitchen, sitting
on the floor. She was okay but it was close. It hit a crab apple
tree thirty feet from the kitchen window.

Some people in town were reminded of Benny Barnes, who was
hit by lightning six times. After three, he was nervous when a
storm approached, and got in his car and drove fast, but it got
him the fourth time, and the fifth time it was sunny with just one
little cloud in the sky and, *bam*, lightning again. He had burn scars
down his legs and his ears had been ringing for years. After the
fifth, he quit running. The sixth one got him sitting in the yard
on an aluminum lawn chair. After that he more or less gave up.
When the next thunderstorm came through, he took a long steel

pipe and stood out on the hill, holding it straight up. He had lost the will to live. But just the same it took him fifteen more years to die. It wasn't from lightning: he caught cold from the rain and died of pneumonia.

Daryl wished the bolt had come closer to his dad. His dad has a character flaw that drives Daryl crazy: he hates plans. The trip to Seattle was planned before Thanksgiving, letters were written to relatives, calls were made; June 30th was the date set to go, but the old man gets uneasy when plans are made and feels trapped and cornered, even if the plans are his own, so one night after chores he said, "Well, I don't know about that trip to Seattle, I might be too busy, we'll have to see about that," which made everybody else want to shoot him.

Daryl jumped up. "How can you say that? Are you crazy?" No, just nervous about plans. Always was. To agree to do something and have people expect you to do it: it bothers him. When his kids were little, he'd tell them, "Now, I'm not promising anything, but maybe next week sometime I could take you swimming, up to your uncle Carl's, but don't count on it, it all depends." As next week came around, he'd say, "I don't know about that swimming, we're going to have to see about that. Maybe Thursday." Thursday the kids would get their bathing suits out and he'd say, "We'll see how it goes this morning, if I get my work done we'll go." Right up to when they got in the car, he was saying, "I don't know. I really ought to get to work on that drain pipe," and even when he stuck the key in the ignition, he'd hesitate. "Gosh, I'm not sure, maybe it'd be better if we went tomorrow." He couldn't bring himself to say, "Thursday we swim," and stick to it. Daryl and his brothers and sisters learned not to look forward to things because Dad might change his mind.

The old man is the same with his grandkids. He says, "Well, we'll see. Maybe. If I can." But the Seattle trip beats all. Ruby got the train tickets and had the suitcase packed three weeks ago, then he said, "I don't know how I can leave with the corn like it is." Ruby put her head in her hands. He said, "You know, the Grand Canyon is a place I always wanted to see, maybe we should go there." She sighed, and he said, "You know, I never agreed to this Seattle trip, this was your idea from day one." And then Ruby went to Daryl's to talk to Daryl and Marilyn. They sat drinking coffee and getting madder and Ruby said, "Oh well, you have to understand Dad." Marilyn stood up and said, "I do not have to understand him. He's crazy. He doesn't just have a screw loose, the whole top has come off."

She is reading a book, *Get Down and Garden*, about getting tough with plants. She has yanked a bunch of slow movers out of her flower garden, the dullards and the dim bulbs, and it's improved her confidence. Now she often begins sentences with "Look," as in "Look. It's obvious." She used to begin with "Well," as in "Well, I don't know," but now she says, "Look. This is not that hard to understand."

She said to Ruby, "Look. It's obvious what he's doing. He wants to be the Grand Exalted Ruler and come down in the morning and hear his subjects say, 'What is your pleasure, sire?' and he'll say, 'Seattle,' so they head for the luggage and then he says, 'No, we'll stay home,' so they sit down, and then 'Grand Canyon' and they all jump up. As long as you keep jumping, he'll keep holding the hoop up there."

Not only does Old Man Tollerud hate to commit himself to trips, he also likes to stay loose in regard to drawing up a will or some other legal paper that gives Daryl and Marilyn some right to the farm that they've worked on for fifteen years. When Daryl mentions it, his dad says, "Well, we'll have to see. We'll talk about it in a few months." Daryl is forty-two years old and he's got no more ownership of this farm than if he'd gone off and been a drunk like his brother Gunnar. Sometimes he gets so mad at the old man, he screams at him. But always when he's on the tractor in the middle of the field with the motor running. Once he left a rake in the yard with the tines up, hoping his dad would step on it and brain himself.

Last April he saw a skunk waddling toward the barn and got a can of catfood and lured the skunk into the tractor shed, hoping his dad would start up the John Deere the next morning and get a snootful. He fed the skunk day after day, waiting for it to do the job for him. Sweet justice. Blast the old bastard with skunk sauce at close range so nobody would care to see him for about a year. Then the skunk started following Daryl, who fed him such rich food, so Daryl quit and the skunk disappeared.

Daryl got some satisfaction at the Syttende Mai dinner at the Lutheran church in May, Norwegian Independence Day, where his dad went through the buffet and loaded up and was heading for a table when his paper plate started to collapse on him. He balanced his coffee cup on his wrist to get his other hand under the plate, and it was *hot*—the meatballs had sat in a chafing dish over a candle. The old man winced and looked for a place to dump the load; then the hot gravy burned right through the paper plate and he did a little tango and everything sloshed down the front of his pants. Daryl watched this with warm satisfaction.

But that was months ago, the satisfaction has worn off. The day after the lightning strike, Daryl drove up to the house to have it out once and for all. He practiced his speech in the pickup. "You don't treat me like I'm your son at all, you've never treated me like a son." He got to the house and found a note on the door: "Gone to Saint Cloud for windowshades. Back soon. Clean the haybarn."

Clean the haybarn! He ripped the note off and wadded it up and drop-kicked it into the peonies. He stalked to the end of the porch and back and stood and yelled at the door: "You don't treat me like I was your son, you bastard, you treat me like I was a—" And then the terrible truth dawned on him. His mother had said, "If anything happens to us in Seattle, I left you a letter in my dresser drawer. I've been meaning to give it to you for years." So he wasn't their son. He was adopted. That's why his dad wouldn't make out the will.

Daryl had wondered about this before, if he was his father's son. He thought, "I'm forty-two, it's time to find out." He walked in and climbed the stairs, step by deep purple step, and turned and entered his parents' bedroom, the forbidden chamber, and walked to the dresser and heard something move on the bed. He turned—it was their old tabby cat, Lulu, on the bed—his hand hit a bottle and it crashed on the floor. She didn't jump at the crash, she sat up and gave him a long look that said: "You're not supposed to be in here and you know it. You ought to be ashamed of yourself. You're no good, and you know it. Shame on you." He clapped his hands—*Ha! Git!*—and she climbed down and walked away, stopped, looked over her shoulder, and said: You'll suffer for this, you just wait.

He picked up the shards of perfume bottle and opened both dormer windows to air out the room. Unbelievable that his mother would ever smell like this, it smelled like old fruit salads. He dug down into the dresser drawer where he'd seen her stick old pictures, under her stockings and underwear. There was a book, *Sexual Aspects of Christian Marriage: A Meditation* by Reverend E. M. Mintner, that he'd read when he was twelve, and he dug beneath it to a packet of envelopes tied with a thick rubber binder, *tight*. He slipped it off: they were his dad's pay slips from the Co-op; each envelope held a year's worth; there were more than thirty envelopes.

He sat on the bed, feeling weak. Of all his parents' secrets, this was the darkest: how much money did they make? They would no more talk about that than discuss sexual aspects of marriage. One Sunday little Daryl piped up at dinner and asked, "Dad, how much money do you make?"

His dad has several different voices, a regular one ("So how come you went down there then when I told you I needed you? I don't get it") and a prayer voice ("Our Father, we do come before Thee with hearts filled with thanksgiving, remembering Thy many blessings to us, and we do ask Thee now . . ."). When he discussed money he used the second voice and he said, "I don't care to discuss that and I don't want you to discuss it with anyone else. Is that clear?"

Oh yes. We don't talk about money, that is very clear. Except to say, "I got this window fan for four dollars; it's brand-new except for this scratch, and you know those things run ten, twelve dollars." Bargains yes, but salaries no.

So here was the secret. He opened the first envelope, 1956. Forty-five dollars. That was for a whole week. Not much for a good mechanic. Forty-five dollars and five kids: it explained all that scrimping, his mother darning socks and canning tomatoes. When the old man forked over their allowance, he counted the two quarters twice to make sure he wasn't overpaying. It explained why he was such a pack rat, saving tinfoil, string, paper, rags—once Daryl looked around for string and found a box full of corks, another of bits of wire, and one box with hundreds of odd jigsaw-puzzle pieces, labeled "Puzzle: Misc."

It dawned on him that he wasn't adopted, he was their boy all right. He'd inherited their frugality and stoicism. If his paper plate fell apart, he'd try to save it, even if his hand was burning. Same as his dad. They raised him to bear up under hardship and sadness and disappointment and disaster, but what if you're brought up to be stoic and your life turns out lucky—you're in love with your wife, you're lucky in your children, and life is lovely to you—what then? You're ready to endure trouble and pain, and instead God sends you love—what do you do? He'd been worried about inheriting the farm, meanwhile God had given him six beautiful children. What happens if you expect the worst and you get the best? *Thank you, Lord,* he thought. Thank you for sending me up here to the bedroom. It was wrong to come, but thank you for sending me.

He heard Lulu tiptoe in, and when she brushed against his leg he was sorry for chasing her out. He scratched her head. It didn't feel catlike. He looked down and saw the white stripes down its back.

The skunk sniffed his hand, wondering where the catfood was. Then it raised its head and sniffed the spilled perfume. It raised its tail, sensing an adversary. It walked toward the window. It seemed edgy.

"Easy, easy," he said. If he opened the window wider, it might go out on the roof and find a route down the oak tree to the ground. He was opening the window wider when he heard the feet padding up the stairs. He hollered, "No, Shep, no!" and raised his leg to climb out the window as the dog burst into the room, barking. The skunk turned and attacked. Daryl went out the window, but not quite fast enough. He tore off all his clothes and threw them down to the ground, and climbed back in. The bedroom smelled so strong he couldn't bear it. The skunk was under the bed. He ran down and got the shotgun and loaded it. Daryl was almost dying of the smell, but he crept into the bedroom. He heard the skunk grunt, trying to squeeze out more juice. Daryl aimed and fired. Feathers exploded and the skunk dropped down dead.

He carried it out on a shovel and buried it, but that didn't help very much: the deceased was still very much a part of the Tollerud house when his parents arrived home a little while later. Daryl sat on the porch steps, bare naked except for a newspaper. He smelled so bad, he didn't care about modesty. Ruby said, "Oh dear. Are you all right?" She stopped, twenty feet away. She thought he looked naked, but he smelled so bad she didn't care to come closer.

His dad said, "You know, Daryl, I think you were right about Seattle."

And they left. They didn't take clothes with them. They went straight out the driveway.

That was Tuesday. Daryl has been living at his parents' house all week. But life is good. I'm sure he still believes this. Life is good, friends. It's even better if you stay away from Daryl, but basically life is good.

Lyle's Roof

It has been a quiet week in Lake Wobegon. On Tuesday, Carl Krebsbach's brother-in-law Lyle tried to start his lawnmower, which had died because the grass was so high that he hadn't cut sooner because it'd rained so much, and a shingle fell off his roof. He looked up and another one slid off and almost creamed him. There was white mossy stuff on the underside of the shingles, and though it was asphalt, it was soft, like a living thing, and it crumbled in his hands. It had held on to the roof as long as it could and then it died. A dead shingle.

People have been mentioning the roof to Lyle for years, in a roundabout sort of way. You can't stand and flat tell a man his house is falling apart. Carl says, "You know, if you'd like me to, I could climb up on your roof and check some of those shingles, they look like they might be loose"—but Lyle is leery of accepting help lest the person helping him think the reason he needs help is that he's stupid.

Lyle thought he better climb up and have a look. He doesn't have a long enough ladder, and he didn't want to borrow Carl's and involve Carl, so Lyle thought he'd go to the attic and look at it from underneath. He looked for his flashlight. He had an idea he'd left it in the corner of the basement when he looked at the water pump. It was dark in there, so he couldn't see if the flashlight was there or not, and he didn't want to go in there, because he could hear water running and the pump is electrical. So he went to put in a fuse so the light would work and he could look for the flashlight. He found a couple dozen old fuses on the fusebox, waiting to be healed, and none worked, so he unscrewed one from another socket and put it in and there was screeching and screaming behind him. He turned and saw a skillsaw making sparks on the concrete floor coming straight for him, and he grabbed for the fuse and touched something that made his whole body feel for one moment like a piece of history, pulled his hand back, and the saw came to the end of its cord and yanked it and stopped. It was all quiet except for the water-pump moan—the same sound he'd gone to check on when he left the flashlight back in there. But now it was louder. And it smelled of something burning.

Five disasters in five minutes, including attempts on his life by a shingle and a skillsaw, and all on a *summer* afternoon. Now comes fall, and after that life starts to get serious. He went to start the lawnmower again and had an idea: why not dig up this sod and put it on the roof? He'd seen that in the *National Geographic*, from Iceland or somewhere, some cold country. If the roof could grow moss, why not grass? People would laugh at him, but then they laugh at him now—so what's the difference? The difference is that, in a couple years, they'd see what a brilliant idea it is.

He would have to give this some careful thought.

He couldn't think while mowing, so he sat down to think in his lawn chair, and soon he was dreaming: something about green grass but not on a roof.

One man who's noticed Lyle's roof is Clarence Bunsen, who takes long early-morning walks for his heart. At 6:00 A.M., in the early light, this little town is so shining and perfect, so fresh, so still,

if you took eleventh-grade English from Miss Heinemann you
would think of Wordsworth:

> There was a time when meadow, grove, and stream,
> The earth, and every common sight,
>   To me did seem
>   Appareled in celestial light,
> The glory and the freshness of a dream.
> It is not now as it hath been of yore;—
>   Turn wheresoe'er I may,
>   By night or day,
> The things which I have seen I now can see no more.

Clarence walks up Taft Street to where it becomes the road
to the dump, and on mornings when he feels worse he walks farther.

This summer Bunsen Motors isn't taking in enough money to
keep four people on the payroll: Clarence and Clint Bunsen, and
Stanley and Earl, plus Marlys Diener doing part-time bookkeeping. They're not selling the Fords they used to. People are driving
forty and fifty miles to buy a car at a big dealer, they don't have
the loyalty to the home town that they used to have, and they're
not even ashamed to display the foreign dealer's nameplate on the
trunk: there it is, big as sin, *Ogilvie Toyota, Saint Cloud.* Who
is Ogilvie? Does he go to the Lutheran church? Does he go to any
church? They don't know him. For all they know, he could be
in Las Vegas, running around with showgirls and eating spoon-
fuls of cocaine; meanwhile, Clarence, their neighbor and friend,
who if they were suddenly in deep water he'd be there to help,
is in some fairly deep water of his own. He's got to borrow
seven thousand dollars to get through September. Wednesday
he saw parked in front of the Chatterbox a brand-new red Ford
Bronco 2 that Harold Diener, husband of Marlys, had bought in
Minneapolis. Clarence was sick. It broke his heart. But he
tried not to show it. He admired the car. "That's nice, Harold," he
said. "That's real good. Four-wheel drive. That'll be handy when

winter comes. You sure know your cars, Harold. I oughta hire you as a salesman."

> The rainbow comes and goes,
> And lovely is the rose;
> The moon doth with delight
> Look round her when the heavens are bare;
> Waters on a starry night
> Are beautiful and fair;
> The sunshine is a glorious birth;
> But yet I know, where'er I go,
> That there hath passed away a glory from the earth.

You live in a small town, you learn about people. You learn that certain people, if they say they'll be there to teach school on Tuesday, they'll be there, and some people won't, and if you call them up Tuesday evening, they'll say, "Oh, you meant *this* Tuesday." It's always the same ones who are prompt and faithful and dependable, and if they're ten minutes late you should call the police, and always the same others who say, "Are you sure today is Tuesday? But yesterday was— Oh yeah, it was Monday, wasn't it? Well . . . do you still need me?"

School started on Tuesday and suddenly it became awful quiet. All the air went out of the tire, the kids disappeared with their goofy ideas and dumb jokes and there was nothing left downtown but business, and not much of that. There was hardly a car on Main Street, you would've had to wait around to get in a traffic accident. At Krebsbach Chev, Florian was in a dark mood. Clarence came up and poured himself a cup of coffee, and Florian got ready to say, "Whatcha put cream in coffee for? Ruins it. I thought only women did that." But Clarence took his black, leaned against the parts counter, and said, "Jeez, what a week. Only Tuesday and it feels like Friday. I'll bet I don't sell one car."

That afternoon, at a quarter of four, Florian stepped out of the Chatterbox Cafe and turned to his left to go up to the garage. As he turned, he heard wheels behind him. He looked back and there was the Best boy coming on fast on his ten-speed. Florian ducked to his left, the Best boy went to his right, and they crashed. Florian fell over and the boy landed a little ways away. Florian sat up, making sure he was not killed, and asked, "Are you all right?"

The boy waited for Florian to yell at him and, when Florian didn't, went home to be yelled at by his folks for riding on the sidewalk and knocking down an old man, but they didn't either, and at school on Wednesday he was still waiting to be yelled at. He thought that perhaps Florian would be the speaker at assembly and talk about bike safety. He was sure Florian would write a letter to the editor—"I was walking along the sidewalk one day last week when one of our grade-school boys attempted to kill me. Isn't it time we stop coddling these vicious children and start putting some of them behind bars as an example to the others?"

The reason he didn't get yelled at is, ever since Florian forgot Myrtle at the truckstop on their way to the Cities, he's expected something to happen to him, and being knocked down by a bike was much easier than other things he imagined.

It's a primitive sense of justice: you do bad, and your Creator smacks you one—but there it is. One day you're daydreaming at the wheel, you smash into someone's rear end. She gets out of her car, looks at the busted taillight, and smiles. She's relieved; she says, "Well, it could've been a lot worse." You've just run into a guilty person. She did something in the past twenty-four hours that made her think the universe would land on her with both feet. She'd be covered with boils, wrapped in burlap, sitting in the ashes, flies on her, and lightning coming closer and closer, but all it is is a taillight. Not bad. She smiles and drives away. Now *you* start to feel guilty. Days later, the Best boy is still hearing footsteps, waiting for the big hand to grab him and spin him around and the voice to say, "Why you—"

Sometimes it's hard to get into trouble in this little town. There was an old guy years ago got so depressed he decided to kill himself, and he got a flask of whiskey and went down to the lake to throw himself in and drown. But he couldn't cut a hole in the ice. It had been a cold winter. He had some whiskey and he banged on the ice with his ax but couldn't cut a hole. He had more whiskey, and then he opened up a hole big enough to stick his hand in, and he drank the rest of the whiskey and took off all his clothes except his boots. He hiked off naked into the dim winter night and felt sleepy and then heard voices—women, he thought—and was scared he'd be seen and ran back and got his clothes on. He went home, slept, and woke up with a hangover worse than death and was resurrected from the hangover and decided to live. That's a true story from long ago. I believe it's true, except about the boots, but he died in 1978, so it's too late to check.

It rained more this week, a heavy rain that fell straight down, and eventually Lyle found his flashlight and looked up in the attic under the roof, which has been leaking for a long time into the plastic buckets in his daughters' bedroom, and he was astounded how awful it looked. Not just wet but slimy, slippery, like a place where mutant creatures come from, shiny green things with empty eyes reaching out for us. For two years Carl has told him he ought to fix his roof, which made Lyle furious but it also made Lyle nervous because Carl knows about these things. Lyle teaches science at the high school; he knows about the stratosphere, the ecosphere, the atmosphere, genetics, the cosmos, but not about roofs.

He climbed down from the attic, and he went downstairs to the furnace room and poured himself a stiff drink. No ice cubes or soda down there, just the bottle in the workbench. He wondered what to do. He didn't want to ask Carl for help, he was tired of him helping, of coming home from school and finding his brother-in-law had got his sink apart—*Lyle's sink*. He had another drink. Poor kids, living in a house that might fall down on their heads because their dad doesn't know what to do.

He felt like going to bed but he went up to the bedroom and called someone. He took the phone to the end of the cord, took it into the closet, sat down on a pile of shoes, and tried to disguise his voice to make it sound sober.

"Father? Is this Father Conway? This is Lyle. You don't know me but I live up here in Lake Wobegon, and I hate to bother you with something like this but I can't talk to my priest about it, it's something I've been embarrassed about for a long time— Yes? Well, I appreciate your saying that. I do. I'll try. It's just hard to find the words to say what I've been going through over this, but, anyway, it's about my roof.

"No, I said 'roof.' It's my roof. The roof on my house."

There's a story about Lyle's house, as there is about most houses in town. That's why old people walk so slow, because they're remembering all the stories. I'm not that old but I know a lot because I used to hang out with old people back when there used to be real old people. Now everyone is sort of my age or younger, and most people don't know much more than I do. It's disappointing to become a leading authority in the field when you still have so much you want to learn. But I do know that Lyle's house was built in 1889 by a carpenter named Swanson who started a milling business to make door and window frames.

He was tall and sported a fine black mustache and had three daughters who worshipped the ground he walked on, and after he died, they lived in the house, adoring his memory. When they got old, about thirty years ago, they couldn't bear the thought of anybody else ever living in their father's fine house. An ordinary two-story wood frame house to everyone else, but to them it was their father's realm, the embodiment of his life and wisdom and goodness, and they wrote in their will that, after the last of them deceased, the house would be torn down.

Then they died: one, two, three, close together. Each death seemed to drain the life from the survivors, and the family collapsed, and a few weeks later, the heir to their estate, a nephew, the son of their ne'er-do-well brother, young Victor rode into town, his long black hair combed high on his head, and a lawyer at his side, to claim what was rightfully his. The entire town came to despise both of them within twenty-four hours. The town couldn't decide which one they despised more. People had never agreed on anything so unanimously and heartily as that young Victor was despicable, heartless, and deserved to be cheated, and they set out to deprive him of that house.

The sisters' will provided that, if the house wasn't torn down within sixty days, then he wouldn't inherit the rest of the estate, about forty thousand dollars in cash in the First Ingqvist State Bank. The town didn't want to see the house torn down. It was a nice house, and if Victor didn't tear it down, the forty thousand dollars went to the library. Victor said it was his house and he started to rip the roof off. The town council made him stop while they studied the matter, looking through the municipal ordinances hoping that their forefathers in their wisdom might have passed something usable that they could hammer him with, and found an odd little law, passed in 1889, that said that the demolition of a building must be completed within fourteen days. Victor had torn some roof off about five days before, and it was a week until the next council meeting. That left two days to tear it down in, and one of those days was a Sunday, so all he had was one day.

He did his best. He arrived early and his lawyer with him, with crowbars and big hammers, but his grandfather had built the house better than he knew, and by noon Victor could see he wasn't going to make it. He'd made a lot of dents in it, busted windows, beat the dust out of it, pried off some boards, but he wasn't going to be able to level it by nightfall, and so he would lose forty thousand dollars. He started to yell and run around like a madman, which meant he got even less done. His lawyer saw that he wouldn't get paid and turned quiet and gloomy, and Victor went to pieces. He yelled out the window: "I'll give you two thousand dollars to help me tear my house down!"

A little gang of men stood out in the dusty street. They seemed interested, so he made another offer: "I'll give you three thousand dollars to help me tear my house down."

"Would that be per man or for the whole bunch of us?"

"Three thousand dollars apiece."

"Could we see some of that first?"

So the sun went down and he left town and the bank sold the house to Lyle: a good house, well built, but one that had sustained some violence, so he has problems with his plumbing, his wiring, his drainage, his roof, that other people might not have. And he has a problem with three ghosts who don't feel good about him being there.

He talked to Father Conway for about an hour—about roofs but also about football and about fall and what a fine season it is. Lyle went off to work the next day to talk about the quiet but passionate life of amoeba, but at noon Mr. Halvorson asked if he could give up his lunch period and take Miss Peterson's speech class—she had had lunch and went home sick—and Lyle said, Sure.

He walked into the speech room and smelled intense fear. Twenty people seventeen years old sat in three rows, facing a low platform. Fifty-five minutes in the class period, each student to speak impromptu for three minutes about himself or herself, so there'd be no more than eighteen speeches, so two would escape till the next day, and of the twenty, about sixteen were hoping to be one of the two.

An impromptu speech about yourself . . . "Well, what is there to say?" one boy said. "I don't know. I was born and I have a family, of course, and I'm in school and—I don't know, what am I supposed to talk about?"

"Just tell us about yourself," Lyle said from the back.

"But there isn't anything important to tell."

"Let us decide that. Just talk about whatever comes to mind."

"What if nothing comes to mind?"

There were terrible silences when a speaker froze in mid-sentence and the audience looked down out of decency, studied their fingernails, while the poor person took a deep trembling breath. Lyle sat in back, and a few feet away, his daughter Mary. He began to feel ill himself. Finally it was her turn and she stood up, her face red, and he closed his eyes and put his head in his hands. *Ah, youth.*

"I was born in 1969," she said, "in Minneapolis. We were there visiting some relatives, I guess. I don't know—I wasn't there, of course." Laughter. Silence. Lyle remembered that weekend when she was born, and tears came to his eyes.

"My first memory is of a day when we had a blanket on the

grass and my mother and dad and I were sitting on it—I don't know where this was, but the sun was shining and dogs were barking far away, and I had this feeling—and I guess I've always felt this—that my family was very close to me, always near, even when they were gone, so I've never really been that afraid. Not even now."

In his head, Lyle heard a voice, and it said, "Lyle, now have your roof fixed. Keep your house in order."

The bell rang. The two who didn't give speeches let out their breaths and relaxed, not knowing that one thing worse than giving a speech is thinking about giving a speech. Lyle went to the office and called Carl. "Carl?" he said. "Uh, I was wondering if you had any time free tonight to come over and have a look upstairs—I've decided I really ought to go ahead on that roof project and not pursue some of these other options I was considering, so I think we ought to get it down before it snows."

Pontoon Boat

I̲t has been a quiet week in Lake Wobegon. It's been hot and dry, and everyone was extremely touchy, so when you walked in the Chatterbox for lunch and sat at the counter and got your cup of coffee and looked at the menu and finally ordered what you have every day anyway, a bowl of chili and a grilled cheese, and turned to Ed on your left and were set to say something, you hesitated. Even to say, "Boy, she's a hot one," might start something. So you make it a question and ask, "Say, I wonder how hot she's supposed to get today anyway?" And he says, "How the hell should I know? What? You think I sit listening to the damn radio all morning?"

That's how hot it was. So hot you didn't dare ask, and no rain, but muggy so the dust sticks to your face. It doesn't seem fair for the Midwest, the nation's icebox, to be the nation's oven too. It's like living in the Arctic but spending your summers at Death Valley. Even at the Sidetrack Tap, where men sit in air-cooled comfort in dim light and medicate themselves against anger and bitterness, they were touchy too.

It's so good to step out of a hot dirty day into a cool tavern and hold a bottle of Wendy's but two or three Wendys later, it's so awful to go back out. After an hour in the dark, the sunlight hits you like a two-by-four, and the beer in your head heats up, the yeast grows, the brain rises. When a man on a hot day who's enjoyed an hour of fellowship gets up to leave, he knows he has dug a hole for himself.

The portly gent in the cool dark behind the bar, Wally, recently bought a boat, a twenty-six-foot pontoon boat with a green-striped canopy, a thirty-six-horsepower outboard, four lawn chairs, and a barbecue grill, which arrived Sunday by flatbed truck and was put in the water off Art's fishing dock. It was christened the *Agnes D.* after his mother. He and Evelyn took a maiden voyage in the twilight. It was cool out there under the canopy, with a nice breeze off the lake. Wally stood at the tiny wheel amidships, wearing a white skipper cap. His ship was only a piece of plywood, twenty-six by twelve, on two steel pontoons, but to him, standing, steering it, it was majestic. He wanted to hang lights on it from bow to stern, on port (left) and starboard (right) sides. He gunned it. "Not so fast," Evelyn said, "you don't have to drive the boat so fast."

"My love," he said, "you do not *drive* a boat. You drive a *car*. You *sail* a boat. And when you *sail* a boat, you need to find out what she's got under the hood." She'd never heard him talk like that.

He didn't talk like that in the Sidetrack—he didn't want anyone to think he was showing off—so when guys asked what was this they heard about him buying a boat, Wally frowned, he shook his head, he said, "Yeah, I don't know. I got a deal on it from a guy I know, but I tell you, it's a headache. Insurance and the upkeep and worrying about the thing—did you know that if some fellows stole my boat to commit crimes with, if they got hurt I could be liable? It's true! But you and the wife oughta come out with us some evening. Wouldn't that be something? We could grill up some steaks, have a beer. . . ."

He invited about a hundred couples aboard the *Agnes D.* in three days. An occupational hazard of being a tavern owner is that you have an awful lot of extremely close friends, men who've become very intimate and told you confidential things they wouldn't even tell their close friends, so that makes you their closest friend, although you barely know their name.

When he invited Mayor Clint Bunsen to come for a cruise, Clint said, "You know what you ought to do? There's a bunch of Lutheran ministers coming through on a tour Friday, we oughta give them a boat ride so they get a nice look at town."

How and why twenty-four Lutheran ministers were touring rural Minnesota is a long digression that I'd rather skip, dear reader. People are so skeptical, they force a storyteller to spend too much time on the details and not enough on the moral, so I'll just say that the five-day tour, "Meeting the Pastoral Needs of Rural America," was organized by an old seminary pal of Pastor Ingqvist's, the Reverend J. Peter Larson, who called him in April and said, "You know what our problem is, we're so doggone theological we can't see past the principles to the people, and the people are hurting, so I'm organizing a tour of a hundred ministers to go and look at rural problems and I want to visit Lake Wobegon in mid-July."

Fine, said David Ingqvist, who forgot about it until, last Sunday, his wife, Judy, said, "What's this on the calendar for Friday? 'Tour/Larson/here'?"

"Oh that," he said. "Well," he said, "I was meaning to discuss that with you," he said. "It's some Lutheran ministers coming through town and I thought we could have them over for a picnic supper in the backyard."

"How many?" she said.

"I don't know exactly, but certainly no more than a hundred."

"Well, I think your best bet would be wieners. You probably just want to boil them. Maybe you could get someone to make you some potato salad."

Rural problems was what Pete wanted to see, but you can't take a crowd of ministers around to someone's house and point to him and say, "There's one. He's in trouble. I don't give him long. No sir. He's headed down the chute." Clint Bunsen thought it was strange. If a minister visits, you hide your problems, and shine up your children and put them through their paces. And you talk about other people's problems. But he agreed to talk to them about municipal affairs, and then he got the brilliant idea of the boat trip. When they arrived, tired and hot and dusty at five o'clock on Thursday, that was the plan: boat trip, speech on board and roasted wienies, and fellowship at the Ingqvists' (four gallons of wine, $4.39 apiece).

They got off the bus and Clint thought: *Ministers.* Men in their forties mostly, a little thick around the middle, thin on top, puffy hair around the ears, some fish medallions, turtleneck pullovers, earth tones, Hush Puppies; but more than dress, what set them apart was the ministerial eagerness, more eye contact than you were really looking for, a longer handshake, and a little more affirmation than you needed. "Good to see you, glad you could be here, nice of you to come, we're very honored," they said to him, although they were guests and he was the host.

"Down this way! Let's go! Down to the lake!" Pastor Ingqvist wore yellow Bermuda shorts and sunglasses. "It's been an incredible trip," Pete said. "Really amazing." They strolled down from Bunsen Motors, down the alley behind Ralph's, and along the path between Mrs. Mueller's yard and Elmer and Myrtle's. Myrtle's cat lay in a limb of an apple tree, its long gray tail hung down and twitched at the tip. Mrs. Mueller's cat sat in the shade of an old green lawn chair, its gaze set on the birdbath. "I tell you," Pete said, "I really feel we've gotten an affirmation of Midwestern small-town values as something that's tremendously viable in people's lives. But there's a dichotomy between the values and the politics that is really critical at this point. It's a fascinating subject."

Wally had gone all out. The *Agnes D.* was hung with two strings of Christmas lights, the kind that twinkle on and off. He had laid in five cases of pop, a keg of beer, and enough hamburger patties to feed the freshman class. The twenty-four men trooped up the plank and on deck, and she sank lower and lower in the water. Clint was the last aboard. He thought, "I'm not sure about this." But how do you tell some ministers to get off? The Church invites us all, the concept of "That's enough for now" isn't part of Lutheran teaching, so Clint stepped lightly aboard, trying not to put all his weight on it, and felt water slosh in his shoe.

The boat was riding low, no doubt about it. Wally thought, "I'm not sure about this," but he didn't want to sound worried like an amateur. A true sailor would be hearty. He yelled, "Cast off the bow line!," and Pastor Ingqvist leaned over to cast off, and the *Agnes D.* tilted to starboard. Wally gunned the engine, she righted herself, and off they went, at about four mph, with little waves lapping at the sides, so low in the water that to people on shore it looked like a miracle.

One problem with twenty-four men on a twenty-six-foot boat is that in the Midwest we need to stand about twenty-eight inches or more from each other, otherwise we get headaches. With the steering post, lawn chairs, motor, canopy, pop cases, barbecue grill, and card table, there wasn't room. Men herded forward and to the sides; there was clearing of throats and "Excuse me"s as twenty-four men edged away from each other and into each other, and that was before the coals got hot.

Wally poured half a can of lighter fluid on them and lit them just before departure. As the heat rose, ministers standing near the grill edged away toward the bow. There were too many Lutherans squeezed into too small a space, and the barbecue shooting up sparks and men ducking and edging—Wally thought, "If we'd just get up more speed I'll bet that bow would come up a little."

Pete was saying to Pastor Ingqvist, "Dave, I don't have the answers, but I think that all of us will come out of this with a feeling of unity of concern," but David was feeling his own concern: they were sinking and he didn't know how to mention it in a way that wouldn't seem negative. Wally at the wheel, calling, "Steady as she goes!," and twenty-four nervous ministers in earth tones and suede shoes edging, shifting, herding, trying to be good listeners and share concerns as the fire got hotter and hotter, driving them toward the bow, which was sinking, but all of them trying to keep a good positive attitude, and then Dave said, "Somebody put out the fire! We're sinking!"

Five men took their beer cups and leaned over to dip up water and the *Agnes D.* tipped. The left front pontoon went under and the *Agnes D.* stopped dead in the water and turned to port. They had reached the edge of the laws of physics. They lurched to the starboard side and both pontoons went under and there—in full view of town—the boat pitched forward and dumped some ballast: eight Lutheran ministers in full informal garb took their step for total immersion.

As the boat sank, they slipped over the edge to give their lives for Christ, but in only five feet of water. It's been a hot dry summer.

Eight went over, and then the *Agnes D.* came up again, a little, and the survivors grabbed to hold on, but then the grill tipped over and they turned to see hundreds of burning coals sliding down the deck toward them—the Book of Revelation come to life!—and they plunged overboard like a load of hay bales. The *Agnes D.*'s bow rose, and Wally turned to Clint hanging on to the canopy and said, "I think I got her under control now."

The ministers stood perfectly still in the water and didn't say much at all. Five feet of water, and some of them not six feet tall, so their faces were upraised to the bright blue sky. They didn't dare walk for fear of dropoffs, their clothes were too heavy to swim in, and they couldn't call for help because their voices were too deep and mellow. So they stood, faces upturned, in prayerful apprehension. Twenty-four ministers standing up to their smiles in water, chins up, trying to understand this experience and its deeper meaning.

Clint's little nephew Brian waded out to them. "It's not deep this way," he said. He stood about fifteen feet away, a little boy up to his waist. They followed him out single file, twenty-four dripping clergy, their clothes hanging heavy as millstones, but still looking interested, concerned, eager to get on to the next item on the agenda. It was fellowship at Paster Ingqvist's home, but he was still aboard the *Agnes D.* with Wally and Clint, so they sat down in a circle under the trees to await further directions.

State Fair

It has been a quiet week in Lake Wobegon and it's a great pleasure to be here at the Minnesota State Fair. I've come every year since I was five, and that's more than twenty years. Every August my mother said, "Well, I don't know if I care to go to the Fair this year or not." Nobody had so much as mentioned the Fair, we were too busy canning vegetables and perishing of the heat and the steam from the pressure cooker— a burning hot day and us stripping skins off tomatoes, slaving to put up a hundred or so quarts of a vegetable we were rapidly losing our appetite for. She said, "There's too much work to do and we can't afford it, it's too crowded, and anyway it's the same as last year. I don't see how we can do it. I'm sorry."

It was her way of lending drama to the trip. So we'd come to the Fair, the roar of engines and the smell of grease, and Mother marched around the Home Activities building looking at competitive cakes and jams. One year we shook hands with Senator Ed Thye, and another time we won a roll of linoleum by guessing the number of agates in a toilet bowl. One year we wandered into the Education building and saw a demonstration of television, an interesting invention: people stood in a crowd and looked at a picture of themselves on a screen. When they moved the picture moved—interesting. Hard to see why you'd want one if you had a mirror, but it was entertaining for a few minutes.

I came with Mother and Dad, and because we were Christians we gave a wide berth to the Midway, where ladies danced and did other things at the Persian Palms and Harlem Revue tent shows. We avoided sin, but it was exciting for me to be so close to it and see flashing pink lights and hear barkers say, in a voice like a talking dog's, "See Miss Roxanne just inside the gate, just beyond that tent flap, she's waiting in there for you, she wants to show you a *good* time," and I tried to see beyond the flap, not wanting Miss Roxanne to be disappointed by my lack of interest in her. It was exciting to hear bands playing slow raunchy dance tunes and to walk past the freak show with the two-headed boy, where the gypsy ticket-seller looked at me with a haughty look that said, *I know things you'll never know, what I've seen you'd never understand.*

I loved the Fair, the good and the bad. It was good to get out of our quiet town into a loud place with bad food and stink, music and sex blaring—listen—it's gorgeous. Dad gave me three dollars and I walked around not spending it, just gaping at the sights. Once I saw a sad midget stand and smoke a cigarette, holding his dog's leash, a big dog. Once I saw a man necking with a fat lady behind the Tilt-A-Whirl. He was running the ride. People were getting tossed around like eggs in a blender, and he was putting his hands up her shirt. Once I saw the newspaper columnist Olson Younger sitting in a booth under the sign MEET OLSON YOUNGER. He was puffier than his picture in the paper and more dejected. He sat drinking coffee after coffee and scrawling his autograph on free paper visors. He led a fairy-tale life in his column, meeting stars of stage and screen, eating meals with them, and even dancing once with Rita Hayworth, and he shared these wonderful moments with us through "The Olson Younger Column." The bad part was that I had to wear fundamentalist clothes to the Fair, white rayon shirt, black pants, black shoes, narrow tie, because we had to sing in the evening at the Harbor Light gospel tent near the Midway gate. We sang "Earnestly, tenderly, Jesus is calling, calling for you and for me," and fifty feet away a man said, "Yes, she is absolutely naked as the day she was born, and she's inside, twenty-five cents, two bits, the fourth part of a dollar." I held the hymnbook high so nobody would see me. I wanted to be cool and wear a T-shirt. In the pioneer days before polyester, a rayon shirt was like wearing waxed paper.

When the service was over, we got one ride on the ferris wheel, rising up over the bright lights into the dark night toward the stars, and falling back into our real lives. On the long ride home I slept, and when I woke up I was in a classroom that smelled of floor wax; Mrs. Mortenson was asking me to explain the Smoot-Hawley Act.

In 1955 my uncle Earl saw an ad for the $2,000 Minnesota State Fair Cake Baking Sweepstakes, sponsored by Peter Pan Flour, and he entered my aunt Myrna. He didn't mention this to her because he didn't want to upset her. She was a nervous person, easily startled by a sudden hello, and he was right, she made the greatest chocolate angel-food cake on the face of the earth. (To call it devil's food would give Satan encouragement so we didn't.) She also kept the cleanest kitchen in the Christian world. I liked to walk in, say hello, and when she recovered, she sat me down and fed me chocolate angel-food cake. As I ate it, she hovered overhead and apologized for it.

"*Oh,*" she sighed. "I don't know. I ought to throw this out for the dog. It's not very good. I don't know where my mind was—I lost track of how many eggs I put in, and I was all out of the kind of brown sugar I always use." I looked up at her in a trance, confused by the pure transcendent beauty of it, and she cut me a second, larger piece. "My mother was the one who could make a chocolate cake," she said, and then she allowed herself one taste of cake. And frowned. "It's gummy," she said. "It's like pudding."

"No," I said. "It's the best chocolate cake I ever tasted."

"Oh," she said, "your mother makes cake just as good as that." Once my mother heard that and smiled at me, hopefully, but all my life I've tried to tell the truth, and I replied honestly, "Sometimes she does, but not often."

Aunt Myrna was one of the few truly slender women in town. She set an impossible standard for the others. "She's small-boned," they said, but the truth is that she was so critical of her cooking, which was head and shoulders above everyone else's, that food didn't satisfy her. She was supernatural that way, like an angel. Angels who visit earth don't feed on corn dogs and pizza. Heavenly creatures have low metabolism, a little bite of something perfect is more than enough. Like her cake. An angel visiting Minnesota to do research on sweet corn could go for a week on one thin sliver of Aunt Myrna's chocolate cake.

When, in early August, Uncle Earl got an invitation from the Peter Pan Flour people, none of us was surprised she was chosen, she was so good. She was mad at him when he broke the news; she said, "I can't bake in front of a hundred people. Stand up and make a cake and have them stare at me like I was some kind of carnival freak. I won't do it."

He considered that for a minute. "I was thinking of it," he said, "as an opportunity to witness for the Lord. If you win the bake-off, I'm certain that you get to make a speech. You could give that Scripture recipe, 'Take four cups of 1 Corinthians 13 and three cups of Ephesians 4:32, four quarts of Hebrews 11:1. . . .' "

"I don't know if I would be up to it. . . ."

"I can do all things through Christ which strengtheneth me. Phillipians 4:13."

She practiced for two weeks and baked about forty cakes, most of them barely edible. She was experimenting with strange ingredients, like maple syrup and peanut butter, marshmallows, cherry bits. "You can't just stand up in front of a crowd and bake an ordinary chocolate cake," she said, but we convinced her that hers was good enough. She baked two of them that Friday, both champs. On the big Saturday she packed her ingredients, cake pans, mixer, and utensils in a cardboard box and covered it with a cloth, and they drove to the Cities, stopping on account of car trouble in Anoka and transferring from the Dodge to the bus. The bake-off was at three o'clock.

They arrived at two-thirty. She had assumed the bake-off was in the Home Activities building and then she discovered it was here at the grandstand. Peter Pan Flour had gone all out. The bake-off was part of the afternoon grandstand program, which also included high-wire acts, a big band playing Glenn Miller tunes, and Siberian tigers jumping through hoops of fire. She and twelve other women would stand on stage and bake cakes, and while the cakes were in the oven, Joey Chitwood's Thrill Show would perform daredevil stunts on the dirt track, and Olson Younger the newspaper columnist would judge the contest and award the prize. We helped Aunt Myrna to the stage. She was weak and moist. "Good luck," we said.

I stand here and look up at the grandstand and can see how nervous she must've been. I remember sitting up there in the forty-ninth row, under the pavilion, looking down at my tiny aunt in the green dress to the left of the saxophones while Joey Chitwood's Thrill Show drivers did flips and rolls, roaring around in white Fords. She stood at a long table whipping mix in a silver bowl, my aunt Myrna making a cake. She was mine, my relative, and I was so proud.

And then the cakes came out of the oven. The State Fair orchestra put down their newspapers and picked up their horns and played something from opera, and the radio-announcer emcee said that now the moment had come, and Olson Younger pranced around. He wore a green suit and orange tie and he waved to us with both hands. It was his moment of glory, and he sashayed from one entrant to the next, kissing her, rolling his eyes, and tasting her cake. When he tasted Myrna's cake, she shrank back from his embrace. She said a few words to him and I knew she was saying, "I don't know. I just can't seem to make em as rich as I used to—this isn't very good at all. It's gummy." It was the greatest chocolate cake in the world but he believed her. So she came in tenth.

A woman in white pedal pushers won because, Younger said, her cake was richer and moister. He had a hard time getting the words out. You could see the grease stains from her cake, beads of grease glittered in the sun. Uncle Earl said, "That's not cake, that's pudding he gave a prize to. This is a pudding contest he's running. He wouldn't know chocolate cake if it came up and ate him." And he was right. When Younger waltzed over to give Aunt Myrna her prize, a bowl, you could see he didn't know which way was north. It wasn't fair. She was the best. We waited for her in front of the grandstand. We both felt bad.

But when we saw her coming, she was all smiles. She hugged us both. She hardly seemed like herself. She threw her head back and said, "Oh, I'm glad it's over. But it was fun. I was so scared. And then I just forgot to be."

"But it wasn't fair," I said. She said, "Oh, he was drunk. It was all whiskey cake to him. But it doesn't matter. It was so much fun." I never saw her so lighthearted and girlish.

That night an old man came forward at the Harbor Light gospel meeting. He was confused and may have been looking for the way out, but we latched onto him and prayed for him. When he left, he seemed relieved. He was our first convert and we were thrilled. A soul hanging in the balance, there in our tent. Heaven and hell his choice, and he chose heaven, with our help, and then Dad lent him busfare.

That night, I said to my mother, "This is the last time I wear a rayon shirt, I hate them." She said, "All right, that's fine." I said, "You're not mad?" She said, "No, I thought you liked them, that's all."

I went up in the ferris wheel for a last ride before being thrown into seventh grade. It went up into the stars and fell back to earth and rose again, and I had a magnificent vision, or think I did, though it's hard to remember if it was that year with the chocolate cake or the next one with the pigs getting loose. The ferris wheel is the same year after year. It's like all one ride to me: we go up and I think of people I knew who are dead and I smell fall in the air, manure, corn dogs, and we drop down into blazing light and blaring music. Every summer I'm a little bigger, but riding the ferris wheel, I feel the same as ever, I feel eternal. The combination of cotton candy, corn dogs, diesel smoke, and sawdust, in a hot dark summer night, it never changes, not an inch. The wheel carries us up high, high, high, and stops, and we sit swaying, creaking, in the dark, on the verge of death. You can see death from here. The wind blows from the northwest, from the farm school in Saint Anthony Park, a chilly wind with traces of pigs and sheep in it. This is my vision: little kids holding on to their daddy's hand, and he is me. He looks down on them with love and buys them another corn dog. They are worried they will lose him, they hang on to his leg with one hand, eat with the other. This vision is unbearably wonderful. Then the wheel brings me down to the ground. We get off and other people get on. Thank you, dear God, for this good life and forgive us if we do not love it enough.

David and Agnes,
a Romance

It has been a quiet week in Lake Wobegon. Cool weather and, down at the football field, twenty boys are working out under the cool eye of Coach Magendanz. After fifteen laps and three rounds of pushups, it doesn't feel so cool, and they lie on their backs, imagining it's a beach, and a woman says, "Did you really play football?" and you say, "Oh, yeah. Sure." Coach says, "You wanna sleep, go home." She says, "Honey, who is that big ugly loud man?" Coach says, "All right, up, ten laps, come on, ladies!" And you jump up; the woman is gone, so is the beach blanket and the frozen Daiquiris. It's just hot sun and a cinder track and a big man yelling at you.

Cool nights, getting down around fifty, and it has all the farmers murmuring over their coffee cups at the Chatterbox. Farmers are worriers, and even though it's been the best year anyone can remember—record crops of oats and wheat, rain has been perfect, a half-inch a week—still, Rollie says, "I don't know, she's been so cool at night now. It makes you wonder if maybe it isn't going to be an early frost this year. It sure isn't doing the soybeans any good. Sure, the oats and wheat were real good, but the price went down, you know. And we could use a little more rain, to fill out the ears of corn." Things are real good but they could be better, because, you know, you never know. Right? "*Ja*, that's right, I know what you're talking about."

That's what they were talking about, but other people were talking about an item that appeared in the *Herald-Star* on Thursday. It read: "THANK YOU. I would like to thank my family and friends for their prayers, visits, flowers, gifts, food, when I was recovering in the hospital. I will never forget your love and generosity. Mange takk. Florence Tollefson."

Virginia Ingqvist read it and called up Arlene Bunsen. "Has Florence been in the hospital recently?" Arlene didn't think so. Neither did Irene when Arlene called her, or Marlys Diener or Marilyn Tollerud. Virginia called her nephew Pastor Ingqvist. He ought to know, and he said he didn't think so either, but then, Val Tollefson has been upset with him, so maybe if Florence went to the hospital, Val got another minister for her, who wouldn't sneak in liberal doctrine at bedside when she was too weak to resist. Virginia called Arlene back. She felt terrible to think maybe Florence had been in the hospital and nobody knew and she had felt so abandoned she put the ad in the paper to shame them. Arlene said, "I don't think Florence would do that." But it did seem to both of them that, about a month ago, they hadn't seen her for a while. Florence is so quiet, though, it was hard to know. Virginia ran into her Friday at Ralph's Grocery and said, "Florence, I've been thinking about you. How are you feeling these days?"

It seemed like an odd question to Florence, one that a number of people had asked her since Thursday. She looked down in the freezer chest among the hams and wondered if something was the matter with her. Did she look that bad? She's a little heavier, but then she always gets a little heavier during the summer months, especially if she's put on some weight over the winter.

It was Arlene who finally came right out and asked. Florence said, gosh, no, she wasn't in the hospital. If she had been, she'd have made sure people knew about it. It's the Christian way: if you need help, you tell people, so they won't feel bad for not giving it. That thank-you item was ten years old, from Florence's old appendectomy. Harold Starr put it in the paper because it was on his desk. He's got stacks of stuff on his desk, some of it going back to childhood, and once in a while you open the paper and a piece of old news jumps out at you: here's the honor roll from high school a quarter-century ago and I'm still not on it, years later, and no smarter. And here's an obituary: your poor old grandma has died, again; once should've satisfied her, but no, she wanted to reperish.

So Florence was fine. Arlene still wondered: wasn't she gone for a few days about the middle of July, she and Val? Seems like we didn't see them—well, I suppose they were around somewhere.

In fact, Val and Florence had planned to go to Mount Canaan, Washington, in June, to pick up a trunk of books and papers and things that had belonged to Val's father, David Tollefson, who died last April. Val had not attended the funeral. He hadn't told anyone that his father died. Most people thought his dad died long ago. Val meant to go west in June, thinking there might be some important Tollefson family history in the trunk, and then he got cold feet and told them to ship the trunk to Minnesota. It arrived around the middle of July. That was when Florence and Val disappeared for a few days. They were in the house reading his dad's papers.

Val's parents were David and Mary Tollefson, married in 1927, and Valdemar was the oldest boy, born in 1928. His father was a carpenter, and in 1946, when Val was eighteen, his father went to work on a house down the road from them that belonged to the Hedders. David added on a bedroom and a living room with a stone fireplace. It took him two months, even with Mr. Hedder's help, and about Labor Day, when he finished the job, he came by the Hedders' house late one night in his Ford coupe and picked up Mrs. Hedder and they went off together and never came back.

They left seven children behind, two of hers and five of his, and drove west, all night, and were married the next morning in South Dakota, which made them guilty of bigamy, but perhaps they thought adultery was worse. They continued west and wound up in Mount Canaan, and he got work there as a carpenter, and ten years later he tried to get back in touch with his family in Lake Wobegon.

Nobody in town had so much as mentioned his name for ten years. The space he occupied was a blank. He was a popular man; men thought he was a real good worker, women thought he was polite and handsome, and children loved him, even little kids who didn't know him—they'd run right up and he scooped them in—but when he left five children and a wife in the middle of the night, there was no doubt which side Lake Wobegon was on, and he was put out of mind and his name disappeared. Ella Anderson was his younger sister. He wrote to her and she wrote back. One Sunday, Ella, talking to Mary after church, mentioned that David was well, and Mary shot her a look of pure bitterness and walked away and wouldn't speak to her again for more than a year.

Val was eighteen and he never forgot. Nobody's father ever left, not in that town; a father was as permanent as the color of your eyes. Val took everything his father had ever given him, every gift, books, bicycle, even a new deer rifle, and he threw them away. He took the rifle down to the lake and swung it around by the barrel, and it flew out over the water, and he heard the splash and crumpled to the ground and lay there and cried.

The trunk that came in July was the first thing of his father's he had seen in forty years. He hauled it down to the basement and it sat by the fruit jars for a week before he opened it. When he looked through the first layer, Val realized that of *course* there wouldn't be any Tollefson family history in it—his father had taken none with him. David's history in the family stopped when he turned the key in that Ford coupe. There were old brown Sunday-school magazines on top, books on Scripture, hymnals, a certificate thanking David for years of faithful service to the Zion Lutheran Church of Mount Canaan, and a Bible. In the front of the Bible was his father's name and the name of his second wife, the former

Mrs. Hedder. Val had never known the name of the woman his dad ran off with. Her name was Agnes.

Agnes. Val sat down on the trunk, feeling a little weak to have her name after all these years. *Agnes.* It felt unfaithful to his mother to know that name. He was surprised how curious he was to know who that woman was. He knew the story about his dad working on the house. He imagined them glancing at each other as the walls started to go up. Perhaps she helped him. His dad hammering, planing, sawing lumber—fresh lumber smells—and her coming out to ask how everything was going. Perhaps she made him a good lunch every day and they talked, and what did they talk about? What sort of man would do this: as you work on a man's house and build him a new bedroom, to be planning to run away with his wife?

In an old Folger's coffee can, Val found letters, dozens of them, addressed: "Dear Mrs. Hedder," then "Dear Agnes," and some "My darling Agnes," all written in pencil, in a handwriting he recognized right away, even forty years later. Val thought, "I don't want to read these," but he did. The letters had been folded into small squares. Maybe he had hidden them for her to find.

"Dear Agnes," he read, "Something has taken hold of my heart, a wonderful feeling, and I cannot turn away from it or I would die inside and be no use to anyone. This feeling leads me to you, my dear lady, and though I know that what you say is wise and true, still I know what is in my heart and I want you to come away with me."

Val cringed. Always the story had been that the Hedder woman lured his father away. But it wasn't true.

He spent hours that day and the next in the basement, by the washtubs, sorting through the layers, laying stuff out on the long table where Florence sorts clothes. It was frightening, like opening a grave sealed shut for years. He reached in and picked up a maple box he knew his father had made, plain wood but so well fitted, and inside, in twelve compartments, were twelve fishing lures his father had tied, more beautiful than jewelry. Pictures of his father and the woman . . . Agnes. Val couldn't look at them more than two seconds, they were so ordinary, like any other married couple standing by a car, sitting on steps. And a poem David had written her—his father had never written him a poem, but here was a poem. Val read it and felt weak. He had to go sit upstairs and turn on the radio. It was like a cave-in down deep in the earth under your house, an event so far in the past he never thought about it, now moving, and his own life shifted and sagged, and he felt afraid.

He went for a walk, and Florence descended the stairs and looked over the mess. It was clear that when David Tollefson arrived in Mount Canaan, Washington, with Agnes in 1946, he got down to business and set about to become a good citizen, and clearly the people in Mount Canaan thought he was and they loved and admired him and said so. But what Florence looked at over and over were the love letters. She held them in her hand— written in pencil on cheap tablet, faded in places to where you couldn't read them:

"My darling Agnes," she read, "This is harder than anything I ever did, but I know it is for our happiness and that is worth more to me than their opinion. When I am with you, I feel quick and happy, and when you aren't near it is sad and empty, I walk out of the house and up the road so I can say your name out loud."

And she found the poem.

> A love so true sings out to me
> I know that if I turned away
> I'd hear the song until my dying day,
> Hear the words—forget the melody.
> It's a song you sang while you were working, dear,
> Patching shirts, and I was outdoors
> Bracing the kitchen wall with two-by-fours
> And heard the song and stopped, it was so clear.
> It said we should open our hearts and be free.
> Love has power over doubt and fear.
> I put down the hammer, leaving the wall to be
> Built by someone else, and so—here

I am waiting for you, knowing I belong
To one who knows it too, the old sweet song.

Val came back and they sat together on the basement steps. He said, "I decided to burn it. Everything. I've looked at it, that's all that matters. Nobody else has to see it."

"Well, if that's what you've decided. It's yours."

"That's what I want to do. He had his life and I don't need to judge him, God will judge him, but I don't need to keep his memory alive either. When he left here, he gave up his right to that sort of thing."

"You're going to burn the poem too? It was a nice poem."

"Everything."

"All right," she said, and she helped him load it all back into the trunk and carry it up to the car. They drove up to the dump, to the back corner behind the birch trees. He tipped the trunk over and put a match to the pile and it went up like straw. Everything was gone in a minute. Except the trunk—he saved that. And the lures—he could use those. The rest he burned. Except for the poem—Florence had snuck that out and put it in her purse. She couldn't see destroying it—"A love so true sings out to me"— seemed to tremble when she looked at it. She felt better knowing Val had saved something too, though she knew he'd be furious if he saw the poem in her purse, and that made her feel guilty. All these years she's had so few secrets, and no guilty ones. It made her think maybe this was the beginning of the end of her marriage too. It was like a precious stone you find alongside the road; it's somebody else's, you can't keep it for yourself. So she took it in to Viola at the historical society the next morning. "Viola," she said, "here's a poem somebody around here wrote; it looks old, but it's nobody I know, but maybe it's worth saving." Viola put it in an envelope and wrote "Poem, Unknown" in black marker. Later she took it down the basement. Back in the corner, behind a commode, under boxes of license plates and trophies and high-school yearbooks, was an oak file cabinet (itself historic, thought to be the first file cabinet in L.W.), a cabinet now full of letters, in English and German and Norwegian, about weather and crops and worries about money and children, everyday business, and she stuck it in. The poem he wrote with a trembling heart lies between the pages of an old account book of the Co-op Elevator Association, from 1902, showing that the oat and wheat crops were good that year also, thanks to good rainfall, but that, of course, they could have used a little more.

The Killer

It has been a quiet week in Lake Wobegon. It was cloudy and rainy and pretty chilly, and in a town that's plain to begin with, when it gets wet and cold you lose most of the charm you didn't have in the first place. Some storytellers would take one look at a little town on a cold wet fall day and tell you about a family on a vacation trip through the Midwest who wonder why this town seems so deserted and get out of their car and there on Maple Street, coming at them with a pitchfork, is a gigantic man with no eyes and chunks of his face falling off and big clods of brown dirt stuck to his bib overalls, but I am a storyteller who, for better or worse, is bound by facts, so I simply observe that nobody was out walking because it was raining, a steady discouraging rain. But there were strange cars driving through.

A culvert had washed out and the roadbed collapsed on Highway 9, just south of the Pet the Tame Deer Park, and the twelve-mile detour led straight past the Co-op grain elevator through town. There was heavy traffic, and Skoglund's Five & Dime held a Detour Sale, 10 percent off on all items, and Clifford at the Mercantile

125

put out a sign, "Fall Eyewear—Slashed in Half—Big Savings"—
but nobody stopped. Ten percent is nothing nowadays. And when
you put the word "Eye" close to the words "Slashed in Half,"
people don't slow down and look for a parking spot, not in a cold
wet little town; they think of the guy with the pitchfork. (Did that
sign say "Big Savings" or "Big Savage"?)

For one morning and two long afternoons, Clarence stood in
the Bunsen Motors showroom watching the traffic cruise by, imagining a car might stop and a guy get out and say, "I'm looking for
a 1986 Pinto, two-door, straight-stick, no factory air, kind of a
dark puke color—like this one right here!" But the cars streamed
past, faces peering out the windows, and you could see what they
were saying:

"Where is this?"

"How should I know? You still want to stop for coffee?"

"Not here. What is this anyway? I'm sure glad I don't live here.
I don't know how people could stay in a place like this. What a
dump. How far to Minneapolis?"

"How should I know?"

Coming home from a meeting in Albany, Mayor Clint Bunsen
noticed that the "Welcome to Lake Wobegon, Gateway to Central
Minnesota" sign had fallen down sideways, and he sent Bud out
to fix it, but when Bud unbolted the one surviving bolt, the sign
fell down and broke into three pieces, which Bud hauled back and
piled behind the fire barn. He said, "You could nail em back together, I suppose, but I donno. . . ." His voice trailed off into a
sniff that said, *What's the point of it?* Our town is not shown on
maps, so why not be anonymous too? Nobody thinks that we exist
anyway. (We've never seen proof of *their* existence, or much need
for it either. But what the hell.)

So the detour passed without benefit and then the trees started
to turn color, especially some maples who got overexcited and
went bright yellow. It seemed early for fall, considering all the
work we have to do before winter. We're not ready for it. Mr.
Berge said to Wally in the Sidetrack, "Shees, it's bin cool out,
don't you think. I thought dey said it was supposta warm up a

little, fer crine out loud." Wally said, "It's almost October, Berge. It's going to be getting a lot cooler from here on out right through the end of the year and into next. It's not going to warm up any time soon."

It's easy for Wally to be a realist. He spends his days in the Sidetrack like a bear in a cave—a cave with green and orange and blue neon beer signs and a bevy of older bears leaning against the bar and belching beer breath. Wally stands in the dark, listening to the bears grumbling and mumbling, and he doesn't know much about how the lovely world outside can raise our hopes. How Tuesday morning, when the sun briefly shone, could excite a person, and how, walking along Elm Street on a morning simultaneously damp and cool and bright and smelling of smoke and sunshine, a person could feel that this was permanent—that God in His grace had removed our town beyond the force of time, beyond change, and placed it on a hill by a blue lake on an eternal perfect day in mid-September where those whom we love will always be as they are now. And then Tuesday afternoon it was dim and rainy and cold. We felt a cold chill. We wondered if there is a God or is the universe only one seed in one apple on a tree in another world where a million years of ours is only one of their moments and what we imagine as our civilization is only a tiny charge of static electricity and the great truth that our science is slowly grasping is the fact that the apple in which we are part of one seed is *falling*—has been falling for a million years and in one one-millionth of a second it will hit hard frozen ground in that other world and split open and lie on the ground and a bear will come along and gobble it up, everything, the Judeo-Christian heritage, science, democracy, the Renaissance, art, music, sex, sweet corn—all will disappear into the black hole of a bear—that was how Wednesday felt.

A big mood swing, from belief in eternal happiness with a loving God to atheistic nihilism and despair in twenty-four hours in a town of less than one thousand population. Fall is a powerful season.

In fall when I was young, I thought, This year I will do better in physics. Study hard, listen, take good notes, and when he calls on me, I'll give the answer in a loud clear voice, and not just a good answer but a brilliant one, possibly an answer that illuminates some dark corner of physics. I'll be not only a good student, I'll be a genius. "SEVENTEEN-YEAR-OLD RURAL MINNESOTA BOY POSES NEW THEOREM OF LIGHT THAT PROVES DOCTRINE OF JUSTIFICATION BY FAITH—GRACE OF GOD EXPRESSED AS MATHEMATICAL CERTAINTY BY BOY FORMERLY CONSIDERED SLOW LEARNER."

Then October came and I didn't understand anything. I was scared that he'd call on me and fear made the air around me hot and dry, creating teacher suction, and he drew close to me and said, "Go up and see what you can do," so I stood at the blackboard, looked at the problem, and thought, "God, take this chalk and write the answer. Or make the blackboard fall off and kill me. Please." I wrote a few faint numbers and the smart kids laughed. He said, from the back of the room: "We talked about this last week, Mr. Keillor! I assumed you were paying attention! Your eyes were open, as I recall! Your head was up off the desk!"

One fall years ago, I was elected president of Young People's Bible Study, which in the Sanctified Brethren there are only five young people total, including Mel, who is thirty-four, but it's an honor and I promised myself that this year I will organize our Bible study as never before and prepare the lesson outline early and meditate prayerfully on it, and then one Saturday night I got a last-minute date with *this girl*, and so it wasn't until Sunday morning I examined Paul's first epistle to Timothy and had to meditate fast, and when Mel stood up to pray to open Bible study, I thought, "Go long, Mel," and looked down at Paul's exhortation to Tim to avoid false teaching and was thinking how I could develop this thought in such a way as to take up twenty minutes ("Let's start by defining our terms. What do we mean by 'teaching'? by 'false'? What exactly is an 'epistle'?") when suddenly Mel was praying a strange prayer—"And now, Lord, it's on my heart this morning to pray for, uh, *one in our midst* who has, uh, taken up with *impure companions* and, uh, neglected Thy precious truths for the pursuit of, uh, *pleasures of the flesh*—Lord, we would ask . . ." In a group of five people, it didn't take much imagination to know who he meant; it wasn't himself, and Larry and Joyce were married, so that left me and my cousin Roy, and Roy didn't have a driver's license. My face burned. Here I was about to lead Bible study and Mel was cutting me down in prayer. Maybe I had *pursued* pleasures of the flesh, but I had failed, and didn't that count for anything? We had sat in the car up at the gravel pit drinking Cokes with vodka poured in them, and I had contemplated two or three times the buttons on her lovely blouse, and then she said, in a strange choked voice, "Oh no, oh no," and grabbed for the door and the handle came off, and I said, "What's wrong, Ann?" and she said, "Oh no," and turned toward me. It was her turning toward me that, one moment later, ruined the evening and my tan corduroy jacket, and now here I was being prayed for as a backslider and what did I have to show for it? "Lord, touch his heart . . . give him strength to witness for You."

It was October 1977 when my classmate Marnie Montaine (*née* Barb Diener) returned to Lake Wobegon, the first one in town history to become a movie star. In her honor, they combined Homecoming and Halloween to make one big celebration, with an afternoon parade and school kids in costumes, and the band stood and played "Anchors Aweigh" under a "Welcome Home, Marnie! (Barb)" banner as she swept past the crowd in a black dress and red shoes. "Oh hi," she said, "nice to see you again! How are you?"—not calling people by their names and looking them straight in the forehead . . . but it was nice. And at the Bijou, Bernie had fixed the magic lantern that made clouds move across the ceiling and put new bulbs in the stars, more than two hundred. Her movie, *The Hand Under the Bed,* was shown there to a full house.

Barb Diener had left town for good in 1968 after coming and going for a few years, trying one thing and another. She headed for California and landed in Sonoma and joined a commune that made belts out of feathers and changed her name to Starflower Moonbright and hooked up with a young man named World Anderson. They went to Los Angeles to see the son of a famous singing star, who had promised a recording contract for World's songs, which were mostly humming—he called them Breathing Songs, they were thirty or forty minutes long, and he could perform more of them in an evening than most audiences would choose if it were left up to them. She left World to go with a theater troupe called "U," six actors who didn't so much put on plays as stand in front of the audience and confront them with their hypocrisies, and then she got into a jeans ad, and she became Marnie Montaine, and one night in 1974 her family saw her in a TV commercial for Papa's Popcorn, though you had to watch close to see her—she was a kernel and she popped pretty fast.

She wasn't exactly the star of *The Hand Under the Bed* either. She played the clerk at the lonely motel who, when the couple arrived on the dark and stormy night and said, "Please. We saw the No Vacancy sign, but wouldn't you have something—we'll take anything," Marnie said, "Well, gee, there's cabin eight, but we haven't used that—not for thirteen years since the night— *hey*, isn't this the anniversary of that night when—" and they said, "We'll take it!" That was Barb's one and only scene. Bernie ran the film back a couple times and people clapped and Barb stood up and made a speech about the movie business and how what looked simple on the screen was actually terribly complicated and how absolutely nice the director Phil Fontinella was, and he was going to use her in his next picture, a bigger part, and then she said she had to leave—Thanks so much, goodbye, you're beautiful—and we all stood up and clapped. And then we weren't sure what to do.

The show was over, really, with Barb gone, but there was an hour left of the movie with the couple and their four children and cabin 8, so Bernie started it up and we watched for a while. People died right and left, hacked to death by something lurking just off camera, it was hard to keep track of. The clouds were lovely, though, and the little stars twinkling in the ceiling, just like when

I snuck down there with girls and sat in the dark with their moist hand in mine.

Later in the movie you finally see the killer, a guy in bib overalls, pitchfork, empty eyes, face falling off in big chunks, but of course with Barb gone it wasn't that good, so most of the audience left early, except for some young people in the back, who were too scared to move and who were trying to be a comfort to each other.

Eloise

It *has been a quiet week in Lake Wobegon.* It was warm and bright and the trees were in full color, magnificent, explosive, like permanent fireworks—reds and yellows, oranges, some so brilliant that Crayola never put them in crayons for fear the children would color outside the lines. Maple trees the color of illicit romance, blazing red sumac and oaks and aspen, such color that you weren't sure you were in this world but perhaps had stepped through a seam in the tapestry and walked into a magical wood. But the only trail through there is a cowpath, so you have to watch where you step.

Florian and Myrtle Krebsbach went driving Tuesday to look at the beautiful trees, which neither of them enjoys, but they go because they've done it for years. Myrtle gets carsick more easily now since she bumped her head on the cupboard. The bright colors only made her dizziness more vivid. Florian was grumpy because he hates to see the odometer roll on his '66 Chev (like new, only forty-seven thousand miles on her). Low mileage is a form of youth to Florian, it means plenty of mileage to come. He drove slowly toward Millet and back and Myrtle hung on to the strap. She said, of the fall colors, "Well, if this don't prove to them there's an Almighty, I don't know what in hell will." They drove 6.2 miles at twenty-five mph and returned to home base, where he wiped the engine clean with a rag soaked in gasoline. The smell of gas makes Florian perk up.

The leaves reached their peak about Thursday and then, in late afternoon, seemed to dim. Friday morning we woke up and could see that we had passed our apex and were heading for the nadir.

It was still warm, though, so when Ranger Steve came to the third grade with a boxful of snakes, they were pretty lively. Snakes are our friends, not slimy, not evil, but really very beautiful and nothing to be afraid of, he said. "I'm sure Mrs. Hughes isn't afraid of snakes—look," he said, and draped a black one on her shoulder as her body shrank and then stiffened. "See? Snakes aren't slimy at all. Actually their skin is rather dry—right, Mrs. Hughes? This is called a bridle snake; it bites, but only if you bother it."

Ranger Steve smiled. "It's all right, there's nothing to worry about," he said to Mrs. Hughes, whose eyes were shut, and took the snake in his big manly hand, and set it on his broad shoulder. Instantly the harmless reptile dove into the V of his collar and disappeared. Ranger Steve said, *"Oh God,"* and grabbed at it. He was wearing a green jump suit, with no belt for a roadblock, and he turned his back to the children and bent over and tried to grab the bridle snake in the jump suit. It was warm under there and the snake was excited, and the children heard a cry, and Steve staggered and the snake came out his left pants leg. They all helped catch it. Steve talked more about snakes but his smile had slipped to the side and gone out of focus. The passage of the bridle snake through the jump suit had worn him out, the exertion of being cool and hysterical at the same time.

Afterward, some of the boys did an imitation of Ranger Steve with the snake in his pants, and Mrs. Hughes said, "I don't consider that one bit funny," even though it was hilarious.

That's what wears out a grown-up person: the contradictions.

After school, a girl from the third grade jumped on her old blue coaster bike and tore off toward the woods to find snakes and put them on her brothers. Then, coasting down Branch Street, she saw her little brother standing looking at their dog Fatso lying by the tree, covering him up with leaves. She swerved and headed straight for the innocent little child and yelled, "I can't stop! No brakes! I can't stop," but he stood there like a stone so she stopped. She said, "You coulda been killed. Why'ntcha move? That was a close call, y'know." Fatso stood up and tottered around back of the tree but the little boy was too scared to move. "You're dumb, you know that? You're as dumb as a dog." Fatso blinked. The little boy's eyes filled with tears to hear his sweet sister talk to him like that, two pools of pale-blue tears in his blue eyes, and then he made a decision that certainly changed his life: he took one step toward her with his left foot and with his right he kicked the big jerk in her ankle as hard as he could. He held back nothing. A swift hard kick.

More happened then: she chased him, caught him, threw him down, pounded him. But it wasn't important. He had done something. (The wrong thing—it's wrong to kick your sister—but sometimes the wrong thing is exactly the right thing to do.) His mother ran out and hauled her off him. "What is going on out here?"

"He kicked me—here," said Amy, and to show how much it hurt, her big brown eyes filled up with tears.

"What did you do to him?"

"Nothing. I was riding my bike."

"Paul! How could you do a thing like that?"

He looked up at his mother. He wasn't sure.

"Just for that, you come inside."

That was fine with him. He preferred inside.

These are Florian and Myrtle Krebsbach's grandchildren and their daughter Eloise, who lives around the corner from Carl. She's got three kids, these two plus a tall lonesome boy named Charlie, one in a long tradition of tall skinny lonesome boys who grew up there. Eloise's name is Best. She married Chuck Best out of high school, a handsome friendly boy, and three years ago he decided he'd been married long enough to her. He came home to pack his bags.

Eloise cried and then, when he went to the garage for his golf clubs, she locked him out of the house without so much as a warm jacket. She told him she was going to give all his clothes to the church clothing drive. When he asked for his car keys she laughed at him through the letter slot. "You want to start over, then *start* over," she said. "Don't be such a drip. This isn't a halfway house, mister, this is my home. You want to go away, go ahead, but don't ask me to give you a ride."

This took place on Greener Avenue South in Minneapolis one bright summer day in 1983. The neighbors were out working on their yards, and when they noticed the Bests' conversation—the shouts from the slot, the man in the blue blazer and tan slacks saying, "Please. Ellie. Try to control yourself"—the neighbors shut off their mowers and got busy doing quiet things. They studied trees for signs of drought, snipped at a hedge with silent little snips, quietly pulled crabgrass.

"Ellie, please. Let's discuss this. Let me in and let's talk."

"I am talking!" she said and called him a bunch of words that moms don't use. "All right," he said. "That's it. That's all I'm going to take from you." And he walked gravely and respectably down the walk. He stood at the end of his walk, glancing left and right, then turned left as she opened the door and yelled, "You . . . are a . . . lousy lover!" Her voice echoed off the frame and brick houses—"lousylousylousylousyloverlousyloverlover-lover"—far up the pleasant street where they'd had a sweet comfortable ten years, and he heard the lawn sprinklers whisper, "It's true, it's true, it's true, it's true."

More happened then. He came after her with excellent legal talent and pounded her pretty hard in court, and she wound up in a two-bedroom tumble-down stucco house in Lake Wobegon, where, well—to be a single woman with three children, you might as well paint the house chartreuse and convert to Islam and make it complete.

Her mother, Myrtle, says, "Eloise, you're the first one in this family ever to collect a welfare check, it's a disgrace. People talk about us. Do you know that? They never useta, and now you can hear em all over town."

She said, "Mother, don't get too ashamed now, because I've got a long way to go."

"I don't see why you can't get yourself a job."

"I'm trying."

"Try harder."

So last Thursday her little ad appeared in the *Herald-Star*. Harold himself called her Sunday and asked, "Is this legit?" So there it was: "Dancing Taught in My Home or Yours. Individual lessons. Polka, Waltz, Foxtrot, or Lindy. Eloise Krebsbach Best."

Ella Anderson called her Thursday night. "Ellie," she said, "I didn't know you could dance."

"Well, Ella, you never asked me."

"I wonder if this wouldn't help my bad hip."

Ella is old and has a hard life taking care of herself and Henry. People don't visit them, because they're embarrassed to see him, a man once important in our town, now old and sleepy. Suddenly he'll sit up and talk about your horse and somebody named David and where did the girls go? The girls went away and became middle-aged a long time ago. Ella is lonely. Her daughter Charlotte called one night and suddenly said, "Well? Mother? Do you want to or not?" And Ella couldn't remember the question. Charlotte said, "Just say yes or no," and Ella said, "Yes." And now she wonders what she said yes to.

"What's it like to be old?" Ellie asked her.

"Old age is like birds in the winter. It's hard to keep going. But you still have your good days, and one good day makes you want to keep on. I used to get so upset if any little thing went wrong. Now everything goes wrong and it doesn't bother me, and some little thing is so wonderful—if my son writes me a letter, that's wonderful. And if he puts in a picture of my grandchildren, then that's just about everything."

Ellie rolled up the old rag rug and pushed back the coffee table and chairs. "What'll it be, a waltz?" she said. A waltz it was, the

"Blue Skirt Waltz," and if you walked by on Thursday night and saw in the window two women dancing, one with white hair and the other with red, smiling, turning, would you have thought it was strange? Would you have stopped? Or would you have walked on, taking the sweetness of it to heart on a fall night turning cold, the bright colors, magnificence and glory all around us everywhere in the air.

The
Royal Family

_____

G*race Tollefson graduated from Lake* Wobegon High School in 1938, a thespian and debater and member of the Order of the Shining Star, a quiet and sensible girl who surprised everyone and ran off with a man by the name of Alex Campbell. He was a handsome green-eyed fellow, the driver of a 1936 Singer coupe, who performed magic tricks with quarters and napkins, told jokes and tossed kids in the air, and seemed to have no prospect in this world. He kept a bottle of whiskey in the trunk of his car and he laughed too loud. The Tollefsons were united in opposition to him but Grace married him and moved to Saint Paul. Years went along, and people heard bits of news that she wasn't entirely happy with him. A child came along, and another. And a third. He left her in 1948. As some people told it, he came home drunk and she locked him out, but it didn't matter. There was nothing for her to do but get a ride back home and live off the charity of her family and the Lutheran church.

Her younger brother Lawrence bought her an old green mobile home and moved it into the yard behind his house, next to the garden. Lutheran ladies came and cleaned it up and donated old furniture, a three-legged table, a very nice green sofa with large holes chewed out of it, some rickety chairs, a reproduction of Larsson's "The Last Supper." People were nice to them, as you'd be nice to anybody who was very peculiar. Divorce in that town was as odd as a purebred dog. Grace could see what people thought as she walked down the street: *We were right, we told you, now look at you.*

The oldest boy was Earl, her daughter was Marlys, and the little boy was Walter, who was only three and couldn't remember his father. When he asked his mother, she only said that Alex was a handsome man descended from Scottish nobility, that he had a weakness but it wasn't anybody's fault. When he asked his grandma Tollefson, she said, "Huh! Those Campbells were all alike. There wasn't one of them worth mentioning. But it's not your fault, Walter. You didn't ask to be born into this world, now did you?" He didn't ask again.

It was hard living in a mobile home, living off contributions. At night, when the four of them cleared the supper table and did dishes, when she was feeling especially sad, Grace said, "Well, what are we going to do when our ship comes in?" That was the cue to quit feeling sorry and to talk about what they'd do when they got rich. They'd have a big white brick mansion in Saint Paul with a stone wall around it, a crystal chandelier in the dining room, fireplaces in the bedrooms. Oriental rugs. A swimming pool. They'd have six servants, six ladies from the Lutheran church, to fix their meals and clean up. Earl had simple tastes and wanted a pony to ride bareback around the streets of Saint Paul and a .22 rifle. Marlys wanted a large dollhouse for her dolls, Mr. and Mrs. Parker Whitehurst and their children, Jacqueline, Lorraine, and Kathy.

Walter went along with what they wanted, but one thing he didn't say was that he hoped when the ship came in his father would be standing in the bow in a white uniform and a blue cap with gold braid.

One day they got a letter from a man in Philadelphia doing research on Scottish nobility, who asked who their ancestors were so he could look it up. He needed the information for a book he was writing. He enclosed a check for $15. So Grace wrote down what she knew about Alex's ancestors and sent it off and didn't think more of it until another letter arrived from Philadelphia five days later.

She opened the envelope. It was addressed to Mrs. Grace Campbell, but the letter was addressed "Your Royal Highness." He wrote: "Today is the happiest day of my life as I greet my one true Sovereign Queen." And went on to say that their branch of the Campbell family was first in the line of succession of the House of Stewart, the Royal Family of Scotland. She passed it to the children and they each read it carefully, as if it were spun gold and if they dropped it, it would shatter into little pieces. She was quiet a long time. Then she said, "It can't be true but we'll find out. Meanwhile, you're not to tell a soul. You don't tell anybody." They promised.

A few days later, the Philadelphia man, whose name was D. R. Mackay, sent them a chart that unfolded bigger than their kitchen table. In the upper-left-hand corner were King James the Seventh, King James the Old Pretender, Prince Charles. There were several lines of counts and marquises, and in the lower-right-hand corner, skirting the clans of Keith and Ferguson, the lines led right straight to them: Earl, Marlys, and Walter. The Royal Family of Scotland living in Lake Wobegon in a green mobile home, furniture donated by the Lutheran church.

They were astounded beyond words. Disbelieving at first, afraid to put their weight on something so beautiful, afraid it was too good to be true, and then it took hold—this was grace, pure grace that God offered them. Not their will but His. Grace. Here they were in their same dismal place but everything had changed. They were different people. Their surroundings were the same, but they were different—and there were times in the months that followed when Walter wished he could tell somebody that he was a prince of Scotland, particularly his cousin Donna who lived in the house the Campbells lived behind and who made complex rules about who could play in her yard and for how long and what they had to do for her, as if she was royalty. Walter longed to tell her. One day D. R. Mackay wrote to Walter, "Your Royal Highness: Discovering you and your family has been the happiest accomplishment of my life. And if God in His infinite wisdom should deny me the opportunity to meet you face to face on this Earth, I should still count myself the luckiest of men for this chance to play a part, however small, in restoring Scotland to her former greatness. Please know that you are in my thoughts and prayers every day. And that I will work with every ounce of my being to restore you from your sad exile to the land, the goods, and the reverence to which you, by the grace of God, are entitled." A boy doesn't get a letter like that very often. He kept it under his mattress, he knew it by heart. He lay in bed and thought, over and over, "the land, the goods, and the reverence to which you are entitled."

The Tollefsons and other people in town, of course, had gotten wind of those letters from Philadelphia and were curious; they tried to pry the secret out of the children, but they wouldn't tell, and then some people began to resent them for keeping a secret. Lawrence said to Grace, "You know, Grace, sometimes you act like you think you're too good to walk on the same ground with us." She told him that she figured she was at least as good as anyone else. He said that if she was, maybe she'd like to try supporting herself. "Gladly," she replied.

They packed up to move back to Saint Paul. Lawrence packed their old donated furniture in a trailer but at the last minute Grace said, "Take it off. I don't want to take that with me. That's not mine. That belongs to the church."

"You might need it. Don't be so proud," he said. She looked at him. She said, "Lawrence, what I need in this life is understanding and love. And I need style. And I won't be carrying it with me from Lake Wobegon. I'm going to have to find it where I'm going." The children sat in the back seat and looked at the neighbors who'd come to look at them as they left. Marlys held the Whitehursts on her lap. "Someday, when we're the Royal Family, they'll have a parade here in our honor. And I'm not going to come," she announced.

Life in Saint Paul has not been easy for them. Earl moved away a few years ago, he was tired of the whole business. He went to school to study bookkeeping and got a job in a salvage yard, as a bookkeeper. Grace had him sign a paper relinquishing all rights to succession. Marlys is twenty-four and still lives with her mother in their apartment near the State Fair grounds and so does Walter, a student at Hamline University. Over the years they've read all the histories of Scotland, learned its geography, and studied over and over the sad story of the House of Stewart, from which they're descended. That the English in 1688 overthrew their true and rightful king, James the Seventh, and brought in the Dutchman William of Orange, and when William and Mary bred no successor, the Stewarts were waiting in the wings, glad to forgive the English and come and be King and Queen again. But no, England sent to Germany for a motley bunch of princes from the House of Hanover. Brought them in and made them royalty. In 1746, Bonnie Prince Charlie came over from France and rallied his brave Highlanders and marched south into England and won battles against the English, then, for some reason, turned around and went back. And in April, at the Battle of Culloden, his army and his hopes were torn to shreds, and the Stewarts went over the hill into history.

Whenever Grace saw an article about Queen Elizabeth in the paper, she bit her lip and shook her head. Usurpers was what they were, all of them. *Germans*, sitting on the Royal Throne of Scotland. It wasn't right. It wasn't even decent.

Year after year, month after month, letters arrived from D. R. Mackay: he was forming a committee for the restoration of the House of Stewart to the throne, he was enlisting the help of other governments—secret meetings had been held and overtures made and some very encouraging signals had been received, *extremely* encouraging—he didn't want the Family to be troubled with details but he had been encouraged by the French, the Spanish, the Portuguese, and even the Americans had indicated an interest— so it could happen any time, they should prepare themselves. Whenever their faith was low, Grace read the letters out loud and she turned to Walter and said, "Walter, tell us what it'll be like when we get the call."

He said: "It'll come at eight-thirty in the evening on a summer day. August. We'll have eaten sweet corn and tomatoes and hot dogs for supper, and the phone rings and they tell us to be on a plane the next morning. We'll be too excited to sleep. We'll go to the airport, exhausted, and get on the plane. Mother is wearing her good navy-blue dress, Marlys her silk bridesmaid dress from Nancy's wedding, I have my dark wool suit on. We land in Glasgow. There are huge crowds of people. Six men in blue pinstripe suits get on the plane, they're from Scotland Yard, they escort us to a helicopter. We fly to Holyrood Castle on High Street in Edinburgh. We're taken in to freshen up and have a light lunch and we can hear a low roar outside, and after a while we'll go up to the balcony—there is the balustrade, with thirteen microphones. And down there are a hundred thousand Scots. And we walk forward and speak."

"You do it, Walter. I'm too nervous," said Grace.

He often thought what he would say. Perhaps something humorous like "How much is all this costing?" Or "Nice to see ya." But he'd aim for something royal and dignified. It was wonderful to imagine being restored and going to Scotland and being the Royal Family, though more modest than the Germans down in Buckingham Palace—they wouldn't need a private yacht or jet planes or new dresses to go off to fancy balls in—the Scottish Family didn't need all that. They'd be a good royal family, thrifty and sensible and plain. Having known poverty, they would eschew excess; whatever was satisfactory would be good enough.

Two weeks ago they received a telegram from their father, saying, "Wire money. Five hundred dollars. Need desperately. Signed, Alex." Grace didn't know what to do. Alex! What if he— Walter said, "Don't do anything. If he can wire us, he can call us." Three days later he called. Walter had never heard his father's voice. It said, "Walter! This is wonderful. So good to talk to you. I think about you every day. How old are you?"

"Twenty-four, Dad."

"My God. It doesn't seem that long ago."

"Well, I get a year older every year, just like everybody else."

"Walter," he said, "I need money. I don't need five hundred dollars. I need more like five thousand. I've been indicted for mail fraud. I didn't do anything wrong. Nothing to hurt people. But they want to put me away for ten, fifteen years, and Walter, I'm too old to go to prison. I gotta leave the country."

"What is it you did?"

His father said, "I was in the genealogy business. I made up family trees for people. But I can explain—let me tell you, son—" Walter's face went flat and numb. He said, "You didn't! God. You did this to us. Why did you do this?"

"I meant to tell you before this. I really meant to tell you. It was meant as a gift, I wanted you to be proud. I knew how those Tollefsons would pity you—I wanted you to be so proud of the Campbell family that I wouldn't have to come crawling back. I hoped you would come and find me."

Walter said he'd send him as much money as he could, and put down the phone. Grace said, "You didn't tell him then about our secret." Walter said, no, there'd be time to tell him later.

She said, "Oh, Walter, what would I do without you? You're so strong. You're so good to me. You're a prince, you know. They can put a crown on a dog and call it a prince, but you are a prince through and through. They may not know it now, but they'll know it soon. Next year we'll be in Edinburgh with the bands playing and the flags flying and the crowds cheering."

Homecoming

It has been a quiet week in Lake Wobegon.
It was Homecoming on Friday, the Leonards vs. Bowlus Friday
night at Bowlus—an away game, on account of Leonard Field has
developed a sinkhole about ten feet in diameter that suddenly
sank two feet between the ten- and twenty-yard lines, not that
the team used that part of the field very often. Coach Magendanz
and Mr. Halvorson decided to fill it with clay, and found that filling
it made it sink deeper, and removing the fill made it deeper yet.
So they are keeping the hole under observation and Homecoming
had to be moved to another location.

The parade was in town, though, and the Homecoming dance
last night, reigned over by Queen Carla and King Jim, royalty
elected by the senior class under the supervision of Mrs. Hoffarth,
who eliminates inappropriate candidates. The drawback of secret
ballots is the tendency on the part of a few to vote for the wrong
person when nobody is looking, and once a girl other than the
Queen got more votes for Queen, but those were not informed
votes. The voters didn't know what Mrs. Hoffarth knew, or else
they didn't have the best interests of Lake Wobegon High School

at heart. The girl in question had been to the gravel pit, parked in a car with a boy and drinking beer, and Mrs. Hoffarth maintains that when you've been to the gravel pit, you shouldn't expect to wear a tiara and ride a convertible down Main Street. A Queen should be above gravel-pit business. "If you climb down off the pedestal, don't expect to climb back up," she says. "A pedestal is not an elevator."

For years, ever since I was in school, because Mrs. Hoffarth's brother Gerald is a colonel of the National Guard, the Homecoming Queen has ridden on a Sherman tank borrowed from the Fighting 308th armory in Freeport. She rides in the forward hatch, below the cannon, and a squad of Guardsmen march in front of her. It made a deep impression on me to see a beautiful classmate in a pink gown smiling and waving from a tank and may have warped my feelings about women, particularly beautiful ones. I talk to them and hear bolts slam in the carbines and combat boots scrape on the pavement. Fear of death isn't the best basis for a friendship. It's an okay basis, but not the best. But that is personal stuff I never told anyone, so keep it under your hat—I don't want to be asked about it by every amateur psychiatrist in town. It's a little odd thing in my makeup that comes from coming where I'm from, no stranger than thinking about death every time you put on clean underwear, one of those quirks a person can live with.

What's hard to live with is not the trash floating in your head but the ordinary facts of life: mortality, knowing that you'll die, and frailty, knowing that when we've got it figured out we don't, and indignity, knowing that if we manage to put up a good front we still have the backstage view. I suppose that's why I don't go home for Homecoming. They know stories about me that I can't explain away and call me by a nickname that I left home in order to lose. Wild horses couldn't drag it out of me now. But I'll tell you: it was Foxfart.

The Queen of Homecoming, Carla Krebsbach, has no odd nicknames to escape, no humiliating secrets, and she made a terrific Queen. She looked like a million dollars, wearing a white spangled dress you could get married in if you wanted, but with a dress like that, why get married and ruin your good looks? The soft contacts made her eyes glisten. She had her hair cut so her posture is improved. When Mrs. Hoffarth walked slowly across the stage holding up the tiara and the other four girls in line squeezed their eyes shut, Carla looked straight ahead, as if she knew for a fact whose head was going to be crowned. Hers. When it was, she didn't cry or hop up and down, she looked as if she was *ready*. The tiara dropped on her and it fit like Cinderella's glass slipper. She blinked and smiled a smile you could feel in the back row of the auditorium.

Unfortunately, her dad, Carl, couldn't be there to see it. He was at his folks' house, Myrtle and Florian's, south of town, looking into the matter of their septic tank, which had reached an emergency status the night before. Florian noticed a problem last week when he raised the extension ladder and climbed up to install storm windows. He climbed up seven rungs and was only two feet off the ground. The lawn was soft as a trampoline, and the ladder sank down into it. "Well, it'll freeze soon, and then I can get around to it," he thought, but it didn't freeze soon enough. Thursday morning the ground around the ladder had sunk three feet. "Well," he thought, "these things happen." He could put in roses there. A sunken garden. Be quite attractive. Friday morning the toilet overflowed, an event that he dared not overlook. So he called Carl.

People often call Carl in this sort of situation. It's what comes from being handy. Sometimes he envies the incompetent. He inspected the sinkhole, went back to town and borrowed the backhoe from Bud, and came back and started digging.

Even he was surprised by what he found. It appeared at first to be—and as he went deeper it actually turned out to be—a 1937 Chevy coupe that someone had buried there to use as a septic tank. Whether they couldn't afford a concrete one or just had a low opinion of that car, there it was in its subterranean glory, the roof caved in, the passenger compartment pretty well loaded to capacity.

You'll notice how gracefully I tell this story, slipping elegantly around the unnecessary or too-vivid details, touching only the high points, but I must tell you that Carl moved the backhoe around upwind and went at it from there. It had to come out—that was the only spot for a new tank unless he wanted to cut down two oak trees or put a new tank uphill of the house, which isn't the textbook way—so he hauled out this monstrosity, getting more and more curious to know who had put it there. Florian has owned the place since Carl's grandpa died. Florian had gone to town with Myrtle to watch Homecoming. Carl loaded the Chevy onto a hay wagon and didn't bother to tie it down: if it fell off, it fell off. He hitched up to the tractor and started his lonely drive to the dump, on the other side of town. By then he was not in a good humor. "Honor thy father and thy mother," yes, but did it include this? Hauling away thirty years of family history? The Chevy septic tank had lost most of its load but with the wind at his back it was suffocating.

That may have been why he didn't ask himself why so many cars were parked along McKinley Street. He didn't see a soul around and figured the coast was clear—he wasn't getting much oxygen to his brain, only the fumes of his heritage. He chugged past the high school and the Lutheran church and had to make a right turn to get the wind off his back, because now his eyes were full of tears. He hung an emergency right onto Main Street, and suddenly he was a feature attraction.

The entire population was lined up three deep on either side of Main between McKinley and Taft, and straight ahead and coming his way was the marching band and the tank behind it. The other tank.

He imagined he could make it to Taft and turn left and avoid the parade, but the old Farmall didn't have much acceleration with that load of Chev, and he and the National Guard put on the brakes and met nose to nose directly in front of the Chatterbox Cafe. The band had melted away to the side. About half the crowd began to move off toward a more distant vantage point, and the other half followed them. A strong aroma of Chev got in the ventilator of the Cafe, and the patrons silently put down their forks and emerged from the rear. Queen Carla sat on the front of the tank, her eyes almost level with her father's where he sat, in front of the old family heirloom. "How could you do this to me?" Her lips formed the words.

She was a Queen. When Queen Victoria once noticed pieces of toilet paper floating in the Thames and asked what they were, one of her counselors, the privy counselor perhaps, said, "Madam, those are printed notices saying that swimming is forbidden." Rank has its privileges, and one of them is ignorance.

The tank couldn't turn around there, the sergeant told Carl, so he had to turn the tractor and wagon. Backward and forward, backward and forward, back and up and back, and now people were cheering and clapping. First gear, reverse, first, reverse, first, reverse. Damn. Damn. Damn. Damn. "If this falls off," he thought, "I'm going to leave it and leave town." The band began to play again, "Anchors Aweigh." When the Farmall got turned around, the band fell in behind it and the three units paraded north to the statue of the Unknown Norwegian, where the second and third units turned left. The Unknown watched the Krebsbach float chug off to the dump.

In a way, it was the most memorable Homecoming ever. Graduates who heard about it later wished they had been there, because of course it won't be repeated. It was a one-time event. Which was how Carl looked at it hours later, when he'd taken a bath and was sitting in the Sidetrack enjoying a cold Wendy's. He said, "Well, if it had to happen, I'm glad it happened where everyone could see it." That's how I feel. Who needs dignity when you can be in show business?

Brethren

It has been a quiet week in Lake Wobegon. Halloween was last night. Children went out trick-or-treating, dressed as hobos or rich glamorous people, and some kids went as grownups: wore dark dowdy clothes, walked stiff, talked funny, and got sore at everybody. The candy they received, and sweet rolls and apples and quarters, they richly deserved. It was the end of October, when the long dark places between houses seem to reach out for you, poor innocent child, and draw you toward the shadows.

Those are places in the dark where the children live who lie in the cemetery, and where Mr. Geske lives, who always loved children and who used to visit the cemetery every day after his beloved mother died. He lived with her for forty-two years. After her death, he went up the hill and tended the flowers on her grave. A prim little man, chubby, who walked like a pigeon. He spent time up there and people didn't think much of it until one day the grave looked different. "I planted a bed of petunias," he said, "that was Mother's favorite." Bud said, "It looks like you dug kinda deep to put in petunias." Mr. Geske looked down at his shoes like he couldn't remember that. He looked away up the hill. He said, "I had to clean out the weeds and the roots went so deep, you know. They go right down there—all the way to where she is, I didn't want the roots to go in where she is."

They found her body on a chair in the kitchen. He had set a cup of coffee in front of her and a piece of lemon meringue pie. There was meringue on her lips. He had turned on the radio to her favorite station. There was more that Gary and Leroy wouldn't talk about. Mr. Geske was shipped to the loony bin, where he hung himself with a bedsheet two years later, that nice middle-aged man who used to help out at Boy Scouts. The hobos and the rich glamorous people thought of him standing in the dark. Standing and holding his shovel and clearing his throat the way he used to do. "Hi, kids. How are you doing tonight?" he says.

Most of the trees have lost their leaves, except one old maple across from Clint and Irene Bunsen's, which was slow to turn color, a luminous phosphorescent yellow—at night, with the streetlamp behind it. It was so bright you could read by it. Most other trees were bare, so sound travels farther, and last night, in the middle of supper, you could hear a door slam half a block away and hear seven fast sharp footsteps, X X X X X X X. The door whanged when it hit the frame and bounced back open, and there were seven slow footsteps going back to shut it. *Thunk.* Everyone around the supper table stopped chewing. A man's voice: "Get in here! It serves you right!" And a boy: "I can't talk to you, you're crazy!" Forks hovered and everyone around the table held their breath, waiting for the gunshot. The door was opened and closed, and there were muffled angry voices. My mother sighed. "I always dread the week before an election," she said.

She is one of the peacemakers, like so many women, though she could get awfully angry—in fact, she hit me with a broom once. I was about fourteen, and though she hit me with the bristles and not the stick, it shocked me so much I forgot what had happened prior, whether I might possibly have said something that upset her. But she was a peacemaker at heart and her anger was brief. Once she yanked me by the wrist, yanked me almost off my feet, and hissed at me. She said, "You little b——." She made a clear *b* sound. I had never heard her use the word she almost used, and it shocked me. I don't recall what led up to it.

Women in our family, as mad as they got, they always made up right away. There was shouting and banging back and forth, then weeping and gnashing of teeth, then a little silence, and finally a little talk and more tears, and then you had your arms around each other and peace was made. Men were different. No noise, no shouting, only a quiet bitter voice saying, "I'm not angry. What do you mean, 'angry'? I'm not one bit angry. I'm hurt, yes, but that's all right, I'll get over it." A soft violent voice. "I can't believe you would say that to me. No—don't apologize. You don't need to apologize. You said what you meant, and I'll just remember it." And you knew that he would. It would be weeks before he'd get over it.

My mother is a peacemaker, though peace and quiet makes her nervous. In disaster she is calm and resolute. A child climbing a tree gives her the jitters, but when our neighbor put his hand into a circular saw and staggered out of the garage one summer day holding something that dripped bright red, she didn't blanch. My own blood drained from my head and I turned and sat on the ground, but she went straight to him. She took off her apron and tied it around his arm, and called to his wife, "Millie, come out here right away."

In the Sanctified Brethren church, a tiny fundamentalist bunch who we were in, there was a spirit of self-righteous pissery and B.S.ification among certain elders that defied peacemaking. They were given to disputing small points of doctrine that to them seemed the very fulcrum of the faith. We were cursed with a surplus of scholars and a deficit of peacemakers, and so we tended to be divisive and split into factions. One dispute when I was a boy had to do with the question of hospitality toward those in error, whether kindness shown to one who holds false doctrine implicates you in his wrongdoing.

Uncle Al had family and friends on both sides of the so-called Cup of Cold Water debate, and it broke his heart. The dispute was really between two men, Brother Wm. Miller and Brother Jas. Johnson, who had dragged others into it, and so, one fine August day, Uncle Al tried to make peace between those two marbleheads and prevent a great deal of unhappiness for the rest of us. He arranged for them to meet at his and Aunt Flo's one Sunday, a few Millerites and a few Johnsonians, not to discuss the hospitality-to-error doctrine but simply to enjoy a dinner of Aunt Flo's famous fried chicken.

It took weeks to arrange. Uncle Al worked through an intermediary, Brother Fields, who had never shown hospitality to anyone, whether in error or not, and who therefore was neutral on the question. Finally, one Sunday, they arrived, in two cars, both Fords, the Brethren being united on the General Motors question. Out climbed, slowly, some gaunt flinty-eyed thin-lipped men in dark floppy suits and their plump obedient wives, and they came in the house and sat in awesome silence in the living room until the call to dinner, and they trooped in around the long dining-room table, extended with two leaves so they wouldn't have to sit close, and the Millerites and Johnsonians bowed their heads in prayer.

Prayer was a delicate matter. Brethren were known to use even prayer before a meal as a platform, and so Al the peacemaker, concerned lest one brother take prayer and beat the others over the head with it, said, "Let us bow our heads in silent prayer, giving thanks for the meal," and they bowed their heads and closed their eyes and—a long time passed; the old clock ticked on the bureau; a cat walked in and meowed and left; a child snickered and was stifled; cars went by; there were dry sniffs and throat-clearings; and soon it was clear that neither side wanted to stop before the other: they were seeing who could pray the longest.

Brother Miller peeked through his fingers at Brother Johnson, who was earnestly engaged in silent communion with the Lord, who agreed with him on so many things. His forehead almost touched the plate. So Brother Miller dove back into prayer and the other Brethren stayed under too, sneaking glances around the table to see if anyone else noticed how *long* it was. Minutes drifted by. Heads stayed bowed, nobody would come up. To stop praying might imply a weakness of faith.

Al said "Amen," to offer them a way out of the deadlock, and said it again: *"Amen."* Brother Miller looked up and saw Johnson still bowed, so he went back down just as Johnson put his periscope up and saw Brother Miller submerged, so down *he* went. It was becoming the longest table grace in history, it ground on and on and on, and then Aunt Flo slid her chair back, rose, went to the kitchen, and brought out the food that they were competing to see who could be more thankful for. She set the hay down where the goats could get it. Tears ran down Brother Johnson's face. His eyes were clamped shut, and tears streamed down, and so was Brother Miller weeping.

It's true what they say, that smell is the key that unlocks our deepest memories, and with their eyes closed, the smell of fried chicken and gravy made those men into boys again. It was years ago, they were fighting, and a mother's voice from on high said, "You two stop it and get in here and have your dinners. Now. I mean it." The blessed cornmeal crust and rapturous gravy brought the memory to mind, and the stony hearts of the two giants melted; they raised their heads and filled their plates and slowly peace was made over that glorious chicken.

Thanksgiving

It has been a quiet week in Lake Wobegon.
Thanksgiving was Thursday, a cold, gray, windy day, and the
Thanksgiving service at the Lutheran church was packed, to Pastor Ingqvist's great surprise. He expected a small turnout, like
last year's, and hadn't prepared a complete sermon, only a couple
index cards, one with a text from the Psalms and the other only
said "Conclusion." He sat thinking hard through the opening hymns.
Halfway into the reading from Ecclesiastes, the fire siren went
off two blocks away, and everyone who had left a turkey in the
oven sat up straight in their pews and had a vision of flames
engulfing their home and the roof collapsing in a shower of sparks.
All the firefighters jumped up and left and came back a minute
later: it was nothing. Bud had accidentally jostled the siren switch
while reaching back into the joists for something. Time for the
sermon. It was a nervous and turbulent sermon, he felt, with a
bumpy landing due to the loss of one engine, but afterward people
shook his hand and said it was one of the finest they ever heard.
Beautiful. Do you have a transcript of that? some people asked.

He thought, *You got to be kidding,* but the Lutherans of Lake

Wobegon don't use much irony, like they don't use much curry powder: some, not a lot. There stood the tall, slope-shouldered pastor in humiliation for a performance that one person after another said was wonderful, even Val Tollefson. "Well, I wish I'd prepared more, and tried to develop it a little better," he said, blushing, and thought, *Thank you, Lord, very much. Tusind takk, Lord.*

Clarence Bunsen wasn't in church. Arlene went, but the mister stayed home, because he wasn't very thankful. He got up that morning and stepped on a screw and tried to levitate off it and strained his back. His back didn't go out but it felt weak. He didn't want to slip in the bathtub, so he took a bath instead of a shower, and felt like an old vet at the Vets' Hospital, and climbing out, he slipped and strained his back again, another part. While he was combing his hair, a clump came out, from the bunch that he's been combing across the top in hopes it would take hold. He came down to the kitchen feeling that life had turned against him.

Arlene said, "Have a cup of coffee, that'll perk you up," and usually that's all a Norwegian needs. Norwegians have often been revived by this method, including some whose EKG showed a flat line—a sip of coffee on their lips and the pen jumped. Clarence felt like coffee wouldn't make much difference.

He didn't tell Arlene that he'd talked to daughter Barbara Ann on the phone Wednesday night. She was going on and on about this, that, and the other thing, and suddenly he had a premonition that the real reason she was coming home for Thanksgiving was to make an important announcement, of her divorce. She and Bill, married for ten years, the poor thing. He could understand, he always knew that Bill wasn't good for her, he didn't have Barbara Ann's undying enthusiasm, he was too serious, worked too hard, and earned far too much money. Clarence could understand her unhappiness—not that she said anything, she didn't, it was what she didn't say. He wanted to stay home from church and be alone.

One other thing: one day in October, Arlene had said, "How about we go to Minneapolis for Thanksgiving and stay at the Curtis and have the buffet in the Cardinal Room? I hear it's fabulous."

And Clarence said, "Naw, let's stay home. If you're tired of making dinner, I'll do it." He heard himself say these words and heard her say, "Fine. Good. We'll stay home, and you make the dinner." One more reason he didn't go to church. Another was his fireplace, recently repaired by a man from Los Angeles named Curtis Olson. Byron recommended him as a man who knew about fireplaces and chimneys, but when Olson left, Byron said, "No, I was only repeating what others had said. I forget who they were, but they said he was pretty good." Clarence didn't want to see Byron for a while, and Byron would be at church.

Olson came with full-color brochures about fireplace inserts and how for a low sum you could have a liner put in the chimney, guarding against chimney fire *and* improving the efficiency of fireplace and furnace by 50 to 70 percent. He installed a unit at Clarence's and suddenly a fireplace that had worked pretty well started to go to hell. Smoke poured out into the living room and the heat went up the chimney. Olson looked anguished. He paced up and down, wringing his hands, and said, "This is terrible; I didn't know your house had a problem with convex airflow. You have an inverse ratio: weren't you aware of it? *I* don't live here, it isn't my house, you couldn't expect *me* to know about your convexity problem. Now look, I've gone and made a mistake, walked into a minefield, and what am I going to do about it? I feel miserable. I came in here feeling good about myself and in two days you've managed to completely destroy my confidence."

Clarence said, "I'm sorry you feel so bad. Why don't I have Carl come and look at it?" "Well, all right," said Olson, "but I still feel like you don't have respect for me." "No," said Clarence, "no, not at all."

Carl came and looked down the chimney. He said, "Whoever was here knocked some bricks loose and he had to pound harder to get the liner in, so now you're got a wad of sheet metal stuck in there, tight; I don't know if it's going to come out or not."

Olson called from Minneapolis. "I'm too upset to work right now," he said. "I feel threatened and embarrassed. I need some time alone." And there was seven hundred dollars gone, *click*.

Thanksgiving morning, Clarence built a small fire in the fireplace with an electric fan on the hearth to push the smoke up the chimney. He heard the door open and a familiar voice said, "Hi, Daddy," and there she was: tall, lovely. He put his arms around her and had to go to the kitchen. Norwegian men cry privately and dab cold coffee on their eyes to get the redness out. Poor child. Thirty-four, about to be alone in the world.

"Can I help, Dad?" said Bill, roaming into the kitchen.

"No, of course not. Fix yourself a drink."

"What do you have?"

"I don't know. It's in the basement."

"Care for something yourself?"

"No, I can't drink while I'm cooking."

He cooked. Basted the turkey, boiled yams, peeled potatoes, checked the pumpkin pie in the oven—thirty minutes, forty, forty-five, an hour, still it wasn't done. Then the crust caught on fire. He chipped off that part. The house smelled of smoke but he was doing pretty well. That's what Arlene said too as she cruised through from time to time: "You're doing awfully well, dear. I'm proud of you. Are you boiling these potatoes here? Then you probably want to put some water in the pot—ah, the turkey smells good. Mmmmmmmm. Want me to put some aluminum over it? It's up to you, but in a four-hundred-degree oven it might scorch after a while."

It was hard but far from impossible, and it felt good to cook and be in charge and not sit, as he had for years, in the living room with a silent son-in-law, saying, "Well, Bill, how's the real-estate business?" "Oh, not bad." Well, that took care of fifteen seconds, a couple hours more and we can wrap it up. He cooked and cooked, waiting for the news to drop, rehearsing his calm reaction. ("Well, kids, that's your decision. I can't say that I approve but I certainly can sympathize. Arlene and I have been together for forty years but there have been times . . .") Then she told him. She said, "We have an announcement. We're going to have a baby. In April."

He almost said, "Well, kids, that's your decision. I certainly can sympathize. Arlene and I have been together for forty years but there have been times . . ." and then the happy news dawned on him and tears came to his eyes and he had to blow his nose.

The happy news lit up the afternoon. An unseen child, in the house with them, a child sleeping inside his daughter. It was a quiet happy dinner, and a quiet afternoon washing dishes. Arlene took a nap, Clarence washed, Barbara Ann dried.

"I remember when I knew that your mother was expecting you. It was right around the beginning of July. A hot beautiful day. I felt so good I walked downtown in my undershirt and bought a panatela cigar and smoked it standing on the corner by Ralph's, and then I walked up to the Co-op and bought four rockets and took them down to the swimming beach and stuck em in the gravel and shot em off, one, two, three, four, way out over the lake. Gosh, that was a day."

He could almost see those rockets bursting in air. Then Bill said, "Say, Dad, something's wrong with your fireplace." Clarence dashed out. Arlene was asleep on the sofa and starting to cough. Smoke filled the room. He opened the window and pitched burning logs out on the grass and heard a faraway siren, and in less time than it takes to talk about it, the old red truck came chugging up the driveway. "Thanks, boys," said Clarence, "no emergency, everything's under control."

They backed out and Bill decided he'd like to go for a long walk. Arlene went back to sleep. Clarence and Barbara Ann were in the kitchen when she felt the pain.

"*Mmhhhh,*" she said.

"What?"

"Nothing, a pain in my side. Mmmhhhh."

"Let's go," he said. "I'll get your coat."

"No, it's not that. It'll go away."

"Let's go. Now. I'll get the car out of the garage."

"Daddy, believe me. It's not that."

"Honey, there's no sense in taking a chance. Let's go."

And they went, but backing out of the driveway, he heard the foolishness of those words: no sense in taking a chance. What else is having babies about if not taking a chance? They headed for the Saint Cloud Hospital, but she felt better and the sun was setting, the pain was gone, so instead they drove to Saint John's and back. What a fine chance to take. A lot of cars headed south from town, foreign cars going back to a life in the city that he did not understand: silent fathers, exhausted mothers, children sitting happily and politely with little headphones on their heads. We took a chance when we produced these people and it looks as if we'll have to wait a little longer to see how it comes out.

Darlene
Makes a Move

It has been a quiet week in Lake Wobegon. It was cold this week and windy. At the Mercantile, Clifford hung blue Christmas lights around the front window, draped blue cloth behind it, and on Charlotte, his old mannequin, whom he has given new brown hair, he hung a cool green satin dress. It made an elegant picture on Main Street. Everyone traipsed by and looked at it, even Senator K. Thorvaldson, who has been holed up with a book for weeks. The dear old man gets in a mood sometimes and disappears with an armload of literature. In September, at the school rummage sale, he purchased a boxful of paperbacks by Ramona Jean Jensen, the romance queen of Sweden, and since has been engulfed in a tide of liquid prose about the lissome, nubile, and (thus far) chaste (but barely) Dianne Dahl, including scenes that made the old gent blush and wipe his glasses.

There on her lingonberry plantation south of Göteborg, one suave nobleman after another has made a play for Dianne and nothing was left between her and disgrace but some gossamer-thin fabric and a dim recollection of something her mother told her before she kicked the bucket. Senator K. said, "I never thought I'd like it and now I hate myself for liking it as much as I do." But it made him think of a lady in Maine and soon he was on the telephone, ringing up more than fifty dollars in long-distance, according to people who know.

That was one piece of news, the other was that Darlene is leaving her job at the Chatterbox Cafe as of January 1, after thirteen years of waitressing. The news hit the old guys at the lunch counter hard because she is like a second wife to them. She pours their first coffee in the morning, brings their eggs and hash browns. Maybe they woke up and got in a fight with the old lady and she said, "I'm not fixing your breakfast, you fix it yourself, you big dummy," and he said, "I'm not hungry. Things you say to me, you make me so upset, I could no more eat than I could I don't know what," and *slam* the door and go to the Chatterbox; there's Darlene; she says, "Hi, honey—coffee? How about a sweet roll? Fresh baked, made em myself. You still take your eggs sunny side up? You want those basted a little or real runny—okay. Bacon, ham, or sausage? Say, how you been? I missed you yesterday. It's good to see ya." No wonder they'll miss her. She's the girl of their dreams. A little heavy and she oughta do something about her hair, but she's young and that's the main thing: thirty-eight. A peach.

She sets down $1.15 change in front of Mr. Darling and gives his old hand a pat and the tremor stops—the old goat is healed for a second—with a steady hand he reaches for her but she's gone, she pours coffee for Chuck, her hand brushes against his, and he trembles.

No wonder they always inquire about her husband, Arlen.

"So," they say, "how's Arlen?"

"All right, I suppose."

"Don't you see him?"

"Not lately."

"Hmmmm. You're still married, aren't you?"

"Of course."

"When'd you see him last?"

"I donno. Last time he was up. Last Christmas maybe. I don't remember."

"Hmmmm. Ya miss him?"

"Not lately."

It's hard to remember Arlen, it was hard to remember him when he was here. If he were missing and the police needed a description, she wasn't sure she could give one. Medium height, brown hair, two eyes, nose. He was a sweet man but vacant. He never noticed things, didn't say much, was content to just be around. Once they were watching a Perry Como special and during a commercial break she asked, "How come we never do anything or go anywhere?" "Well," he said, "what do you want to do? Nothing stopping you, it's a free country." Then the special started again and she remembered thinking to herself: Maybe we oughta get a divorce.

Arlen was from a religious family but he and Darlene never went to church. Sometimes he mentioned it on Sunday morning, but then there was the Sunday paper all fresh and colorful, and he was a slow reader, and pretty soon it was dinnertime. His brother Erling was an evangelist and once they drove all the way to Moorhead in a red Pontiac with no muffler to see him preach.

He preached in a parking lot between a Red Owl supermarket and a liquor store, standing on a flatbed trailer behind his old van with a green neon cross behind him. He kept his engine running because the loudspeaker was hooked up to the battery. It was sunset, and beyond them was flat prairie for a thousand miles, and around them were seven people listening to the sermon, but Erling didn't seem to mind. He wasn't preaching to this bunch, he was talking to the world. He said: "For what shall it profit a man if he gain the whole world and lose his own soul? You are the light of the world! So let your light shine before men that they may see your good works and glorify your Father who is in heaven."

Afterward he wrapped the cross in a plastic bag and shut off the engine and they went to Perkins Pancake House for dinner.

Erling talked about the world being in the last days, signs all around pointing to Christ's imminent return, maybe tonight—though tonight he was driving to Williston. His family lived in Oak Park, Illinois, and he said he didn't see them as often as he liked. Darlene didn't ask how often he'd like to see them. Erling didn't seem like a homebody. He was restless just sitting eating a burger and fries, he wanted to go. He said to Darlene, "I'm praying for you," and she wanted to tell him to stick around and see if they're answered. He was the opposite of Arlen, maybe Erling got all the juice in that family and Arlen was left with the pulp.

He was from north Minneapolis and that's where he went back to after he lost his warehouse job at the Co-op. She planned to go with him, but she was waiting for him to bring it up and ask her to, and he didn't, he just stood by the car looking at the tires, so she said, "Well, see ya," and he said, "Yeah, see ya," and drove away. He came up on weekends for a few months and then not so often and then it didn't seem important.

She's been married to him for thirteen years, as long as she's had this job. This job is like being married to Arlen: you wait for something that isn't going to come. It's taken her too long to find this out. Fifteen years ago she got up the courage to go to Minneapolis and try to find something for herself, and what did she find? Arlen. Came back home with him, and now, thirteen years later, she's right where she started from.

"Oh honey," her mother said, "why don't you do something with yourself? You could do so many things if you'd try." So she went to Minneapolis and got Arlen. She met him at the Bon Ton Scandinavian Snackshop on Johnson Street N.E., where her uncle Bob got her a job through his sister-in-law Myrtice, that was in 1971. Darlene moved into a furnished studio apartment over the Snackshop and went to work, 6:00 A.M. to 3:00 P.M., Tuesday through Saturday, $1.56/hour, and first day at work in came Arlen. She didn't notice him but he saw her and started coming to the Bon Ton every morning for some doughnuts, some scones, a bismarck, a piece of pie—he weighed 176 at the time, and eight pounds later he asked what her name was, and when he tipped 195 he took her to a movie at the Hollywood Theater, put his arm around her in the pale light off the big screen, and he kept coming back for more, as they say. Back to the Bon Ton day after day, and when she said, "Have another slice of pie? Care for some cake? Fry you up a burger?" he'd say, "Sure," and when he reached 200 he kissed her, and he got to 204, and 208, and somewhere between 200 and 210 he proposed, and he married her at 218 and her dad got him a job at the Co-op.

When they moved home, Darlene felt bad. She'd been in Minneapolis eight months, working her tail off, and had never been to the top of the Foshay Tower, never saw Lake Harriet or the Como Zoo, never made it out to Southdale, got a Penney's charge card and hadn't even used it. Back in Lake Wobegon, they moved into her parents' basement, to a rollaway under the stairs with a hot plate next to the laundry tubs, and the bathroom upstairs. Her mother would come down and iron, Arlen would go up and watch TV with her dad.

"Oh honey," her mother said, "why don't you do something with yourself? There's so many things you could do." Other people have said the same and she's thought about it herself, but—everything she's thought of doing, she knows of somebody who did exactly that thing and isn't happy at all. Thought of going to California but she knows two girls who went and they say it isn't at all like what you expect and the people act creepy, especially men. Thought of going into hairdressing but her friend Denise knows a couple girls who did and they say they don't really make all that much money. Thought of going to college but her girlfriend Therese went and look at her, she's all confused and stuck-up on top of it, a unique combination. So Darlene stuck to waitressing. "Better the devil you know," they say. No sense going looking for trouble. The grass is always greener. Learn from other people's mistakes.

"Oh honey," her mother said, "why don't you do something with yourself?" But what? It's a jungle out there. Just look at a newspaper and you'll see the tragedy that comes from making a wrong choice: people who made the mistake of going on *that plane—*

walking down *that street* right then, driving across *that bridge*—
it ought to teach you to be careful.

And then after Thanksgiving her mother said, "Oh honey, why
didn't you ever do something with yourself? You could have done
so many different things."

It was only a change of tense but it felt like a door shut, and
Darlene got up and went in her room and bawled. The next morning she got up at four and went to work at the Chatterbox and
she took out her pack of Alpines and nailed it alongside the door
to the cooler. She wasn't so nice to the old guys, she said, "Yeah?
What you want?" After lunch she gave notice to Dorothy and last
week she drove down to the Cities to look for a job in a department
store.

Last Sunday morning at Lake Wobegon Lutheran Church, when
Pastor Ingqvist looked out over the faces and said, "Any additional
announcements this morning?" (which, of course, there wouldn't
be, because you're supposed to tell him if you're going to stand
up and make one, and nobody had), Darlene's mother stood up in
the third row and turned around and faced the congregation and
said, "I have an announcement of a personal nature."

She was nervous and reached to brace herself on Earl's shoulder
but he was bent over low in a prayerful position. She said, "My
daughter Darlene, a member of this church, will be leaving after
Christmas to accept a position of employment in Minneapolis, and
since there isn't much time and this is such a busy season for
everyone, I have decided that in lieu of a going-away shower,
those who wish to go in on a nice gift for her can see me after
church. I would like to send her to Minneapolis with at least one
nice dress. There is no pressure put on anyone to do this, it is
purely a matter of individual choice, but if you'd like, you may
see me after church. Thank you."

She sat down, breathing hard. Several women in that church
could've shot her on the spot, they were so furious. To stand up
and announce a collection for your own daughter!—hard to believe. But those Lutherans were nailed and they knew it. She
planted herself by the exit, where you couldn't miss her, and she

said good morning to everyone on their way out, and if you didn't want to give, you had to be pretty determined.

She got the cool green satin dress. It needs letting out a little bit, but it does look wonderful on Darlene, and she feels lovely in it. She'll wear it for Christmas and take it with her to Minneapolis, where she will find Arlen and wind up her business with him and start something with somebody else, she hopes.

Christmas Dinner

It *has been a quiet week in Lake Wobegon.* Christmas. The exiles were home. It was pretty quiet, though you could hear the gritting of teeth, and there was a moment of poisoned silence at the Clarence Bunsen home that rang like a fire bell. Before the blessing, as they sat around the table and admired the work in front of them, a still-life *Christmas Dinner* by Arlene, before they ate the art, their daughter, Donna, in town from San Diego, said, "What a wonderful Christmas!" and her husband, Rick, said, "Well, if Democrats had their way, it'd be the last one." Silence.

Arlene said that if Rick had his way, the turkeys would be having us. Clarence bowed his head. "Dear Lord, the giver of all good things, we thank Thee." He prayed a long prayer, as a cease-fire. Arlene smiled at Rick: "Have some mashed potatoes." "Thank you, Mom." She winced. He is her son-in-law and she doesn't know why. He is not raising her grandchildren right, he comes to Minnesota and talks too much about the advantages of southern California, he wears silly clothes, he makes fun of Norwegians, he makes fun of women including his own wife, and he says "agenda"

173

in place of "plan" or "idea"—"Did you have a different agenda?" he says. "Let's get our agenda straight." "I sense a hidden agenda here."

He piled his plate with Christmas agenda and chomped a big bite of it. He said, "Mom, this is the best dinner I ever ate. I really mean that." She smiled her brightest smile, the smile she has used all her life on people she'd like to slap silly. She'd like to give him a piece of her mind, but she can't, because he has hostages, her grandchildren. So she kills him with kindness. She stuffs him like a turkey. Fresh caramel rolls for breakfast, a pound of bacon and smoked sausage and scrambled eggs, and two hours later pot roast for lunch and big slabs of banana cream pie. He has gained four pounds since Tuesday. Her goal is twelve. All day he sits dazed by food. "Fudge bars, Rick? I made them just for you. Here, I'll put the plate right beside you, where you can reach them." "Oh Mom . . ." She's found the crack in his armor, and it's his mouth. His Achilles mouth. Her agenda is stuffing him so he becomes weak and pliable and goes into a calorie coma, and she takes the little boy and the girl for walks and tells them about our great presidents, our great Democratic presidents. And did you know they were all Norwegian? Yes, they were, a little bit, on their mother's side, and that little bit was enough to make them great.

At the Tolleruds', Daryl and Marilyn and their six kids went up the hill to the folks' house. His brothers, Gunnar and Fred, and their families were home for Christmas, and Daryl's family barely has room for themselves around their little table.

When Daryl went into farming in partnership with his dad in 1968, he was under the impression that someday soon he and Marilyn would move into the big house and the folks would take the little one, the one that Grandpa Tollerud built when he came from Norway. But nothing has been said about this for a long time. The little house would be fine for an older couple, who tend to sit quietly and not tear around chasing each other. But the old folks sit quietly in the big house, with four empty bedrooms up-stairs. "We really need a larger house," Daryl says. "Well," his dad says. "Soon as we get the pig barn built, we'll see about adding on to it."

Up at the folks' house, Christmas is the exact same as it's been forever. You close your eyes and it could be any time. You might open them and you'd be six years old, not forty-two. The dialogue is the same. His mother complains about leaving the turkey in the oven too long and it being too dry, and every year it is perfect. The men sit in the living room, gently clearing their throats, and when it's time, his dad stands up and says, "Well, I'm going to go see to the horse."

They haven't kept a horse for years. "You boys going to come help me see to the horse?" he says, and they troop out to the barn and he reaches down behind a horse collar and pulls out the bottle of Jim Beam. They pass it around and have a pull, and stand and say some things, and pass it around again, and the old man takes a nail and marks the new level and puts it back, and they troop indoors. Daryl wishes they could just have a drink in the living room, but to his old man there's a difference. He is not the sort of man who keeps booze in his house. The barn doesn't count.

Gunnar was on the wagon again, the third or fourth time. He is the oldest boy and the smartest, he should've gone on and become somebody but drink has cursed him since he was young. He'd go in the Sidetrack and have a bump with his buddies but then he got belligerent and tried to pick fights, which nobody wanted because he was so strong and quick, so they took care of him by giving him more to drink. He'd say, "I'm not going to take that from you. You son of a bitch, you sat down in my chair." They'd say, "Gunnar, I bet you can't drink a whole glass of whis-key. Two dollars says you can't."

"Put it down where I can see it," said Gunnar, and Wally filled up the glass. A beer glass. And Gunnar drank it, and as he drank he forgot about the chair, the two dollars, where he was or why or who. He finished the glass, and they carried him out the back so he could be sick there, and they scraped him up and drove him home. This happened over and over. Then Gunnar skipped the part in the middle, the argument and the challenge, and went straight from the first drink to the last on his own steam.

Gunnar drives a semi and when he's drinking he takes a bottle in the cab to help keep him awake. He quit drinking this time after his last crash, driving a tank truck that jackknifed in broad daylight in the middle of Kansas and overturned in the ditch. The tank had a hole knocked in it and when Gunnar climbed out of the cab he was up to his hips in scrambled-egg mix, a thick yellowish froth. He slipped and went under and thought he was going to drown in egg but struggled to shore and hasn't had a drink for three months.

Daryl has had some close calls himself the past couple of months. He doesn't drink except in his dad's barn, seeing to the horse, but several times he's been in his old Ford about to pull onto a highway and looked left and turned right and suddenly, HONK, a car swerves and jams on its brakes. Or he looks in the side mirror, turns into the left lane, HONK, a car right there! Once he ran a red light. What's the matter with him? Is he losing his peripheral vision? Monday he was out teaching Eric to drive and he heard brakes screech, he'd gone through a stop sign. Tuesday he went to ask Dr. DeHaven about it, who talked about changes in the brain that come with aging, a loss of reflex, a diminution of one's faculties. "This is normal," he said. "Ordinarily we don't see it so much in a person of forty-two, but it isn't anything to worry about. Just relax and slow down and take things at your own speed."

Daryl was depressed for two days. Tuesday night he left a door open in the pig barn, and twelve got out. Recess for pigs. It took him and Eric two hours to get them back in class, but Daryl felt fast on his feet and felt the reflexes working, bang, bang, bang. Wednesday afternoon, not thinking, he walked in the kitchen and opened the fridge and got out a bowl that was full of glop and dumped it in the garbage, and just as the force of gravity was pulling it down he thought, "That's mincemeat pie filling."

How could he do such a dumb thing? Just wasn't thinking. Marilyn was gone to the farm wives' luncheon. It was two o'clock. He had never made mincemeat filling before, but how hard could it be to follow a recipe? Fairly hard, he discovered. Mincing the meat. Beef and venison. Mincing the apples. And then the recipe called for brandy. No brandy anywhere that he could find—where did she keep the stuff? Did she have a secret stash in the laundry room? Finally he took an empty mustard jar in his pocket and snuck up the hill to the barn. He crawled around back through the corn, dashed for the door, got the bottle, filled the jar, made a careful mark with the nail. Heard a door slam. Tore out back. Crawled through the corn to the end of the field, stood up, walked down to the house, whistling. Into the kitchen. Tossed in the whiskey. Mixed it, cooked it up, popped it in the fridge as the car rolled up the driveway.

Thursday, as they came to dessert, Daryl's heart was pounding. He chose pumpkin. Everyone else chose mincemeat, except Gunnar, who chose pumpkin too. The pie was sliced and served and the first forkfuls of mincemeat came to their mouths. "Mmmmmmmm," said his mother. "Oh Marilyn." His dad said, "Oh my, now that's mincemeat." "It sure is," said Fred. "How do you make it, Marilyn?" "Oh, it's just from a recipe," she said. "Do you use brandy in it?" "Oh no," she said. "You don't really need brandy. I just leave the brandy out." "Well, it's the best I ever ate," said Fred's wife. "You ought to have some of this, Daryl." "No," Daryl said. "I got my pumpkin here. I don't care for mincemeat. Keeps me awake at night. I can't take so much rich food anymore. I'm getting old, I guess."

Exiles

It has been a quiet week in Lake Wobegon. Warm and foggy on Tuesday, and late in the day, as the temperature fell, fog froze on the trees and made white bare trees in which the fog appeared ghostly beautiful, as if you could walk into these trees and receive immortal powers of a sort we all want at Christmas: the power to gather our friends and loved ones close around us and prevent suffering and evil and death from touching them.

When I was little, I worried about a group of men I called the Murderers, who had killed before and would kill again because killing meant nothing to them, they had nothing to lose, it was the electric chair for them either way. They were now driving in a stolen black sedan toward a Y in the road where two roads diverged, and if they chose one they'd come to our house and kill us, and if they didn't they wouldn't. I could keep my family safe by prayer. At night I crawled into bed between cold sheets like sheets of ice and prayed for God to keep the Murderers away from us, and as an extra precaution, in addition to prayer, I always got into bed from the left side. I lay on my right side. I prayed the exact same prayer. And although I knew I shouldn't, in the dark I made the sign of the cross, on the odd chance that God was not Protestant. I pulled the blankets up and lay warming my little hollow, listening to the house creak, smelling the Vicks my mother put on me as a precaution, and felt I had kept the Murderers from our door. Then, one night, I got into bed from the wrong side, exposing my family to evil because I was in a hurry, so I got out and got back in on the correct side. But was still afraid. So I took my radio into bed with me. It was the size of a breadbox. I pulled the covers over my head and tuned in Bob Franklin, host of "Music by Moonlite"—the "Old Smoothie," he was called, because he made you feel like you and him were close ("Hello, friends, Bob Franklin here—say, I believe that I know you well enough to say that you're discriminating when it comes to the finer things and particular about the details being just right, just the way you want them, and that's why I know that Jirasek's Dry Cleaning in Albany is just the place for you . . ."). It thrilled me as a boy to hear a man take me into his confidence that way, but instead of old Bob playing Glenn Miller, there was a preacher on the air who wasn't friendly at all and didn't think I was discriminating and didn't think dry cleaning would do me much good one way or the other. He seemed to suggest that the Murderers were standing over my bed about to stab me with an ice pick and that it was exactly what I deserved. What was "Brother Carl and His Wall of Hope Revival Show" doing in place of old Bob and "Music by Moonlite"? Then I checked my clock: it was five-thirty in the morning. We were safe for another day.

Corinne Ingqvist came home for Christmas on Sunday. She came barreling north in her red VW from Minneapolis, arguing with a preacher on the radio, telling him his theology was repressive, when she noticed she was going seventy-five mph. She cruised through the lights of town and turned down the long-familiar driveway to their house by the lake. In the backseat were two tins of tea for gifts and 132 critical essays by her seventeen-year-old students on Robert Frost's poem "The Road Not Taken" ("Two roads diverged in a yellow wood, . . . and I—I took the one less traveled by, And that has made all the difference") that she was planning to grade on Monday. Her parents' house seemed like a quiet retreat with only her and Hjalmar and Virginia for Christmas.

She pulled up the driveway and parked by the old limestone wall. She got out the shopping bag of presents and essays and walked up three steps to the back door and put her bare hand on the cold brass knob and a sudden cold thought came to mind: *This soon shall pass. And it won't be too long.* She swayed slightly and then went in. "Hello," said Hjalmar, and kissed her. "Hello, dear, you look so wonderful," said Virginia. The tree in the same place, beside the old piano, in front of the bright fish tank. Orange and silver guppies seemed to swim among the ornaments, drifting to and fro, like orange and silver snowflakes that never reach the ground, fish in the branches among the lights.

Dozens of exiles returned for Christmas. At Our Lady of Perpetual Responsibility, Father Emil roused himself from bed, where he's been down with cancer since Columbus Day, and said Christmas Eve Mass. He was inspired by the sight of all the lapsed Catholics parading into church with their unbaptized children, and he gave them a hard homily, strolling right down into the congregation. "Shame. Shame on us for leaving what we were given that was true and good," he said. "To receive a great treasure in our younger days and to abandon it so that we can lie down in the mud with swine." He stood, one hand on the back of a pew, and everyone in that pew—children of this church who grew up and moved away and did well and now tell humorous stories at parties about Father Emil and what it was like to grow up Catholic—all of them shuddered a little, afraid he might grab them by their Harris-tweed collars and stand them up and ask them questions. "What a shame. What a shame." They came for Christmas, to hear music and see the candles and smell incense and feel hopeful, and here was their old priest with hair in his ears whacking them around—was it a brain cancer he had? *Shame, shame on us.* He looked around at all the little children he'd given first communion to, now grown heavy and prosperous and sad and indolent, but clever enough to explain their indolence and sadness as a rebellion against orthodoxy, a protest, adventurous, intellectual, which really was only dullness of spirit. He stopped. It was so quiet you could hear them not breathing. Then he said that this was why Our Lord had come, to rescue us from dullness of spirit, and so the shepherds had found and so shall we, and then it was Christmas again.

Dozens of exiles were back, including some whom their families weren't expecting because they'd said they weren't coming, couldn't come, were sorry but it was just out of the question. But Christmas exerts powerful forces. We turn a corner in a wretched shopping mall and some few bars of a tune turn a switch in our heads and gates open and tons of water thunder through Hoover Dam, the big turbines spin, electricity flows, and we get in our car and go back, like salmon.

Larry the Sad Boy was there, who was saved twelve times in the Lutheran church, an all-time record. Between 1953 and 1961, he threw himself weeping and contrite on God's throne of grace on twelve separate occasions—and this in a Lutheran church that wasn't evangelical, had no altar call, no organist playing "Just As I Am Without One Plea" while a choir hummed and a guy with shiny hair took hold of your heartstrings and played you like a cheap guitar—this is the Lutheran church, not a bunch of hillbillies—these are Scandinavians, and they repent in the same way that they sin: discreetly, tastefully, at the proper time, and bring a Jell-O salad for afterward. Larry Sorenson came forward weeping buckets and crumpled up at the communion rail, to the amazement of the minister, who had delivered a dry sermon about stewardship, and who now had to put his arm around this limp soggy individual and pray with him and see if he had a ride home. *Twelve times.* Even we fundamentalists got tired of him. Granted, we're born in original sin and are worthless and vile, but twelve conversions is too many. God didn't mean us to feel guilt all our lives. There comes a point when you should dry your tears and join the building committee and start grappling with the problems of the church furnace and the church roof and make church coffee and be of use, but Larry kept on repenting and repenting. He came up for Christmas and got drunk and knocked over the Christmas tree. That was before 2:00 P.M. He spent the next eight hours apologizing for it, and the penance was worse than the crime.

Eddie the Jealous Boy came home. He told his parents that he wasn't going to come, but they didn't protest enough, and he felt unwanted and so he came up with his lovely wife, Eunice. She is the most beautiful woman ever to leave Lake Wobegon, having been elected Tri-County Queen in 1960, Miss Sixth Congressional District the same year, first runner-up in the 1962 Miss Midwest contest, and then Miss Upper Mississippi Basin by the U.S. Corps of Engineers, and having won them all, she retired from royalty because it made Eddie crazy to see other men look at her and like her. If she so much as touched a man on the arm in a friendly way, it meant she'd later spend hours listening to Eddie's hot dry angry voice and endure days of his silence, and so this funny and lovely woman has tried to please him and make herself quiet and dull and unattractive, but he's more jealous than ever. On Christmas afternoon, when he looked up from a robot he was assembling and noticed that Eunice and her brother-in-law Fred were nowhere to be seen, he tore around in a frenzy, ran outdoors, got in the car (there is no motel in town), and headed for the skating rink. The warming house was open. Maybe they were kissing in there. Maybe they were skating together. Maybe they were off in the woods, naked in the snow. He saw her alone, walking. He jumped out, ran up, and said, "Where is he? Where's Fred?" She stared back at him with a dull look in her eyes. "Fred didn't come for Christmas this year," she said. "Don't you remember? He and Marcie went to Des Moines."

Corinne put off grading those papers until Monday and got busy baking cookies and some little currant buns from an old Norwegian recipe. She hadn't had them since she was little, and now she was baking them herself. Amazing: a delicious smell from childhood that brings back every sweet old aunt and grandma as if they're there beside you, and you do it with just a little saffron. Monday night she made herself start those papers, and then carolers came, and it wasn't until Tuesday afternoon that she really faced up to it, 132 essays of five hundred words each, about seventy thousand words about the poem "Two roads diverged in a yellow wood, . . . and I—I took the one less traveled by, And that has made all the difference." And of those words at least ten thousand were *I*, *me*, or *mine—This poem makes me think of what happened to me when I was ten and my parents said to me* . . . For them, all roads converged into the first person singular. It was hard reading, very hard, and their teacher finally chose the road that led away from the stack of essays toward the Christmas tree and the fish tank. A lovely thing about Christmas is that it's compulsory, like a thunderstorm, and we all go through it together, it's not individual, it's sociable.

Foxy the Proud Boy came home, but now he is Richard to everyone, except among his close pals in the grain-futures business in Minneapolis, where he is Pinky. He drove up in a pink 1987 Ferlinghetti, a car so fabulous that when he sits in it, even en route to his origins in a little house painted lavatory green, he feels attractive and *special*. He forgets his dull seedy relatives, who come out and look at his fantastic car, its red leather seats, the incredible instrument panel that shows you the tides, the movements of planets and galaxies. They peer in the tinted windows and say, "Cheess, there's no room in there, Richard—two seats—what are you thinking of—whaddaya do when you got things to haul?" They don't see that Richard is traveling light, he's secure in himself, and with Vanessa sitting next to him, that's a total reality and his life is complete, and yet— Why does he turn pale when he leads this fabulous woman in a silver-lamé shirt into the dim little house? Why does he tremble? Is it the pictures on the walls: the praying hands, the *Threshers* by Millet, a Winslow Homer ship, needlepoint, "Ve Get Too Soon Oldt and Too Late Schmardt"? Is it his family, who never learned the art of making conversation because they only talk to people they know? A slow and terrible death, asphyxiation in your own past. All afternoon he's dying to get back in the Ferlinghetti and go home. At the first decent opportunity, he begins the long ritual goodbye:

Well, I guess it's time we . . . No, really, Ma. Vanessa has to (lie lie lie). Well, okay, just one, but then we got to (lie). No, I'd like to but we promised these friends we'd (lie lie). Finally, with a wave and a roar, they pull away and she turns to Richard the Proud and says, "They were nice. I liked them." But his eyes are full of tears, from exhaustion and relief and guilt and from pride— he really does love this car, it gives him so much pleasure.

Corinne didn't see Richard, Larry, or Eddie. She stayed home. On Christmas Eve, she and Hjalmar and Virginia sat and talked and listened to the Mormon Tabernacle Choir, both sides, A and B, and their old scratchy record of Lionel Barrymore in *A Christmas Carol*. They watched Midnight Mass from Saint Patrick's Cathedral in New York and ate the saffron buns. In the morning, Hjalmar took their dog, Puddles, for a walk. A mile away, the old dog was exhausted. Hjalmar had to pick him up and carry him home. Hjalmar was too tired to drive into Saint Cloud to the Powers Hotel for the elegant Christmas buffet, and so, because there were only three of them, Corinne said, "Let's not fuss, let's make a little turkey dinner with the microwave Daddy got you for Christmas last year." "Fine," Virginia said, "it's under the bed in the guest room, in the box." They both studied the operating manual. In its attempt to describe the incredible flexibility of the microwave, its various functions and options and alternatives, the infinite variety and joy of the thing, it bewildered them. The control panel had buttons numbered from 0 to 9 and other buttons that said: Over, Stop, Clear, From, Time, Recall, Auto, Memory. Which brought back the memory of how lovely it was to put water in a pot, boil it, and drop stuff in— "No!" Corinne cried. "We can't let electronics defeat us!" They put the frozen turkey-dinner pouches in the microwave, pushed a combination of buttons that made the light go on and the fan whirr, and left the kitchen and went and conversed until the bell rang, but something was wrong: the peas were a bluish green, the pouch of turkey had flecks of silvery ash in it. They had each had two glasses of sherry and were in a philosophical mood. Corinne looked at her mother, her mother looked at Corinne. "Well," said Corinne, "I'll never have babies."

"So," said Virginia, "I'll never be a grandma." "That's life," they said, "let's go to David and Judy's and see what Christian charity really is worth nowadays. They invited us, didn't they—? It was a month ago and we said no, but we didn't know then what we know now, so let's go."

The Reverend David Ingqvist and wife, Judith, were in the midst of an argument when they heard the knock on the door. They were arguing whether she is always wrong or not: she was saying that, yes, she can never do anything right, and never pleases him, and he was saying that, no, she was wrong now but she is usually right and, no, she often pleases him and, yes, he does tell her—when he opened the door, expecting to find someone with a gift in hand, and saw his aunt and uncle and cousin. "Hello," said Hjalmar. "We thought we'd come down." "How are you?" said Virginia. "Merry Christmas." "What're you having for dinner?" asked Corinne. "Aren't you going to invite us in?"

New Year's

It has been a quiet week in Lake Wobegon. A warm dry winter, with no snow for a month, just brown grass and some dead snow, and the Lake Wobegon Weather Bureau, which meets at the Sidetrack Tap, has never seen one like it. They're getting fed up with it. They are storytellers, and it's tiresome to have a phenomenon so unusual it doesn't remind you of one that was similar but more so. A blizzard would make you think of some good blizzards of the past, and you could improve on them, but this January drought is only a novelty. It defeats memory. It brings conversation to an end. We wish it would snow.

The ice fishermen wish it were colder, but they put their fish houses out on the lake anyway, they couldn't wait any longer. Mr. Berge asked Elmer, "You think the ice is thick enough?" Elmer said, "Mr. Berge, ice doesn't freeze from the top, it freezes from the bottom, so the temperature of the air doesn't have much bearing on it. Look, Swanny's got his out, and his weighs more'n yours and mine both." Swanny has the first two-room fish house on the lake, twenty feet long, a mansion. He hauled his out on Tuesday, and Wednesday night there were forty houses out there, a little city of men who know that this is the alternative to divorce.

187

In the dead of winter, a home gets smaller and smaller and a man's natural tendencies become more pronounced. Some days she looks at you and wonders if it was worth fifteen dollars for the license. One day she finds you surrounded by newspaper and empty beer bottles and some dirty plates and bits of spillage and she shrieks in horror—you look down and see your pants are gone, you're dressed in a bearskin skirt, holding a hunk of wood, and dangling from your mouth is the tail of the wounded rodent you're eating for dinner. The lovely woman shrinks away in disgust, and you open your mouth and growl. At this point in the marriage, discussion is no good; you need a place to hunker, and that's your fish house, a little plywood room with a stove, a sleeping bench, table and chairs, and a floor with two holes in it to fish through the ice.

The Boosters Club motto for 1987 is "Onward Ever Higher Our Community Inspire," but so far this year doesn't look any different from last, except that Darlene is gone from the Chatterbox. She hung up her white waitress dress and gave the counter one last swipe with a wet rag and drove to a new life in Minneapolis. Her mother said, "You couldn't spend New Year's Eve with your own family? Honey, after all we've done for you? We were counting on it. Couldn't you just come and be with us for an hour? Is that too much to ask? One hour? A half-hour?" But Darlene said, "Mother, you always said that a girl has to learn how to say no. I'm trying to learn. No."

Senator K. Thorvaldson sat and drank eight cups of coffee Wednesday afternoon, flirted with Darlene, and made remarks about maybe going to Minneapolis with her. He is reading a boxful of novels by Ramona Jean Jensen, a writer of whose *oeuvre* you might remark, "I wouldn't read that trash if I was on a desert island with it," and then you pluck from the paperback rack in Ralph's a thick novel with a picture of a bosomy Viking temptress in a diaphanous gown struggling with a heavyweight wrapped in animal skins, and you read a few paragraphs and suddenly your legs are stiff, you're on page 43, your frozen steaks are thawing and your ice cream is melting; but you sit down on the ledge inside Ralph's big front window to learn how Ingrid will ever escape from Stefan and read a passage about her milky white ——, her young and tender ——, her small, pert ——, her ——. Good Lord, you had no idea people sold this in a grocery store. Then a shadow falls on the page and you look up and there's Ralph. "Want me to put your meat back in the cooler?" he says.

Senator K. looked at his old waitress and thought how much he'd miss her. Her skin was milky white . . . her hands as she stuffed napkins in the holder . . . the special way she filled his coffee cup . . .

"How about that woman in Maine—aren't you still writing to her?" Darlene said. "Oh well, yes, but she can't leave her son, he's sick, some kind of sleeping sickness. And she's been seeing another man. He's younger, seventy-one. That's fine. I don't want to get in her way if she cares for someone else. I don't want to make a fool of myself. It's up to her. Maybe she's too polite to tell me. So I'll just have to remove myself from consideration." He'll leave soon for his little condo in Florida. "Maybe you'd like to go to Florida," he said to Darlene. "It's pretty down there. A lot of old people, but we wouldn't need to bother with them."

The Ingqvists bought their tickets to Florida two months ago, Pastor Dave and Judy; at least that's what she said. They've missed the Annual Ministers' Retreat three years in a row because the civilian leadership at church can't see why their minister and his wife should cavort in the tropics in January. She can see about three reasons, but she can't tell the Board because it's more than they want to know about a minister: it's hard work to stand up and say what people don't really believe but want to think they do; and it's tough when a man of faith suffers from depression in a town where nice people are expected to be upbeat. For a few days on Captiva Island, at the Château Suzanne, around the blue kidney-bean-shaped pool, cool aquamarine in a forest of deep green and fabulous birds of brilliant plumage, some pale plump Lutherans will sit in the sun like lumps of bread dough and say forbidden things. Oh, the luxury of truth when you come from a town of storytellers! The luxury of sitting in sunlight, clasping a gin-and-tonic, wearing two articles of clothing that allow the world to reasonably assume you are a woman, lighting up one of your ten annual cigarettes, and saying openly to other ministers' wives, "It has been hard this year."

"I moved up to the third pew, left side. His idea. I was sitting about in the tenth row, and he said it looked to people like indifference on my part. So there I am in the store window with an admiring look on my face, and he looks up from the sermon and says, 'My wife said a wonderful thing to me the other day,' and I just blanch. It's always some dumb thing—all of us have that ability in a pinch to utter something pretentious and moralistic and false—but he quotes this with a big cheesy smile, and I have to smile up at him in a modest girlish way, when inside I'm thinking, 'You bastard, you didn't even quote me correctly. I didn't say, "The acorn doesn't fall far from the tree," what I said was "I'd know a Tollefson even if the lights were off." ' "

Judy misses her friend Katy, who moved to town with her husband, Merle, six years ago, both of them schoolteachers, both funny and bright. But it was Merle who got a job at the school, and Katy didn't. Katy stayed home, raised their kids, was active in things, and found out that Lake Wobegon didn't like her to be too active. She was . . . too critical. Too sarcastic. At the band-and-choir concert, Katy said, "God, it's awful, isn't it? You can tell where all the accidentals are because everyone misses them. It's like they never saw the music before." It was the truth: the band played rotten, and it was funny to hear someone say so, but Judy was glad she hadn't said it herself. The women who sat with them froze in shock. Katy got cut out. Nobody went to visit her. So she decided to show them—she opened a one-hour photo-developing business in her basement. She'd show them and be successful despite what they thought of her. But they didn't send film to her. You don't send film to someone who you think is making fun of you. You don't want her looking at photos of you and your husband, fat and sleepy and grinning like idiots. She sat smelling chemicals for four months, and got mad at people. Finally she got a job as a schoolbus driver. She had her B.A. in English and was angry to be earning four dollars an hour, and one winter day her bus skidded into the ditch. No one was hurt badly, but by then she and Merle were having troubles, she was in debt from the photo business, and one night she left town without telling anyone. The thing was: she didn't take their new Ford Sonata, she took the old Hornet that was on its last legs.

Their escape to Captiva Island was all set. The tickets arrived. Dave's substitute would be Reverend Bob Olson, a friend, not one of those flashy subs who have one sermon they've performed a hundred times so they talk like it was from the heart like TV ministers and have special drops to put in their eyes to make them gleam—one of those subs, and you return from vacation and feel the disappointment. Reverend Bob is a plodder.

"Do you honestly think we'll go?" she asked him one night over dishes.

"Of course," he said. "Don't even think about not going. Of course we're going. You have to believe in it. All right? What makes you think we're not going to go?"

Advent exhausted them—so much joy and great tidings proclaimed while inside they felt crummy—and before the candlelight service they stood in the vestibule, he in his vestments and she at the head of the children's choir, and they got in a fight and hissed at each other. "How could you say that to me?" she said.

"I never said any such thing."

"You certainly did."

"Oh shut up."

In this little town, as winter descends, we depend on marriage to get us through, because we can't be attractive every day on a regular basis, we need loyalty, money in the bank, and if it's the Church that stands behind marriage, then the Ingqvists' marriage is crucial to everyone. So then they tried hard to be nice to each other, and that was almost worse. To treat your true love like they are a customer. "Good morning, how are you? What can I do for you today?" They needed to sit in the sun and hear birds cry, paradise birds, non-Lutheran birds, with their sharp cries. Lutheran birds wear brown wool plumage and murmur, "No thanks, none for me, I'm fine, you go ahead," but these paradise birds in their brilliant orange-and-green silks are all screaming, "MORE MORE MORE! I want MORE MORE MORE!"

Sunday night she looked at the calendar. "Seven days to go. Can we make it?" The Scripture verse for Sunday was: "By the rivers of Babylon, there we sat down, yea, we wept, when we remembered Zion. We hanged our harps upon the willows in the midst thereof. For . . . how shall we sing the Lord's song in a strange land?" What did this mean in regard to Florida?

Val Tollefson came Monday afternoon, with his old dog, Rick. "David isn't here," she told him. "That's all right," Val said, "I came to put a new circuit box on your furnace." He and Rick went down the basement like it was their house. Val has never liked them, and it took her years to find out why. Val owns the entire series of Joy-and-John books, all sixteen. The inspirational adventures of Joy and John Kendall, Lutheran minister in the town of Littleton, books like *Rejoicing in Him* and *Blessed Quietness*, in which Joy and John meet the challenge of each new day with quiet simple dedication. "No wonder Val doesn't like us," she thought, "we smell, we chew our food—the Kendalls are perfect, they cast no shadow." Val knelt by the furnace. "I don't know," he said. "Seems like we're spending money left and right. 'Stead of going to Florida one week to get warm, seems like it'd make more sense to fix this furnace."

On Monday all of them had fleas. The kids couldn't go to school. She drove to Ralph's and bought groceries and stole two bars of Lysine soap because she was afraid someone'd notice the wrapper said FOR CONTROL OF HEAD LICE AND FLEAS. She slipped them into her purse. An exterminator recommended over the phone that they go to a motel for a week. She started cleaning the house with Lysine. Tuesday the furnace went on the fritz. They didn't dare call Val. The furnace went on if you jiggled the thermostat and dialed the combination fifty-five, ninety, seventy degrees; it went on and got the house up to sixty-two. On Wednesday the flu struck and their two littlest children woke up with hot dry eyeballs and the taste of flu in their mouths. They lay in misery, weeping. The house was cold. "We're a decent home," she thought, "we have a piano, encyclopedias. Now fleas."

She didn't know they had mice too. Rick, who'd brought the fleas, had driven off their old cat, Sam. David discovered the mice after she found the fleas, and he decided not to tell her. He set a corn trap under the basement stairs and disposed of the mice every morning. The corn trap is a bucket with corn soaked in syrup in the bottom; the mouse jumps in and eats and can't get out, and you carry it outside and spin the bucket to confuse the mouse and let it go.

It wasn't that he couldn't kill a mouse, but in winter, when life itself seems so precious and precarious, it is easier to spare the creature. He took away two mice Monday night. Tuesday morning another mouse sat in the trap, who looked like one from the night before. David painted its left front ankle blue. Tuesday night it was in the corn trap again. Despite the triple-reverse spin he had given it, it had found the way back to their home. An amazing mouse, so he named it Moses.

Tuesday night he carried Moses up the hill and deep into Egypt, up to Val Tollefson's backyard. Wednesday morning Moses was back in the bucket. That afternoon David carried him over the hill and into the Tolleruds' cornfield. The mouse lay quietly in his mitten, and David thought about killing him. Maybe a sacrifice would set them free. Kill the mouse and go back to a toasty-warm house with happy feverless children and a lovely happy wife, a wonderful Lutheran family with no fleas. *Kill the mouse.* He set Moses down in the snow and it ran and sat and looked at him.

Thursday the mouse came back. David carried him to the lake, out on the ice, halfway to the fish houses. He said, "Moses, I'm going to miss you. But how can I until you go away? Now go in peace." He dropped him, and Moses put his head up and sniffed and sniffed, and that night he was back at the parsonage, like there was a star overhead. Thursday night was prayer meeting but they didn't go: the house was sixty-two degrees, the kids 103,

Judy had been boiling sheets and blankets, the kitchen reeked of disinfectant, supper was cornflakes in a bowl, and he noticed the big suitcase by the door. Was it theirs or hers?

After supper he put on his jacket and picked up Moses and carried him out across the lake toward the fish houses. "This is our last trip," he said. "If you come back again, I guess we'll have to take you in." The moon shone and smoke curled up from the little shacks. "What if I go through the ice?" he thought. "Carrying a mouse to freedom, I lose my life." The thought made him slip, then he caught his balance. He walked out to Berge's shack. "Here," he said, "you two will like each other," and set Moses down, and the mouse was dead. It lay on the ice, a little piece of gray fur. When he slipped, he must have squeezed his hand and broken its neck. One slip. Tomorrow the mouse would've come back and they'd've kept it there in the land of Canaan. Moses almost made it.

He ran home and called Judy's mother, Clarice. "Come now," he said, "we're going." *How?* Judy asked. "Now," he said. *Tonight?* "If we wait until tomorrow it'll be that much easier to wait until next year." Clarice came in, took off her coat, and told them not to worry. They picked up the suitcase and drove to Minneapolis, slept in a cheap motel on a truck route near the airport, woke up on a gray day, and at seven-forty-five they sat in row 24, seats E and F, in a beige tube full of people that suddenly vibrated and rumbled and tilted up and they rose. Clouds flew past the window, and then a brilliant blue sky. Sunday will be Lay Sunday at Lake Wobegon Lutheran Church, Clarence will be in the pulpit. The Ingqvists are at Château Suzanne, in the sunshine, listening to birds cry: MORE. But that's all there is.

Where Did
It Go Wrong?

It has been a quiet week in Lake Wobegon. The strange weather continues, the warm winter with no snow, the famous winter of 1987—we'll be talking about this twenty years from now: "*Ja*, that winter of 1988, boy that was an odd one." "Nineteen eighty-seven, Grandpa. We read about that. Nineteen eighty-seven." "Shuddup. I was there, I seen it, 1988. No snow, it was warm, and we were all sick from January to March. It almost killed us."

A lot of people *have* been sick in Lake Wobegon, and it could be due to the weather. Norway is a seafaring country and if you have Norwegian blood you're happier and you operate best when you're cold, wet, and sick to your stomach. Misery is what keeps a Norwegian going, and in warm sunny weather such as we've had, they get sick and go to pieces and get a case of Swedish flu caused by weakness on account of a lack of suffering. (Swedish flu is like Asian flu but in addition you feel like it's your fault.)

The Leonards lost three of their starting five to the flu, and eight of the top ten, all of them sick, which is how they normally feel right before a game: weak, feverish with cold chills, nauseous,

achy—these boys felt that bad on Sunday, so on Tuesday, against
Freeport, Dutch's starting lineup included boys who joined the
team expecting they would never have to play. Tall shy boys who
had come to feel comfortable on the bench, whispering, kidding
around, making fun of the poor saps out on the floor: the team
satirists—Tuesday, there they were, warming up, passing the
ball gingerly around the circle, trying not to drop it, trying to look
as dignified as possible under the circumstances, with Freeport
kids yelling humorous things at them, knowing the game was not
theirs to win.

"These are my formative years," thinks a boy in this situation,
"and tonight will help shape the rest of my life. I'll become a
hopeless derelict to begin with and sell secrets to the Russians
and fire a gun into a crowd and turn to cannibalism. After that,
who knows?"

You start out with thoughts like those in warmup, and game
conditions don't make you feel better. The Leonards got greased,
63–34; they were baked forty-eight minutes at four hundred degrees and were had for lunch.

On the long way home, they came down sick with the flu, a
busload of nauseous Leonards and their fainthearted fans on an
overheated bus with bad suspension swaying back and forth barreling sixty-five mph down that bumpy old tar road and the rail-
road tracks up ahead—they knew when they bounced up something
wouldn't come down—and just before they hit, a satirist yelled,
TRAIN COMING!

A wave of cold terror! The brakes screeched, they crashed forward into the seat ahead, the bus banged over the tracks, they
bounced in the air, and then they rode along quietly for about
twenty seconds, not moving, praying: Lord, please do not let this
happen to me, what is going to happen right now—this is what
comes from having a warm winter.

Harold and Marlys Diener were sick in bed; so was their dog,
but not as sick as them. They lay side by side with headaches,
fever, vomiting, diarrhea: a whole new dimension to their marriage. Ordinarily one person is sick and the other one is the kind,
sympathetic, helpful, Christian person, but with both of you down

in bed, you just lie there and look at each other with mounting disgust, your true love looking as awful as you feel, romance receding into the dim corners of memory, and your stomach sinks. And then it rises.

They lay in the tangled swamp of flu for a day and a half. Marlys's mother came and helped, and then she was sick, so Marlys dragged herself out to make breakfast for the kids and got them off to school, and then she lost track of time. She lost track of school, of society, and the idea of parenthood, and went away into the depths of flu, where a person ceases to be an American, where you join the ancient tribe of hairy lowbrowed people who hunker around a cold fire and chew on rancid elk and moan to each other in a dry white tongue: *huhnnnn, hwihhhhhhh-qwertyuiop.*

She lay in the twisted bedclothes, dozing off, waking up, sweaty, weak, dreaming short fast horrible dreams about falling and falling through the air and turning around and around, jumping out of bed and running to the toilet, back to bed, sleep, boys jump on you and hit you in the stomach, up out of bed, run, run. . . .

Later, not sure what time it was, she got up and went to the kitchen. It was dark outside but this is February in Minnesota: darkness is normal. She snapped on the kitchen light—and turned it off. A mess like that, you don't want to see when you're sick. It looked like the cupboards had blown up. It looked like the fall of Rome. Then she heard a hissing sound from the living room, like a gas leak but worse—*sssssssssssssss*—like that scene in *It Came Up the River* about mutant eelpout changed by radioactive wastes from the power plant into immense slithering damp carnivorous monsters who invade Metroville one Friday night, this was the sound the eelpout made from their immense wicked mouths full of lurid bluish radioactive light as they slithered along. *Sssssssssss.* The living room was dark except for the TV. The screen was blank, the sound was turned up high, *ssssssssssssssss*, and there on the floor, in a mess of blankets and empty pop cans and cereal boxes, lay her three kids asleep, their mouths open, their lips crusted with sugar. A living nightmare of What Happens When a Family Falls Apart.

She said, "Up! Come on! Everybody up and brush your teeth

and in your pajamas and into bed!" That one sentence exhausted her. She staggered away to bed, and awoke again, and it was light, sun streaming in, and extremely cold. The front door was open, the living room was a shambles, and she heard dogs in the kitchen eating the remains of the sausage pizza the kids had made for their breakfast. This is the price we pay for a warm winter.

Father Wilmer was down with the municipal virus, so Father Emil, the poor sick old man, did the honors on Ash Wednesday at Our Lady of Perpetual Responsibility. To observe this holy day the same week as half the town has the Swedish flu is to be in a state of redundant contrition, one would think, but Father Emil got out of bed and did his duty. As the faithful shuffled up the aisle to the altar, he dipped his thumb in the bowl of ashes and put the black smudge on their forehead and said the words God said when He threw our parents out of paradise, "Dust thou art and unto dust thou shalt return."

Adam and Eve evidently weren't from around here because the Bible says they went naked and we know that's not right. But they were from a place that was *similar* to this, except warm all the time, like a shopping mall.

They had everything their hearts could desire and all of it exactly perfect, shining, beautiful, and new, but of course they didn't realize it at the time because they had nothing to compare it to. They didn't know what misery and grief and pain were like, they were a couple of wahoos in birthday suits, perfectly happy, but they didn't have two minutes of education between them. So when God made one rule and said, "Don't get on that bus," they had no reason to get on it, but when the bus came, they had no reason to stay.

It was a long silver bus with a shiny apple on the side that said *Minneapolis*, driven by a rather handsome snake, his brown hair slicked back, wearing a little snake mustache and a brand-new suit. He glanced at them with a gleam in his eyes and said, "Minneapolis. Step right up. Bright lights, smart sophisticated people, artists. You're gonna love it. Yethir, yethir. *Board*." They had no reason *not* to get on the bus, except that God had told them not to go, but what did that mean? Adam and Eve didn't understand No. Paradise was the land of Yes, there was no negative around there anywhere.

So Adam looked at Eve with her naturally curly hair, and she looked at him in his green feed cap that said "Let there be light," and he said, "Well, I donno."

She didn't know either. Serpent said, "Hurry hurry hurry hurry. Step right up. And put those adult tickets aside, everybody comes in on the children's price of admission. Free, folks, it's absolutely free."

Well, they were children to begin with. She said, "You want to eat that apple?"

"Well, not particularly, but I suppose I could. It's up to you."

She said, "Well, if you don't want to, that's all right," and he said, "I'm not saying I wouldn't, it's not important to me either way," and she said, "Same here. I could go or not, either one is fine," and he said, "Well, as long as you want to go, then I'll come too, I don't want to spoil your good time, I'd never hear the end of it," and she said, "Well, it's up to you, but that's fine, I'll go." And they went. And it was a one-way trip. How you gonna get them back to paradise once they've been to Southdale?

Darlene went to Minneapolis to find her destiny and to find her husband Arlen so she could divorce him. They were married in 1971 and he left home in 1976 for the Bicentennial, so she had him for five years and was without him for ten. The decade seemed better to her, lonesome but cheerful. For a long time, however, Darlene wondered. All the years she waitressed at the Chatterbox, sitting drinking coffee and smoking Alpine cigarettes—for the coupons, because the more you smoke you can get nice things like TV trays or a clock radio and if you got one already you could give one to your mom. She wondered where did it go wrong and how was it that she and Arlen lost the happy feeling they started out their marriage with.

It might've been when she served him the Szechuan chicken.

She'd never made it before, but he was tired of what she'd been making, so she tried a new recipe and bought some unknown spices and used more garlic in one day than she'd used in six years. These two innocent people raised on the ambrosia of cream-of-mushroom soup and the many hotdishes derived therefrom such as tuna hotdish, the world's most comforting food, sat down and ate the Szechuan chicken, all of it. It tasted bad but they didn't want to admit it and they were brought up to clean their plates, and afterward they lay down and moaned. Nothing seemed the same after that.

It might've been when Arlen came in the bathroom (as a joke) when she was taking a shower, scrubbing, and singing to herself "How Great Thou Art." She had a feeling that someone was watching her and she looked up and screamed—it was their golden retriever, Rex, looking over the curtain bar. Arlen was holding him up, Rex's big brown eyes full of prurient interest peering down at her bare breasts. Afterward they laughed about it, but weeks went by, and every time Rex looked at her, she still felt ashamed. He looked at her through half-closed eyes, leering. "I know you," he seemed to say. She'd be vacuuming and turn and there he was, staring at her. Wake up and he was by the bed. Come out of the bathroom, he waited in the hall: "Hello, baby," he seemed to say. One night she woke up and the bed was shaking, it was Rex trying to climb in. "NO," she said, "NO NO NO." She made Arlen give him away to Arlen's hunting buddy, Jerry, but then, when she saw Jerry, she noticed a look in his eye, like Rex had told him. He said, "Hi, Darlene," looking straight through her blouse. Then one morning she saw it in Arlen's eyes, a strange look. She thought, "Please don't, honey, please," but you can't very well tell someone not to look at you that way; they can't change how they look.

Post Office

It has been a quiet week in Lake Wobegon. The first snow fell Monday and it turned cold. It got so cold Tuesday and Wednesday, you actually saw boys wearing scarves outdoors. The cold snap came on fast. Bud had been meaning to put antifreeze in the pickup—it was his firm intention, and he even mentioned it to Eloise one day—and the next morning the truck was frozen up and Bud was mortified. He couldn't even eat breakfast. She said, "For heaven's sake, what's wrong with you?" He said, "Radiator cracked on the truck, and now I got to spend a day putting in a new one." He couldn't even admit the truth to his own wife.

As the municipal maintenance man, Bud has a reputation for competence and foresight, the man Mayor Clint Bunsen calls first for any mechanical problem. He wasn't about to take his frozen truck to Bunsen Motors and become Clint's joke of the week, so he borrowed Carl Krebsbach's pickup and drove to Little Falls for a new radiator. But first he had to call Clint and say he was going. He had to think of an excuse. "I need to go to Little Falls to . . ." To what? What could he say he was going to Little Falls to get so that Clint wouldn't say, "Oh we got that right here. What size you need?" Had to think of something too odd for Lake Wobegon to stock but not too odd for Little Falls, a town of seventy-two hundred. A trailer hitch. Or tin snips. A piston for his lawnmower. Or a chamfer bit. He'd heard of that somewhere; "chamfer bit" sounded good. Like something you ought to know, so Clint wouldn't say, "What's a chamfer bit?" He'd say, "Oh. Yes. We used to have those but we don't anymore." Unless Bud had the name wrong. Maybe it was a chandler bit. And Clint'd correct him: "You mean a chandler bit." And every time they consulted him on mechanical problems, Clint'd remember and say, "Well, a *chamfer* bit might do the trick," and laugh and slap his knee, and everybody would start chortling and wheezing. *Chamfer bit!* Bud was nervous, and when he got Clint on the phone, he said, "I got to go over to Little Falls to get me some work gloves." "Okay," said Clint, "see you later." Bud said, "They're not just ordinary gloves. They're a special kind." "Okay," Clint said, "that's fine." "Somebody told me about these," said Bud, "so I thought I'd run over and see if they got them there. Nobody has them here. I checked." "All right, then," said Clint, "we'll catch you later." As Bud was pulling away, Carl came running out and said, "If you go by an auto-parts store, see if they don't have a radiator hose, I froze up my car the other night, forgot to put the antifreeze in." Okay, Bud said, I'll do that.

Carl knows, there's not much privacy in a small town. You know so much about other people, and you have to figure they know at least as much about you. What they surmise about you from what they know is, of course, a matter of conjecture.

It was cold. Not historic heroic cold, just plain everyday cold, not even worth complaining about, a fact of life like the flat terrain, though some people complain about that. "It's flat out there," they say, "darned flat. It's a lot of sky to have to keep track of." The furnace broke down at the *Herald-Star,* just when Harold's wisdom tooth was on the fritz and he had it pulled Tuesday. He sprained his ankle at the dentist's when he hooked his foot around the chair, hanging on while the tooth came out. He almost pulled his foot off. When he hobbled to the Chatterbox for a cup of soup, Carl said, "That tooth had a long root, didn't it?" He heard the same joke from others. That night the furnace stopped, two water pipes froze, and the toilet burst, causing a short so the lights wouldn't go on. Harold's blessings were running in the red. He reached for the bottle of Old Overcoat whiskey in the desk and the bottle was empty. Someone had finished it, perhaps himself. He threw it into the wastebasket, or meant to, but had gotten turned around in the dark and threw it through the door instead. Glass shattered on the sidewalk. Water was frozen on the floor, and he slipped and fell on the glass. Some people thought he must be drunk but he only wished he was.

It was cold, and at the Lutheran parsonage Judy Ingqvist said to her husband, Pastor Dave, "This year we've got to try to make the Annual Ministers' Retreat in Florida this January. We really need to. Three years in a row now we have cheated ourselves out of it, and we could use a break."

"It's not in Florida this time," he said, "it's in the British West Indies, I think. They sent a brochure on it. Let me go find it." Off he went, and then from the dining room: "Honey, did somebody fool with this thermostat? It's sixty-two degrees in here."

"What's the thermostat set at?" she said.

"Seventy-five."

"Aha!" she said. "Try turning it to fifty-five. Slowly. Then up to ninety. Then off. Wait fifteen seconds and put it up to seventy. That worked last year a couple times."

For months the building committee has discussed the parsonage furnace, an old coal burner converted to oil that some think needs replacing and others say has a lot of use left in it. Finally, on Monday, the committee traipsed through the kitchen down to the cellar on a fact-finding trip and stood meditating in front of the ancient blackened hulk in the corner and its tangle of pipes. "It sure runs quiet," said Elmer. "I don't think it's on," said Clarence. He glanced at the laundry rack where the minister's wet shorts hung and his wife's brassieres and pantyhose.

"It seems to work fine except that it doesn't give heat," David said. He squeezed past Elmer and stood a few feet from Val, in front of the laundry rack. "It seems to be discouraged by cold weather. Any sudden drop of temperature and it feels like the furnace figures 'What's the use?' It feels doomed to failure. So it quits."

He stood, hands in his jacket pockets, as the men studied the prehistoric furnace, and Judy noticed that he was shielding the laundry rack and her wet underwear—what a lovely modest man—his hands in his jacket pockets so as to spread himself wider to protect her private clothing.

"I don't know," said Val, "my cousin in Canby has one almost exactly like it, he says it's the best he ever had. I just wonder if it isn't a problem up here in the hot-air vents. . . ." And he slipped around back of the laundry rack, peering up into the joists, the minister keeping an eye on him. "But I suppose we could replace it if it comes to that. We could take it out of Foreign Missions—we got nine hundred dollars in the disaster relief fund that we earmarked for Laotian refugee camps and I'd hate not to send it to them, with things down there being what they are, but—I suppose."

He circled the laundry rack, and Dave turned and tried to slide the underwear together, and one pale-pink lacy brassiere fell to the floor. The men all glanced down at it. It was pink because it'd been washed in a batch of red things, but Judy didn't explain that to them. Dave picked it up and dropped it in the laundry tub, a big pink fish. Tears came to her eyes: taking money away from refugees to buy a new furnace and the minister's wife wearing fancy pink lingerie, they'd never get to go to Florida in January, not now.

In the post office, due to the lack of a fifty-nine-cent part for the gas jet in the stove, it was too cold to sort mail. Mr. Bauser dumped the morning sackful on the table and put up a sign, DUE TO NO HEAT, MAIL IS OUT OF ORDER—HELP YOURSELF, and people wandered in all morning and rummaged around for their own.

"I ordered that part six weeks ago from way over in South Dakota, they coulda sent it by congressional committee, it woulda got here by now," Mr. Bauser said, but we didn't mind. It was interesting looking at the mail. To know that Irene Bunsen subscribes to *Northern Spy* magazine with its big black headlines, FLESH-EATING FLAMINGO FOUND IN FLORIDA, NEST SURROUNDED BY EMPTY BABY SHOES. 450-LB. WOMAN MARRIES 78-LB. MAN. GRANDPA, 89, TAKES NITRO PILL AND EXPLODES AT DINING ROOM TABLE AS WHOLE FAMILY LOOKS ON IN HORROR. Irene has been leading the discussion of Ephesians in Women's Circle. WISCONSIN MAN PREGNANT WITH FIRST CHILD. You don't find that in Ephesians, do you.

Mr. Berge had a big creamy envelope from an attorney firm in Houston, their name in black raised letters. What could that be? A legacy from an old rich aunt who died thinking of him as a sweet boy, that grizzled old souse, and here was a check for twenty-five thousand dollars? He was in Texas once, wasn't he, in the Army during the war—didn't he go through basic training there? You don't suppose he committed a crime? Maybe he did and was in prison when we thought he was in the Army, and now time has passed and public outrage has cooled. He is applying for a pardon from that heinous crime, hiring a smooth Houston lawyer to expunge the horrible words from his record. Do you think? *Naw.* He couldn't afford a lawyer with stationery like this. Of course, sometimes a court will appoint you one. What do you suppose he did back then?

"I don't know about this stove," Mr. Bauser said. "Do you know, I bought this brand-new two years ago from a guy from Rapid City; he was driving a late-model van and he had blue aviator glasses and a sheepskin jacket and cowboy boots, and he give me a five-year warranty on it, parts and labor, and now when I write him a letter there's no answer; I don't know, I don't know. . . . You care for some coffee?" He reached over to his electric hot plate and touched the teakettle—"I got hot water right here"—and the rest of us who were looking at Mr. Berge's envelope glanced at the teakettle. Steam curled up from its tin spout.

What sort of crime might he have done in Texas? Now a slick lawyer in a three-piece blue pinstripe suit will get him pardoned by a rich liberal judge who lives in a mansion and lets murderers and rapists go free. If Mr. Berge bludgeoned someone to death on a three-day weekend pass on a Texas back road in 1942, don't we have a moral obligation to our community and our children to steam this envelope and find out? Of course it would be wrong, but if by opening the envelope we could save a life, then shouldn't we? If we think something might be wrong, if there's a suspicion and someone seems to have a tendency?

"I tell you, I start to miss that old woodstove we useta have. That was good heat, wood heat—a real *warm* heat, not drafty heat." And he pulled up his parka and rummaged in the postage drawer for instant coffee. We looked at the teakettle boiling on the hot plate. It seems like it's sat there since I can remember, but I don't recall Mr. Bauser drinking coffee or tea. And yet for years and years he's had water boiling on the back shelf next to where he sorts the mail.

I walked over and helped myself to a clean Styrofoam cup, put a little Sanka in it, and poured hot water in. I tried to catch Mr. Bauser's eye. I wanted to look him in the eye and silently ask him if he ever read my mail, and by the look in his eye, as I thought it, I'd know if he's guilty or not, the old son of a bitch. I wrote about 187 love letters a year ago, and if I thought the old snoop had steamed the flaps open, reading my words to that lovely woman—words I wrote to her, thinking only of her, far away, the beautiful her—should I have been thinking of him, old man with hair in his nose and little red eyes darting across the page, reading my mind, stealing my life . . .

Each person knows how much privacy you need, and you can't accept less, not even in a small town. If you drop by Bud's garage and say, "You putting in a new radiator? What's wrong?" and he says, "A rock came up and knocked a hole in the bottom," you should accept that. When people watch us too closely, it turns us into an actor and kills us, because, frankly, most of us aren't good at acting. I forgave Mr. Berge for the murder he committed. Maybe it was someone who read his mail and he stabbed them with a letter opener.

Out in the Cold

It has been a quiet week in Lake Wobegon. It was cold this week, so cold it brought tears to the eyes of a Norwegian bachelor farmer. Mr. Odegaard's Ford pickup wouldn't start when he came out of the Sidetrack Tap after lunch, so he decided he'd walk home, feeling pretty warm from the lunch, and a half-mile later he decided to hitchhike. He put out his thumb as Mr. Bauser came along in his old green post-office Chevy, and he drove right on by. Mr. Odegaard jumped out on the road. "Tell-witcha!" he yelled. "Goddamn you anyway, I'm never gonna write another damn letter in my life! I'm never gonna even go in your damn post office! I hope you die in hell!"

Mr. Bauser has a lot on his mind. He turns fifty-five in two weeks and is thinking he ought to do something with his life and not just go along in the post office, sorting letters. He's thinking an idea he's had for several years since he bought a Lawn Quest rider mower, and that is: get together some guys to set a cross-country record for rider mowers and get in the *Guinness Book*. He's not sure there is a cross-country rider-mower record to break, in which case they could take it easy and whatever they did would be a record. Maybe a month or two, Los Angeles to New York. Or start from New York. The news media are there, and maybe you'd rather have them present for the start of the event rather than the finish. Mr. Bauser didn't even see Mr. Odegaard.

Mr. Odegaard walked on. If he wasn't so angry, he might've laid down and died, it was so cold. Anger kept him going. He wanted to get home and write to the *Herald-Star* about so-called Christians—"Some of these people you see parading out of church on Sunday, you ought to see them when you are stranded on a highway on a cold day, they pass you by like you was a mailbox." He was mostly done with the first paragraph and thinking about the second.

It was bitterly cold. A group of young evangelists were working door-to-door in town, who came all the way from Bob Louvin Bible College in Blunt, Georgia. They sat in a big blue motor home with "Bob Louvin Bible College" painted on all sides and tried to get warm before they made a run at a house to preach the Gospel.

They knocked hard on the doors with their bare hands and said, "Morning, ma'am, I'm from Bob Louvin Bible College, wonder if I could step in for a minute and share something from Romans?" She said, "What?" They said, "Could I come in, please?" They looked like warm clothing wasn't doing them any good at all. They were too far north, outside of Bob Louvin's cable-TV coverage area, and part of their testimony, once they got in the door, was to play a videocassette of Bob Louvin, and nobody around here had VCRs, so the evangelical team didn't stick around long, about two hours, their motor running, and headed west into the wind. They whipped on past Mr. Odegaard standing on the county road, his thumb out, and he watched them speed away, his finger out, and there were tears in his eyes. ("They are no more Christians than pigs are, or a goddamn fish. Just cause you're underwater doesn't make you a Baptist.") Long after they disappeared, he still yelled things their way, which only time can tell if it comes true or not.

While the motor home was still parked by the Knutes' temple, consumed by a cloud of exhaust, a shiny old black Cadillac with a silver-angel hood ornament slid up to the curb in front of the rectory next door to Our Lady of Perpetual Responsibility school at the end of morning recess, when the herd was just lining up at the front door before they went up the chute. When they spotted the car, most of the livestock broke loose and galloped over to have a look. Sister Arvonne said, "Hey! Inside!" A tall horse-faced man in a black coat and hat slid out the back door and stood up. He said, "Good morning, Sister," and went straight into the rectory. There was a faint smell of cologne and his heels clicked on the sidewalk, then he disappeared. The driver sat in the car with the motor running for half an hour, halfway through algebra. Kids working problems at the blackboard stared down at it. "Keep your mind on your business," said Sister Arvonne, "and I'll let you know if anything happens worth looking at."

What she knew was that, after forty-four years, Father Emil had asked to be relieved of his duties at Our Lady, but she didn't know who the gentleman in black was. Our Lady is a mission church of the Order of Saint Benedict, founded in 1858 to minister to the Indians and then to the German immigrants who were following a map drawn by a Father Schlafmeister, who placed Minnesota several hundred miles farther west than it actually was. When the settlers arrived, they had the feeling they weren't quite there yet, that the mundane fact of longitude had stopped them short of their dream of Minnesota, that it was out where Montana is, and they lost touch with their home base in Pennsylvania. Our Lady has always been under the jurisdiction of the Abbey of Saint Frederic, outside of Scranton, but when Father Emil submitted his resignation, it panicked the Abbot, who had been in office for only eleven years and didn't know he had a mission church loose in Minnesota, rolling around the deck. Father tended not to ask his superiors for much guidance and the file on Our Lady was thin. The Abbot worried that it was one of those crackpot Catholic Second Coming churches with ammo boxes in the basement and the Knights of Columbus in masks, so he got on the horn to Minnesota, to the Bishop of Brainerd, and said, "If you want it, you can have it." That was the tall man in the black coat, Bishop Dennis

O'Bleness of Brainerd. He sat in Father's parlor and balanced a cup of Sanka on his knee and listened to Emil's rocker creak and tried to see the old man's face.

Father likes to put his chair so the morning sun comes over his shoulder. The sun lit up the Bishop while Father sat there like the Ghost of Christmas Yet to Come. The younger man tried to slide his chair southward into the shadows. "Light bother you? I can pull the shade. Just takes a minute, with these knees the way they are—"

"No, that's fine. So. You feel you can't continue—"

"Don't feel. Know. I knew I'd know it when the time came, and now it's come."

"How old would you be now?"

"Seventy-two."

"And what sort of timetable are we looking at here?"

"I would like the privilege of celebrating Easter Mass. I would like to leave on Monday, March 31."

"And what are your plans at that point, Father?"

"My plan is that you will take care of me for the rest of my life."

"Well, I would hope that the Abbey would make some arrangements for you. . . ."

"Whatever. I'll just pack my bag and sit on it and wait for somebody to come."

He still hadn't got a good look at Father. First the hallway was dark and now the sun was in his eyes. He wasn't sure this was on the up and up. *Lake Wobegon:* had he ever driven through here before? It was on the border between Brainerd Diocese and Saint Cloud and, frankly, he couldn't recall discussing with Bishop Reitz whose parish it should be. It was no prize, obviously. A strange town, one that would take a special sort of priest, a man who perhaps couldn't fit in at another parish, a square peg, who would find his voice, his vocation. . . . Well, he'd been giving Father Wilfred some careful thought recently. Poor old Wilfred. Maybe he could find peace in Lake Wobegon. Maybe the Lord had created this vacancy especially to give Father Wilfred a place in the world.

A strange town, the Bishop thought. On the sidewalk outside, a man came up and spoke to him urgently about rider mowers. The old priest with the light over his shoulder: could he have been a ghost? And now this old man ahead on the road—a hitchhiker, but he was standing in the middle of the road, waving his arms— Brother Curt had to veer to the left, almost off the road, to avoid him. They sped away and the Bishop looked back as the man threw something at them, hitting the rear window. The Bishop ducked. ("Catholics are the worst, the bottom of the barrel. A few days ago . . .") The glass didn't break, the object wasn't hard. In fact, it stuck to the window. A few miles farther, Curt stopped and scraped it off, but it wouldn't come off, it spread around.

He thought that Father Wilfred might be just the ticket.

Hawaii

It *has been a quiet week in Lake Wobegon.* It got very quiet when all that snow fell and the weather turned cloudy and cold. A gray sky the color of a tin roof. Then, when they found out I was coming here to Hawaii, things got even quieter than that. Bitterness and envy are never nice to see, especially among Christian people who used to tell me, "Be content with what you have, dear—we should all feel fortunate to have food on the table and a roof over our heads," assuming that someone who tells lies like I do would never prosper. But here I am, cruising up and down Prince Kuhio Avenue in a clean shirt and a pair of shades, at the wheel of an '87 Mirage with unlimited mileage.

I believe I am the first person from Lake Wobegon to make the trip here, though Hjalmar and Virginia Ingqvist were going to come four years ago with their grandson Stanley. I know it was four years ago, because he was fourteen then and he's eighteen now. Almost eighteen, anyway. He'll be eighteen in a month or two.

They picked him up in Fergus Falls and drove to Fargo and

got on an Elks charter flight to Hawaii via Los Angeles. Over South Dakota, Hjalmar had a glass of complimentary pink champagne and began to hum to himself. He patted Shirley the stewardess's hand as she poured him a refill. He carried it with him, strolling up and down the aisle, saying "Call me Hjalmar," glad-handing strangers like he was in public office. Stanley was deeply embarrassed. He shrank down in his seat. Shirley offered another glass. Hjalmar said, "Well, you're the doctor." Arrived in Los Angeles in a mood to entertain, pranced down the concourse singing, "Honolulu Mama, could she dance, in her pink pajamas when she took off her— Oahu! Oahu! Oahu!"

Virginia laughed and laughed. Stanley walked twenty feet behind, as far away as he could get and not be afraid of losing them completely. The poor child was so distracted by grief and shame and worry, he didn't see where he was going and he tumbled down a flight of stairs, holding on to his suitcase, and broke his leg. They came home with nothing to show for it but a souvenir hula doll; you poke her top, she wiggles her bottom. Hjalmar hasn't touched pink champagne since.

Daryl and Marilyn Tollerud were thinking about coming to Hawaii three years ago; their pig operation had done well and they had money in the bank. But then Daryl thought, "No." He said, "Rather than going this year"—after they'd gotten the brochures—"what we'll do is invest that money in building up the herd, get more feeder pigs, and next winter we'll go and take your parents too." So they did. It was in January, he went out one morning and twenty-four pigs had died of a virus. They were lying on their backs in the sun with their little legs stuck straight up in the air. Next morning there were forty-two more dead, and about sixty-eight died about two days after that. And that was their trip to Hawaii.

In February 1957 twelve men from Lake Wobegon Lutheran were going to come to Honolulu for the National Church Ushers Convention, including the finals of the Ushers Team Competition. The guys had raised thousands of dollars for the trip and had been drilling for two nights a week for six months, practicing their silent usher signals, a complicated set of hand and eyebrow signals like this: cupped hands (it means "need additional hymnal in this pew"), or crossed arms and kicking motion ("remove this child"), or fluttering fingers with arms akimbo ("need a new collection plate, this one is too full"), a signal seldom used in church but popular at contests.

Nowadays many ushers use walkie-talkies, especially in big churches, where they're called Sanctuary Security and can be heard during the service, lurking behind pillars and back in the vestibule, beeping each other, talking walkie-talkie talk: "Avenging Angel, this is Deadly Shepherd, we are proceeding now into recessional sequence, ETA on the benny is 1259:30." But back in 1957 they used silent signals and a team of twelve: a head usher, the front four, five linebackers, and two deep safeties. They knew the service forward and backward, they could run it in their sleep and often did. That's when they used their only nonsilent signal, when they looked and saw a buddy resting his eyes and listing to starboard: the sinus toot, *braaaghhhh*, the usher's wake-up call.

The local squad that was coming to Hawaii in 1957, nicknamed the Herdsmen, was headed by Val Tollefson. He wasn't elected—he just happened to be the one who made up the lineup every Sunday, so he got to decide between Cliff Peterson and Cully Kolstad for the twelfth spot on the traveling squad, a tough call that Val made at Wednesday-night practice: Cliff got the nod. All the Herdsmen were standing in the vestibule, buttoning their overcoats and buckling their overshoes. Clarence said, "What? Why Cliff?" Val put on his hat, pretending not to hear him. Everyone was a little embarrassed. "Why did you decide that?"

"It's seniority, Clarence. Cliff's been with us longer."

"No, he hasn't. Cully's been an usher since '46, and Cliff didn't even move here until after that."

Val took a long, slow, deep breath to give himself time to think. Clarence was right. He slowly let his breath out. "It's not *just* seniority, Clarence. Of course it's not. Seniority is just one thing. It's also dedication and teamwork, how a man gets along with other people on the team."

"You can't just pick people you like! It's not right!"

Val put on his gloves. "Well, you know, Clarence, we wouldn't be arguing about this if you hadn't brought it up in the first place." He looked around at the other Herdsmen, and they glanced down at their feet. Val said, "If you want me to step down as head usher, then just say so right now and I will."

He let a few seconds pass. "All right, then."

A silent election. Not as good as guys hoisting you on their shoulders and carrying you around the room, but it meant he was reelected for another three or six or ten or twenty years, until whenever somebody dared to stand up to him again. Cliff got to go on the traveling team instead of Cully, and Cliff got an official Herdsmen's insignia sewn on his suit jacket—the shepherd's staff against a field of blue, blue standing for obedience. As the Lord would have said in the Sermon on the Mount if He had had time, "Blessed are those who arrive early, wait to be seated, and sit where they are told." The ushers at that service would've been called Mounties, and they'd have passed out bulletins ("Peter and Andrew went fishing last week and caught so many that their nets almost broke—way to go, guys!") in addition to loaf and fish distribution.

Cliff got on the team to come to Hawaii for the finals, but people had bad feelings about Cully's not coming. Several guys said, "Cully, you take my place, I don't even care about Hawaii, I don't want to go," but Cully said, "No, I feel that the Lord made this happen as a way of testing my faith and drawing me closer to Him." They voted to take thirteen guys, twelve regulars and an alternate, but Cully said, no, he felt that his faith had been strengthened so much in just a few days, and he was learning about how if you turn the other cheek it actually makes you a stronger person and the Lord comes in and takes away your bitterness and replaces it with love. At that point, morale was so low, the Herdsmen couldn't have organized a two-car parade. They went to Minneapolis for the semifinals and stumbled around in Central Lutheran, a big strange sanctuary, and never got adjusted to triple-aisle formation and scored only 82.12 points. That was as far as they got. No Hawaii for them.

"Wait a minute," you say. "The Herdsmen were paying their own way. They could've gone to Hawaii whether they got into the ushers competition or not, couldn't they?" No, they could not.

This was Minnesota, they were Lutherans, and you didn't just fly over to Hawaii for your own pleasure because you wanted to. It wasn't right. You walk in the Chatterbox and say, "Guess what? We're going to Hawaii!" and someone'd say, "Oh. Say, that's great. Sure wish I could afford to go on a trip like that. That must be nice, being able to take off and go like that." And guilt begins to fall like a gentle rain of rabbit pellets on your head. You shouldn't go and you know it. The extravagance of it. The money you're spending having a good time, while people you love are home, suffering, needing you. How can you do it, you selfish pig? You can't.

Only way you can go to Hawaii is if you can say, "Well, it looks like we're going to go to Hawaii after all. Yeah, I wasn't going to go, but she's got her heart set on it, so—you know. Yeah, her sister and brother-in-law—Annette and Warren? Remember them? The one who had the chemotherapy and lost all his hair. They're going and they got this package deal on a tour where they needed another couple to go in on it with them, so—you know."

You've got to have a good reason to go to Hawaii. "Yeah, well, we're going to see my aunt on Maui. She's going to be in a hotel there. She doesn't live on Maui, she lives in Cleveland, but she's there visiting friends of hers and we figured that, as long as we're going to Portland for the funeral, we might as well go over." And as you explain the web of circumstance that forces you to visit that tropical land of romance and delight, people nod, they understand: "Yeah, well, that's right. God knows you don't want to go to paradise, but you got to. There's no way out of it. It's that kind of a deal."

My people aren't paradise people. We've lived in Minnesota all our lives and it took a lot out of us. My people aren't sure if we'll even like paradise: not sure that perfection is all it's cracked up to be. My people will arrive in heaven and stand just inside the gate, shuffling around. "It's a lot bigger than I thought it was going to be," we'll think. We'll say, "No, thank you, we can't stay for eternity, we'll just sit and have a few minutes of bliss with you and then we have to get back."

We were brought up to work hard, not complain, accept that life is hard, and make the best of what little we have, so when we come to the grandeur and grace of an eternal flower garden ringed by mountains beside the pale-blue coral sea under the continuous sun, we naturally say, "Oh no thanks, it's too much, really, I don't care for it, just give me some ice, please."

When Lake Wobegon Lutheran women walk into heaven, they'll think it's church and look for the stairs to go down the basement, where the kitchen is. When the men arrive, they'll look at the Father's mansions and talk about siding: aluminum vs. cedar shakes.

My people aren't paradise people, but when God loves you, then everywhere is paradise enough. The honeymooners walking along Waikiki Beach are in love, and yet they are uneasy in paradise, not sure their love is good enough for paradise to last. When Daryl and Marilyn saw their dead Hawaiian pigs on a cold January morning, it was enough to break their hearts. If two of you pick up sixty-eight little pig carcasses by their frozen legs and throw them into the pickup and haul them to a landfill and bury them, and if you don't get mad and blame each other, just do the job, and go to bed, your pigs gone and your shirts lost, and turn toward the middle and lie in each other's arms, that's true love. Probably it will last because it has endured so much already.

Hansel

It has been a quiet week in Lake Wobegon. It snowed eight inches on Tuesday and if you'd been there and come for a walk with us you'd know why people in my town love stories so much. There was a fine dim light in the air: the town was full of moonlight, the old streetlamps glowed, the houses were lit, light shone up from the snow, the snow on the trees—it was so absolutely wonderfully shining beautiful, it made you feel that anything could happen now, just as I felt when my uncle Lew sat on the couch and cleared his throat and said in his quavery voice, "Well, I believe this was back in 1906, when I was in high school. . . ."

Anything could happen. George Washington could ride down this snowy street followed by a thousand ragged troops on their way to the battle of Trenton. Angels could descend, saying "Fear not" and scaring the wits out of us. Noah could ride along on an elephant, leading another elephant, and all the other animals strung out behind. Maybe it wasn't a flood God sent, maybe it was winter and they were snowbound, and it wasn't an ark, it was a barn. Forty days and forty nights would be a short winter but . . . In

Uncle Lew's story, a house burned down on a cold winter night and the little children inside ran barefoot into the snow of 1906—some were pitched out the bedroom window by their father—and all were safe. But although I heard the story dozens of times, whenever he told it again I was never sure they'd all get out. And since these children grew up to be my ancestors, I had an interest in their survival.

Just so, walking in the mysterious light of a warm snowy winter night in Lake Wobegon, it's not quite certain what year this is but it is certain that in this world that we think we know so well, and in our life that we're always talking about, there is a great mystery and powerful music playing that we don't hear and stories full of magic, so many stories that life isn't long enough to tell them all. This seems clear from the light in the air on a winter night. A car goes by so quietly on the snowy street; a little cloud of snow falls when we brush by a tree; our feet crunch on the snow. In this big white house are the Kruegers, in their dark living room, watching television, poor things. They sit in the bluish light and from their faces it's hard to tell if they're alive or in a persistent vegetative state—maybe it's time to pull the plug. The Obergs' house is dark in front, a light is on in the kitchen. You can just about make out her plate collection in the dining room, dozens of plates on display on shelves he built for her, and such beautiful china and majestic black-walnut furniture, but the four Obergs always eat in the kitchen. Why have good things you don't use? The next house is Wally and Evelyn's, who own the Sidetrack Tap, and next is this little beaten-up blue house with plastic tacked on the windows.

In the front window, you see Kenny fooling around with his kids in the living room. The room is all torn up, cushions and clothes scattered around, one kid bouncing on the sofa, three kids hanging on to him, and Kenny chasing the littlest boy, who toddles around the dining-room table, his diaper half coming off. He doesn't see that his dad has reversed directions. The little boy walks along laughing and then—looks up—in shock and delight (there is no joy like that again in life until you have a baby of your own)—he trembles and squeals and Kenny picks him up. They dance around and then Kenny lies down on the floor and they crawl on him; the boy jumping on the sofa climbs up on the end table and the lamp almost falls.

The dining-room table is strewn with dirty plates and the dog stands, paws on the table, reaching for the meat loaf. Joanne's at choir practice.

Kenny is a chubby guy with a mustache and the start of a bald spot. You can see he loves them and loves it when they hang on him, and now, just as they're getting a little too wild and tired and about to break into tears, he collects them in his arms and they all lie back in a heap in the messy messy living room, and he will now tell them a story. The dog is licking the meat loaf, but they don't see. The kids curl up close to their dad lying on his back, and before he can start the story, everyone has to get very quiet. Very very quiet—you see how stories have been useful to parents over the years: the children get quiet.

It's the story of Hansel and Gretel, the little boy and his sister in the house in the dark forest; their mother is so sick and she dies and their father is so sad and after a while he comes home with a new mother. . . . That's how the story begins.

Kenny lies there with his kids and tells the story, which is familiar, and yet it's not easy to tell about the dad who lets his wife talk him into leaving the kids in the woods to be eaten by animals. Kenny sometimes forgets a detail but his kids remember each one, and if the bread crumbs on the path sparkle like diamonds in the moonlight in one version of the story, then the next time you can't say they glisten like pearls, you've got to tell it the same way. You can't disappoint them but you also have to surprise them, so each time he'll toss in something new and crazy—maybe the gingerbread house will have a garage this time, made of pepperoni pizzas, and the wicked witch will sit drinking coffee and watching TV—but Kenny has to be careful: next time he can't say the pizzas were sausage and onion. Stories are permanent.

As they lie in a heap, and Hansel and Gretel sit in the clearing and Gretel says, "Don't cry, Hansel, I'll take care of you," and the dog's big black snout reaches for the gravy bowl, and Joanne is putting on her coat in the vestibule of the church after choir practice, on the end table where the lamp almost fell lies a letter in an envelope addressed to Kenny that tells him that his dad has died. The letter is from his stepmother, written in ink now smeared from orange pop; it says, "Just in case Larry doesn't get hold of you, I know that you will be glad to hear that Doc finally passed away at Good Shepherd early this morning, it was very peaceful, he just seemed to let go and take a breath and let that be the last one. I'm too tired to write much, but I am grateful for 31 years with him and know it'll be lonely without him but that is what comes from loving someone, you miss them when they're not here, and we accept that when we love another, that sadness and loneliness will be part of it. What a lovely man. I will write more tomorrow. Love, Ora."

Doc was born in Lake Wobegon in 1910. He helped his dad farm and when they lost the farm in 1927 Doc didn't know how to quit. He couldn't give up his horses, so he hired out as a farmhand. He got the nickname Doc because he liked books. He loved the independence of farming. In pictures of him as a young man, he looks dignified, tall, shy, poor (you can see that from the clothes), but look in his eyes, he looks like a young prince. He worked as a farmhand in North Dakota and led a pretty wild life. He drank a lot and read a lot, played baseball, stayed out all night, worked all day, and knew some women whom he made a big impression on, either because of baseball or by quoting to them from books and pretending it was his own ("I wrote you a poem, LaVerne, I don't know if it's good or not. 'Let me not to the marriage of true minds admit predicaments' "), and one winter, back in Lake Wobegon, he met Dorothy and fell in love. They courted between Thanksgiving and New Year's and were married the first of February 1944. She was a schoolteacher, so he couldn't pretend he wrote that sonnet for her. She saw through his bragging and wildness that other women had loved him for, and loved him for something he didn't know was lovable, that he was gentle and good and when he told the truth he told even better stories. But it wasn't often enough, and after Kenny was born, the third child, in 1950, she told Doc not to come home anymore. He was forty. He drank too much and did other things that weren't good for him, but mostly he just plain worked too hard. He still hired out as a farmhand, being a good farmer, but the work was backbreaking. He hurt, his body was so stiff he could hardly move. He kept going because it was all he knew how to do. Then he was too old and sick, at forty-two. He came to Saint Paul and hung around downtown, walking the streets. He looked like an old wino but he was simply worked out. He met Ora, who was a waitress at an all-night diner, and they married and he got a job as a caretaker in an apartment building. They got a tiny basement apartment, where, in 1969, Kenny, who was nineteen, came to see his dad for the first time in twelve years. It was for Thanksgiving.

Ora was very sweet to him. She made him Swiss steak and french fries and asked him fifty questions about himself, but it wasn't any use, it was terrible sleeping on a couch in the basement in a strange city with a dad you don't know at all. Kenny felt seven years old, lost, scared. He couldn't bear to be around his dad, who had left him. He went for walks around Saint Paul, and one snowy night like this he glimpsed the tower of Montgomery Ward's on University Avenue, a Spanish castle above the used-car lots, and he imagined that a great man lived there who would come and rescue him, a sweet, generous, handsome, strong, and wise man named Montgomery Ward. The next day Kenny ran away from Doc and Ora's little apartment and went home to Lake Wobegon for Thanksgiving. He saw them the next summer, but only for supper, and the next winter Kenny married Joanne. He loved her so much and was so afraid he'd be like Doc, unfaithful, he didn't tell her about Doc or invite Doc to the wedding, but by then Doc was too sick to come. He had emphysema and a liver problem. The great lover of 1944 was beginning to die, just as his grandchildren were being born. And now he is dead, finally. Kenny is lying on the floor, five kids on top of him. Hansel and Gretel have escaped from the witch. Gretel didn't push her in the oven but just turned up the volume on the TV set. She and Hansel tiptoed quietly away.

Their father was overjoyed to see them! They brought home

diamonds and emeralds and pepperoni pizzas. And suddenly there was a tremendous crash and the dog ran down to the basement.

The gravy boat is broken. Gravy all over the carpet. The table not cleared, the kitchen a mess. And the living room—cushions on the floor, papers, dog hair, clothes, pop spilled. And little children half asleep, their teeth unbrushed, lying in a heap. Kenny thinks, "Joanne! She'll be home any minute." And he's right. In fact, here she comes down the street from choir practice, humming "We Gather Together to Ask the Lord's Blessing." In a moment she'll come in the front door and look at this scene of incredible chaos, but she would get too angry if she went in now, so the writer is going to send her around the block. She thinks, "Gosh what a beautiful evening, I'll walk around the block," and walks past just as Kenny gets up off the floor and sees her. *Go, Kenny, go.* C'mon, kids, wake up, brush your teeth. Pick up the cushions, papers, scoop up dirty plates, lay paper over the gravy, *zoom zoom zoom.* Minutes later she walks in. "Honey! What in the world has been going on in here! I can't believe this mess!" But if she can't believe it now, she should've seen it two minutes ago.

They are in love, though, and later, when the kids are asleep and they go to bed, she says something to him that she said fifteen years ago when they first knew each other. She says: "Kenny, you only think about one thing all the time." And he says, as he said then: "Yeah, well—that's so whenever you think about it, then you'll know there are two of us."

And after they make love, they lie in their warm winter bed, their arms around each other, the room full of mysterious light. Anything can happen.

Du, Du Liegst
Mir im Herzen

It has been a quiet week in Lake Wobegon. We didn't make it to the state basketball tournament or even get close, but there's no point talking about that. All those years you watch little guys shooting baskets in the driveway on cold winter afternoons—little guys wearing gloves with the fingertips cut off, sliding around on the gravel, making set shots in the dark—and you think, "Someday these little fellas are going to put our town on the map," and then they grow up and they're not quite good enough. They were good with mittens on, dribbling on gravel and rocks, but a smooth floor and a heated gym seem to throw off their game.

It snowed on Wednesday, a heavy wet snow, and all the men were out to shovel, a sociable job when the snow is heavy and you need longer rest periods, especially us older guys who are heading into heart attack country. You shovel ten feet down the walk and take off your parka and stand and talk to your neighbor. "This is the heaviest snow this year," he says, "it makes you think about getting a snow blower." It would be ridiculous to die from a heart attack shoveling snow. Clarence's cousin Dan died on his front sidewalk. He pitched over from a mild heart attack and died of a concussion when his head hit the clean concrete—some snow might have saved his life.

It's a couple weeks until the exiles return for Easter, and a couple weeks until Father Emil leaves town. After forty-some years at Our Lady, he is retiring and moving south.

People still can't believe that he really is going to leave them. Friday night there was a dinner dance for Gene and Lois Pfleiderscheidt's golden wedding anniversary, and there was Father going from card table to card table in Our Lady's basement, and people thought, "Two weeks and he'll be gone. I can't bear it. It's too sad." Except Father didn't look sad at all. He had a Wendy and soon he was showing a Pfleiderscheidt grandchild how to play a polka on an empty beer bottle, blowing across the top to make the oom-pa-pas. He looked younger than when he was young, and some people felt hurt to see him look so good. A man who's leaving, you'd think he'd have the courtesy to seem confused and pitiful, at least until he gets out of town. They thought, "What's wrong with us, that he's so happy to be going away?"

He told a joke to Gene that made Gene lose his breath and get dizzy. They thought, "Well, if that's how he feels, maybe we don't need to give him a going-away party."

He danced a schottische with Lois and her sister Mrs. Luger, and they danced so hard they almost fell over. People thought, "You know, there used to be more dignity in the priesthood in the old days."

It was a wonderful dinner of roast beef, of course, sliced thick and piled on the potatoes and all of it swimming in sweet salty greasy brown gravy. Everyone came, even people who weren't hungry and who had a small helping but managed to recover their appetites and have a second and third. The Pfleiderscheidts' daughters borrowed half the Catholic card tables in town for the occasion; when you put four big beef dinners on a little card table and add eight big elbows, you have a potential for drama: Gene and his brothers, Louie, Bernie, and Whitey, were seated at one of the head card tables, eating in silence, heads down, and gravy starting to run over the gunwales, and Lois zoomed over and said, "Don't lean on it so hard, what's the matter witcha, ya got brains or not."

Gene looked up at her: "What?"

"Getcher elbows off or you're gonna break that table and everything'll land in your lap."

He started to say, "You can't . . . " Then he got his elbows off. And his side of the table rose and Whitey's plate slid almost off but he caught it with only slight spillage. And the gravy stain on his pants matched the old stains, so no harm was done.

Gene and Lois Pfleiderscheidt have complained about each other to everyone else for forty-nine years, eleven months, and twenty-nine days of their marriage. When she sits down with her sister for coffee, she says, "I could just wring his neck," and he walks into the Sidetrack Tap and says, "I have just about had it with that woman." Over the years they've got hundreds of hours of free counseling and sympathy from people who slowly realized that in some mysterious way Gene and Lois were happy together and their marriage was staying aloft by a law of physics nobody could understand, so advice was wasted on them, and meanwhile some of their counselors' marriages were becoming shaky. Couples who had seemed like a story out of *Catholic Homes and Gardens* suddenly got tight-lipped and spooky; meanwhile, Gene and Lois sailed on, complaining to anyone who'd listen that they'd made a big mistake thirty, thirty-five, forty, and now fifty years ago.

Lois was decked out in a red pant suit with black lace up the legs, a black wig, and bright-red lipstick. Gene had come in khaki pants, a green-plaid shirt, a string tie with a silver clasp, and a green nylon jacket that said "Central Seed Corn" on the back. She said to her daughter Louise, "Look at your father, he looks like he was going to the grocery for a quart of milk, he's trying to get a rise out of me, well, he's got it." He said to his daughter Frances, "Look at her, have you ever seen anything like it—is that a Catholic mother? She looks like you could rent her by the dance."

Father Emil no sooner sat down than Lois grabbed him. She

was steaming. She said, "I can't believe it, I could wring his damn neck. *Boy*, am I mad. It just burns my bacon. The girls give him one little dinky job to do, and what does he do, he makes a mess of it as usual, like he's done all his life. Jesus Mary Joseph—" She snatched her granddaughter going by and said, "Quit that chewing on your hair, Rosemary—don'tcha know you get hair in your stomach, it gets all balled up, and it'll kill you? I mean it. *Father?*" He was gone. She grabbed her daughter Katherine: "How could he do this to me?" she said. Kathy gave her a weak smile.

Gene was supposed to hire the band, so he got Whitey's boy Dennis, a drummer, and his band. They play rock and roll on Friday and Saturday nights, when they're called The Desperadoes, and Sunday nights they are The Happy Hooligans and play old-time, but this was Friday night, and the accordion player, Chuck Weimer, couldn't come, so Denny only had drums and bass and Randy the organist from The Desperadoes, who is nineteen and has hair down to his shoulders. He was just trying to play some chords around the beat and not move his head too much, because it hurt a lot. When Lois said, "Excuse me, when are you going to play the 'Blue Skirt Waltz'?" he winced and said, "I don't do requests, lady. Okay? I'm not into that. I'm a songwriter, you know?"

Dennis hummed the "Blue Skirt Waltz" to him, but Randy couldn't hear it with his headache so bad—he couldn't even shake his head. He said very quietly, "I think I need to be by myself for a little while."

"He's unbelievable. He hires a band that doesn't know the 'Blue Skirt Waltz'! They don't know 'Du, du liegst mir im herzen.' He might as well have got a phonograph and a couple of records."

At an anniversary dance, the "Blue Skirt Waltz" is required. It's a rule, same as if you have coffee, you give people cups. You don't serve it in pails or pour it into people's cupped hands but have actual cups and saucers, spoons, cream, sugar, and some bars. Or cookies. Or cake. And you sit, and after a while you say, "Have some more?" and they say, "Oh no I can't, I gotta run," and you sit and have more. There are rules in Minnesota, this is a civilization here, we don't just do what we feel like doing—it's not like California, it's a civilized place. You must dance to the "Blue Skirt Waltz" and sing "Du, du liegst mir im herzen" at the Pfleiderscheidts' anniversary dance.

"How can he do this to me?" Lois cried to Father Emil. "I send him out for bread, he comes back with bricks. How could I marry someone so damn dumb you'd think he was a Norskie."

She reminds him of Elsie in Maryland, his old pen pal. In 1947, Father saw an ad in *Collier's* for a pen-pal service; he wrote in and got Elsie's address and wrote to her, seeing if she'd like to correspond with him. He didn't mention he was a priest, because it might inhibit her. Instead he said he had just been released from Sandstone Prison for burglary. It seemed like a good act of contrition to be a convicted felon. Elsie wrote back and said she had discussed it with her husband, Vince, and he approved, so it was all right. She was interested in hearing about prison and she was interested in American history and wondered if he knew about raising tomatoes. Thus was born his most wonderful friendship with a woman.

After a few years of letters, Elsie said she and Vince were driving to Glacier Park but they wouldn't stop and visit him because she thought they'd be better pen pals if they never met. Yes, he wrote, I think you are right. Once he tested her and said he was thinking about the priesthood as a possibility, and she said, "Don't do it. I think you were meant to be a poet, not a priest. You are far too original in your thinking to ever be part of a system as rigid as the Catholic Church."

Father Emil likes Lois. She swears a lot and she's been smoking too much for far too long, but she does bring drama wherever she goes. You remember Lois. Father never can remember her daughters' names. After being Pfleiderscheidts as girls, they married men named Smith or Gray or White or Brown, and are pretty and nice, and it's hard to believe they came from this old lady rollicking around in toreador pants, smoking Camels, getting angrier and angrier at her fiftieth anniversary.

Finally a tentative peace is made, thanks to Father Emil, and

Randy is set to play the "Blue Skirt Waltz," which Denny has written down the chords to on a paper sack, and everyone is gathered around for Gene and Lois to dance, but she is still furious. "I'll never forgive you for this," she says. He is mad because she's so mad: "Our fiftieth anniversary and what does she do? She goes and makes a big stink in front of everybody and tries to make me look like a goddamn fool!"

"Dance with her. Please, Daddy. Please."

"I ain't going to dance with anyone who's said the things about me that she has said. I got some pride."

"Mother, please."

"If he thinks I'm gonna apologize to him, he better go get a chair, because it's going to be a long wait."

"Gene, come on. Just dance with her."

"I've put up with this about long enough."

"Lois and Gene, please. As a favor to me. I ask you. Please."

"Well, all right, Father Emil—Jesus Mary Joseph"—and they danced, at arm's length, not looking at each other, looking for a sympathetic face in the crowd, who would understand what he and she had been through and why now, at last, they had finally come to the end of their rope.

They stood at the end of a brief waltz and everyone clapped. Father led them in singing "Du, du liegst mir im herzen." He made them hold hands. They held but they didn't squeeze.

Lois looked fierce, like she was about to give a speech, and Gene looked like he might be silent for the next two weeks.

Their daughter Patty—Smith, or Gray—put her arms around them both and said, one last time, "Please, for our sake."

But this is a play, and they're actors, and they're good at it. And they *do* do it for our sake, that's why they do it so loudly, so we can hear. And now, for our sake, the old man puts his arms around the old lady and looks in her eyes and announces, "I love you, Lois," loud, and she rolls her eyes and blushes and sighs and says, "Well, it's about time."

Aprille

It has been a quiet week in Lake Wobegon. Spring has come, grass is green, the trees are leafing out, birds arriving every day by the busload, and now the Norwegian bachelor farmers are washing their sheets. In town the windows are open, so, as you pause in your walk to admire Mrs. Hoglund's rock garden, you can smell her floor wax and hear the piano lesson she is giving, the tune that goes "da da Da da Da da da," and up by school, smell the macaroni cheese hotdish for lunch and hear from upstairs the voices of Miss Melrose's class reciting Chaucer.

> Whan that Aprille with his shoures soote
> The droghte of March hath perced to the roote
> And bathed every veyne in swich licour
> Of which vertu engendred is the flour;
> Whan Zephyrus eek with his sweete breeth
> Inspired hath in every holt and heeth
> The tendre croppes, and the yonge sonne
> Hath in the Ram his halve cours yronne

And smale fowles maken melodye
That slepen al the nyght with open ye . . .

The words are six hundred years old and describe spring in this little town quite well; the sweet breath of the wind, the youth of the sun, the sweet rain, the tendre croppes, the smale fowles maken melodye: we have them all.

I made a pilgrimage up there last Sunday to visit my family and my family wasn't there. I walked in, called; there was no answer.

I drove over to Aunt Flo's to look for them and got caught in Sunday-morning rush hour. It was Confirmation Sunday at Lake Wobegon Lutheran Church. Thirteen young people had their faith confirmed and were admitted to the circle of believers, thirteen dressed-up boys and girls at the altar rail in front of a crowd of every available relative. Pastor Ingqvist asked them all the deepest questions about the faith (questions that have troubled theologians for years), which these young people answered readily from memory and then partook of their first communion. Later they lounged around on the front steps and asked each other, "Were you scared?" and said, "No, I really wasn't, not as much as I thought I'd be," and went home to eat chuck roast, and some of them had their first real cup of coffee. They found it to be a bitter oily drink that makes you dizzy and sick to your stomach, but they were Lutherans now and that's what Lutherans drink.

The Tolleruds, for example, drank gallons of coffee on Sunday. Church had been two hours long, the regular service plus confirmation, and Lutherans don't have the opportunity to stand up and kneel down and get exercise that you find elsewhere, so everyone was stiff and dopey, and the Tolleruds, when they sit around and visit, are all so quiet and agreeable they get drowsy, so they drink plenty of coffee. Years ago, when Uncle Gunnar was alive, they didn't need so much. He had wild white hair and eyebrows the size of mice, he spilled food down himself and didn't care, he had whiskey on his breath, and if anyone mentioned the Lutheran church he said, *"Haw!"* He was an old bachelor who got rich from founding a chain of private clubs in the Dakotas and Iowa called the Quality Prestige Clubs. They were only empty rooms over a drugstore with some old leather couches and a set of *Collier's Encyclopedia*, and he gave away memberships to men who'd never been invited to join a club before, tall sad men with thin dry hair, of whom there are a lot, and made his money selling them lots of shirts and ties and cufflinks with the QP insignia. Uncle Gunnar got rich and sold the Clubs to an Iowa meatpacker and went to Australia to get into some line of work down there he didn't consider worth mentioning, and the last anyone saw him was in 1962. Presumably he died, unless perhaps he just got tired of us knowing him.

The Tolleruds gathered for pot roast because Daryl and Marilyn's daughter Lois was confirmed. She sat at the head of the table, next to her dad, promoted from the children's table out in the kitchen. She is a tall lanky girl who has grown four inches this year, and it has tired her out. She is quieter than she used to be, a tall shy girl with long brown hair she has learned to tie in an elegant bun, and creamy skin that she keeps beautiful by frequent blushing, which is good for the circulation and makes her lovelier whenever she is admired.

A boy who has sat silently across from her in geometry since September has written her a twenty-seven-page letter in small print telling her how he feels about her (since September he's looked as if he was just about to talk, and now it all comes out at once: he thinks God has written their names together in the Book of Love). But she wasn't thinking about him Sunday—she was blushing to see her Confirmation cake with the Scripture verse inscribed in blue frosting: "Be not conformed to this world: but be ye transformed by the renewing of your mind, that ye may prove what is that good, and acceptable, and perfect, will of God." It was a large cake, and Marilyn used the extra-fine nozzle on the frosting gun—there it sat, lit with birthday candles, and Lois didn't know how to tell them that she wasn't sure that she believed in God. She was pretty sure that she might've lost her faith.

She thought she might've lost it on Friday night or sometime Saturday morning, she wasn't sure. She didn't mention it at that time because she thought she might get it back.

On Friday night, less than forty-eight hours before confirmation, she was sitting on the couch watching television with Dave, the boy who wrote the letter, while her mom and dad were gone to have supper with her prayer parents. When you're confirmed, you're assigned prayer parents, a couple who promise to pray for you for three months prior, and Lois's turned out to be the Val Tollefsons, people she had never liked. To think that every night over supper Val Tollefson had bowed his big thick head and said, "And, Lord, we ask Thee to strengthen Lois in her faith"—the same man who said once, "You won't amount to a hill of beans, you don't have the sense that God gave geese." She could feel her faith slip a little. She felt guilty, because Dave wasn't supposed to be there, and she was supposed to be ironing her confirmation dress, but he had walked two miles from his house, so what could she do? She felt sorry for Dave, he always has a bad haircut and a swarm of pimples on his forehead, but she likes him, he's quiet and nice. They talked to each other at Luther League get-togethers about what it would be like to be someone else, someone famous, for example, like Willie Nelson—you could use your fame to do good—and they went for one walk halfway around the lake, holding hands, and then she got the long letter saying how much she meant to him, twenty-seven pages, which was much more than she wanted to mean to him; it scared her.

She didn't know that Dave was a born writer, that twenty-seven pages is nothing to him, he did thirty-one on the death of his dog, Buff—she told him it would be better if they didn't see each other anymore. Friday night he walked over, full of more to say. She had four little brothers and a sister to take care of, so he sat on the old red sofa with a bottle of orange pop and watched as she fed the baby, and she turned on the TV and lost her faith. Men in khaki suits were beating people senseless, shooting them with machine guns, throwing the bodies out of helicopters. Their reception was so poor, the picture so fuzzy, it was more like radio, which made the horrors worse, and she thought, "This could happen here." It gave her a cold chill to imagine violent strange men busting in, as they had done to Anne Frank. She held the baby, Karen, imagining all of them were hiding from Nazis, and heard twigs crunch outside and knew that this boy could not protect her. She prayed and heard something like an echo, as if the prayer was only in her head. The whole world in the control of dark powers, working senseless evil on our lives, and prayer went no place, prayer just went up the chimney like smoke.

When Marilyn cut the confirmation cake and served it with butter-brickle ice cream, Lois thought, "I should say something." Like "I don't believe in God, I don't think." Nobody would need coffee then.

After dinner she put on her jeans and a white jacket and walked out across the cornfield toward the road and the ravine to think about her faith on this cloudy day, and, walking west over a little rise, she saw, just beyond the ravine, a white car she'd never seen before, and a strange man in a trenchcoat standing beside it. She walked toward him, thinking of the parable of the Good Samaritan, thinking that perhaps God was calling her to go witness to him and thereby recover her faith. He stood and pitched stones up over the trees, and as she got closer, he turned and smiled, put out his hand, and came toward her. She saw her mistake. Something glittered in his mouth. She stopped. He was a killer come looking for someone, it didn't matter to him who it was, anyone who came down the road would do. He walked toward her; she turned and fell down and said, "Oh please no, please God no."

I hadn't seen her for five years. I said, "Lois, Lois—it's me." I helped her up. How are you? It's good to see you again. We shuffled along the rim of the ravine, looking for the thin path down, and she told me about her confirmation, which I have an interest in because I am her godfather. I wasn't invited to church, I reckon, because fourteen years ago I wasn't anyone's first choice for godfather. I was nominated by Marilyn because Daryl suggested his brother Gunnar and she thought that was ridiculous, and to show Daryl what a poor choice he would be she suggested me, and Daryl said, "Sure, fine, if that's what you want," and they were stuck with me.

The baby was named for her mother's Sunday-school teacher, who was my aunt Lois, my youngest aunt, so young she was like

an older sister. She was single when I was a boy and so had plenty
of time for her favorite nephew. She told me I was. She said,
Don't tell the others but you are the one I love more than anyone
else, or words to that effect. We were riding the bus to Minneapolis, she and I, to visit Great-aunt Posie. Lois seemed young to
me because she loved to pretend. We imagined the bus was our
private bus and we could go anywhere we wanted. We were *somebody*.

My favorite game was Strangers, pretending we didn't know
each other. I'd get up and walk to the back of the bus and turn
around and come back to the seat and say, "Do you mind if I sit
here?" And she said, "No, I don't mind," and I'd sit. And she'd
say: "A very pleasant day, isn't it?"

We didn't speak this way in our family, but she and I were
strangers, and so we could talk as we pleased.

"Are you going all the way to Minneapolis, then?"

"As a matter of fact, ma'am, I'm going to New York City. I'm
in a very successful hit play on Broadway, and I came back out
here to Minnesota because my sweet old aunt died, and I'm going
back to Broadway now on the evening plane. Then next week I
go to Paris, France, where I currently reside on the Champs-
Elysées. My name is Tom Flambeau, perhaps you've read about
me."

"No, I never heard of you in my life, but I'm very sorry to hear
about your aunt. She must have been a wonderful person."

"Oh, she was pretty old. She was all right, I guess."

"Are you very close to your family, then?"

"No, not really. I'm adopted, you see. My real parents were
Broadway actors—they sent me out to the farm thinking I'd get
more to eat, but I don't think that people out here understand
people like me."

She looked away from me. She looked out the window a long
time. I'd hurt her feelings. Minutes passed. But I didn't know
her. Then I said, "Talk to me. Please."

She said, "Sir, if you bother me anymore I'll have the driver
throw you off this bus."

"Say that you know me. Please."

And when I couldn't bear it one more second, she touched me and I was myself again.

And the next time we rode the bus, I said, "Let's pretend we don't know each other."

She said, "No, you get too scared."

"I won't this time." I got up and came back and said, "It's a very pleasant day, isn't it? Are you going to Minneapolis?"

Eventually we do. We pretend to be someone else and need them to say they know us, but one day we become that person and they simply don't know us. From that there is no bus back that I know of.

Lois Tollerud asked me, "Why did you stop here?" I told her I had parked by the ravine, looking for a spot where our Boy Scout troop used to camp and where Einar Tingvold the scoutmaster got so mad at us once, he threw two dozen eggs one by one into the woods. Each egg made him madder and he threw it farther. When he ran out of eggs he reached for something else. It was his binoculars. He didn't want to throw them away but he was so furious he couldn't stop—he threw the binoculars and reached for them in the same motion. Heaved them and tried to grab the strap as it went by. We scouts looked for it for a whole afternoon, thirty years ago. Whenever I go by the ravine, I look for a reflection of glass, thinking that, if I found those binoculars by some wonderful luck and took them back to him, he might forgive me.

"That's not true, is it?" she said. "No, it's not."

I stopped there because, frankly, I'd had a lot of coffee, but I couldn't tell her that. We walked for almost a mile along that ravine, to the lake and back, and then I felt like I'd like to visit her family after all.

We walked in. I got a fairly warm hello, and was offered coffee. "In a minute," I said. "Excuse me, I'll be right back." I had a cup and a slice of cake that said "Con but for," a little triangle out of her verse.

Be not conformed to this world: but be ye transformed. Our lovely world has the power to make us brave. A person wants to be someone else and gets scared and needs to be known, but we ride so far on that bus, we become the stranger. Nevertheless these things stay the same: the sweet breath, the rain, the tendre croppes, and the smale fowles maken melodye—God watches each one and knows when it falls, and so much more does He watch us all.

Goodbye to
the Lake

It has been a quiet week in Lake Wobegon.
We got a good rain on Wednesday, a long soaking rain good for
field and garden and lawn. It was so dry, no rain for a month.
The ballpark grass looked dead last Sunday, the lake level fell and
rocks showed in the river. It began to rain in the night, Tuesday.
People woke up and lay listening to it. It wasn't a storm, it didn't
blow, it was just water falling from heaven, trickling off the roof.
Clarence woke up and thought the phone was ringing and imagined
it was his daughter Barbara Ann calling to say the baby was born
and they named it Clarence. But it was rain. Ella Anderson woke
up because Henry rolled over. She lay squeezed half under him and
said out loud, "La Crosse." A city on the river, a transfer point
for train crews on the Zephyr, and a name that for some reason
makes him roll back to his side. His rolling interrupted a dream
of hers in which a young man approached and touched her cheek
and spoke in a musical voice, "Come, come," and she was about
to when Henry woke her up. She lay and listened to the rain.
David and Judy Ingqvist lay on their sleeping porch, the one and
only luxury in the parsonage, each of them awake, looking at the

roof, the rain rattling down. Each of them wishing the other were awake but careful not to move, knowing the other is a light sleeper.

It rained through the morning. Couldn't work in the gardens so kids lay around on the porch and read books. At ten o'clock in the morning. Such luxury, only rich people get to do it, rich people such as you only find in books, but rain gives the poor children a holiday. People in books never work in gardens. The Three Musketeers never had to kneel along a row of peas and weed them. That's why they got in all those swordfights, resisting the call to weed. Princesses didn't weed peas, one pea made a princess black and blue even though it was under forty featherbeds, so weeding peas woulda killed her, poor thing. Laura Ingalls worked in the garden but always cheerfully and only for a sentence or two: "Laura worked in the garden under the hot sun. Soon it was time for supper. 'Laura!' Ma called from the little house." You can't call that hard work.

Brian Tollefson lay on his porch reading *The Case of the Deadly Smorgasbord*, the latest in the Flambeau Family mystery series, in which Nobel prize–winning scientist Emile Flambeau, his wife, Eileen, the star of stage and screen, and their exceptionally bright and happy teenage son, Tony, leave their large tastefully cluttered Manhattan apartment and zoom off to Copenhagen to track down a band of left-wing terrorists who put mood-altering chemicals in the red herring, but that's only a story and what Brian loves is how the Flambeaus talk to each other—they're a family and yet they're also each other's best friends.

" 'Tony,' Eileen said, touching her hand to his cheek, 'what happened between you and Rosemary? Aren't you still seeing each other?' " Brian's mother never touches his cheek except to see if he has a temperature. But Eileen is Tony's good friend as well as his mother, and so much more interesting than Rosemary, a better talker, more understanding, Tony actually prefers his parents to other teenagers. Brian loathes his parents. They sicken and disgust him, they are fat and lumpy and dreary and slow and determined to be dumb. Born to be boring. Emile and Eileen live in large sunny rooms full of plants and piles of books and are easy-going and affectionate and talk intelligently about so many things. "Emile turned and put his arms around his son and held him closely for a long moment. 'You're an important part of my life,' he said softly, 'and you have a right to know that.' " Their lives are not consumed by petty things. The need to pick raspberries and freeze them is not part of the Flambeaus' life on the Upper West Side, nor is gas mileage or back problems or aphids or Lutheranism. The Flambeaus are above that. Probably they are Christian but they don't need to talk about it so much.

Arlene picked up her sister Irene and they drove up to the cemetery and sat in the car. June 10 is the anniversary of their mother's death. Lutherans don't ordinarily observe such days but the girls do because it would have pleased their mother, Mrs. Holm, so much. She was impossible to please when she was alive, but now that she is gone and her spirit recedes into the shadows, the girls are able to satisfy her with this annual trek to sit under the tree that shades her—she always burned easily, Mother did, and always needed shade. The tree's roots reach down where Mother lies, so in a sense Mother is shading herself, like a lady with a parasol. They sat in the car in the rain for fifteen minutes, thinking their own thoughts, and Arlene said, "Seventeen years. Do you know that I still sometimes pick up a phone to call somebody and forget and dial Mother's old number? A couple named Ferguson has it. After years of me saying, Oh I'm sorry, I have the wrong number, we finally introduced ourselves. And do you know, she sounds a lot like Mother."

The rain patted on the roof and ran down the windshield. Irene held a bunch of yellow and blue irises. "Do you know that I still hear her sometimes—I'm washing dishes or ironing, something simple, and I hear her say, *Oh Irene you're doing that all wrong, here let me*, and my hands tighten on the dishcloth, I grab the iron. The simplest things. Putting toast in the toaster. Boiling an egg. *Oh Irene, that's not how to do that, here I'll show you.* I still hear it. Never when I'm trying to do needlepoint, or make a soufflé—always when I'm pulling a weed, hanging a picture. *Oh that's not straight, Irene, here. What's the matter with you? Oh you don't put on a pillowcase like that.*" She began to sniffle. "Oh this is so crazy. I don't know why it has to be like this." She cried and Arlene cried and they held hands, the rain streaming down the glass. And then Irene bounded out of the car and ran up on the grass and heaved the bouquet as far as she could toward their mother's grave. It hit the tree and fell apart in a shower of wet irises and dropped on the grass.

The noon siren went off and a lot of damp happy people trooped in to lunch, including Florian Krebsbach and his son Carl. Carl couldn't work at the Bausers' because of the rain so he went to his dad's garage, Krebsbach's Chev, and helped out with the annual parts inventory. His brother-in-law Lyle was there too. Carl didn't want to work at Bausers' anyway, it was a bad job, taking off their porch and modernizing the house with aluminum siding. The porch sags, so Bob wants it out. Carl ripped out the floor Tuesday, painfully, feeling like a vandal (when a car drove by, he stopped), leaving the roof for Wednesday in case Bob got converted overnight. Inventory was fun. Counting bearings, bushings, grommets and gizmos and thingamabobs, calling out the count for Florian to write down. *121 lugnuts! Three repeaters! A box of shanksnaps! Two extensogrips, one left, one right! One Folger's drip grind coffee can full of nuts and bolts, some iron, some brass!* Like playing Captain May I. Lyle and Ronnie and Ernie and Carl roamed the storeroom, the library of parts, and Dad sat at his old desk, the pigeonholes stuffed full of slips of paper to remind him of things he has to do that he has managed to put off until it was no longer necessary. A trophy shelf of defeated obligations, each hole stuffed with pigeons that Florian the Great Postponer has successfully escaped. The inventory shows once again that Krebsbach's is in chaos. "I donno, I can't figure this out," Florian says, "this don't make sense. Look at this, boys." And the boys look: carburetor parts missing, floormats, doorknobs, wiper blades—all the numbers are there but nothing adds up against last year's inventory. He says, "I donno. It's too much for me. Pop always said it was Frank who had the head for business and Pop was right." Florian is happy. He rips the inventory sheet off the pad and carefully folds it down the middle lengthwise and into thirds, and finds room in the last pigeonhole to stuff it in. He looks up at them and shakes his head. "One of these days I am going to come in on a Saturday morning and get this desk straightened out. Now let's go have some dinner."

Rain fell all morning and everyone was in a festive mood, the Chatterbox was packed for dinner. A bunch of Norwegian bachelor farmers piled into the back booth and had mushroom soup and liverwurst sandwiches. "Looks like this may keep up all day," one said. "Yeah, that's what they're sayin." If a drought were to kill off his crops, a bachelor farmer might be forced to contemplate marriage, the last refuge for men unable to fend for themselves, just as poor Mr. Hauge did in the drought of '59. He married a Saint Cloud woman and died six months later and not from excitement. To them, rain means that life continues, and they cleared their throats like happy lions, *Braaghhhh*.

Mayor Clint Bunsen sat with Rollie and Louise and Marlys Diener and Mr. Berge and By Tollefson, a tight fit. Clint had thought he was going to have to order a ban on watering lawns, it was so dry and the level in the water tower was getting low, or so he thought. Its depth gauge broke back in 1968 when the water level got so low that the float arm snapped, and now Clint tests the level by getting a strong boy to throw a baseball way up there and hit it, the tone telling him how full it is, but this spring he couldn't find a boy with a good enough arm to reach the tank, so Clint himself had to climb up the ladder—Bud gets nosebleeds past twenty feet and has to come down and stuff cotton in his nose—and he climbed high above the roofs and trees and banged on the tank with a hammer. It rang like a deep bell tolling for the dead, *wonnnngggg. Wonnnnnggg*. Now with the rain watering them, the tank is filling up, and soon it'll sound like wedding bells.

Byron was happy, and like a true Norseman he showed it by complaining loudly. "No mushrooms in this soup," he groaned. "It's getting to be like everything else. You got decaffeinated coffee, soda pop with no sugar, pretty soon we'll have chemical sweet corn. Taste fresh year-round, and it'll be flat and round like a cracker. No salt, no sugar, no fat. You wait and see. It's coming.

I'm glad I won't be here to see it but you'll see—I was reading where by the year 2000 they'll be cultivating without tractors, using low-frequency sound waves, and they'll breed a dairy cow with no legs, a rectangular body you can stack a thousand or so in a warehouse the size of the school. It'll give fifty, eighty, a hundred gallons a day on a bushel of grass clippings and a couple Demerol. This story said that when agriculture is fully capitalized for peak efficiency, all of rural Minnesota can be run by three hundred people, seventy-five to raise the crops and the rest to write the reports. I believe it. I believe it."

Mr. Berge didn't hear him, he was looking at Marlys. He took a spoonful of corn chowder and fell in love with her, her lovely bare shoulders and neck, her throat, the lovely spot where the collarbones join together, and he took a bite of liverwurst and tears of love came to his eyes, a brief powerful romance until it ended. "Yeah," Rollie was saying, "we put in the last of the sweet corn yesterday. Two rows. Should take us through the middle of September."

I look at them as I eat my cheese sandwich and don't hear them anymore, they sit like a picture. Specks of rain on the big front window, a cool breeze through the screen door, raindrops in the puddles along the curb, rain out on the lake, which is so misty you can't see the other shore, it's like an ocean. Just as I imagined when I was little and we floated sticks offshore and bombed them with rocks. Now Lake Wobegon looks even more like an ocean, and through that mist I can sail to anywhere, including where I'm going, Copenhagen.

This is my last view of them for a while. If you see them before I do, say hello from me and give them my love. For now I'll remember them as they are this moment, on a Wednesday in June, sitting with each other and listening to a summer rain that may yet save the crops. And the river may rise so that you and I can push our lovely rafts from shore and be lifted up over the rocks and at last see what is down there around the big bend where the cottonwood trees on shore are slowly falling, bowing to the river, the drops glistening on the dark green leaves.